The
IMMORTALS

★ ★ ★ ★ ★

THE WORLD WAR II STORY OF
FIVE FEARLESS HEROES,
THE SINKING OF THE *DORCHESTER*,
AND AN AWE-INSPIRING RESCUE

The

IMMORTALS

STEVEN T. COLLIS

SHADOW
MOUNTAIN

For my parents,
who raised me to build bridges.

And for Asher.
May you build them as well.

Photos and image credits. Pages 15, 23, 76, and 83, public domain. Pages 47, 50, and 144, images recreated by Deseret Book. Pages 53 and 252, photos courtesy of Sharon David. Page 107, Government of the Republic of Poland, Ministry of Foreign Affairs MSZ. Public domain. Page 137, Iconographic Archive/Alamy Stock Photos. Page 151, photo courtesy of Adam Artigliere. Used by permission.

Visit us at shadowmountain.com

Library of Congress Cataloging-in-Publication Data

Names: Collis, Steven T., 1978– author.
Title: The immortals : the World War II story of five fearless heroes, the sinking of the
    Dorchester, and an awe-inspiring rescue / Steven T. Collis.
Description: [Salt Lake City] : Shadow Mountain, [2021] | Includes bibliographical refer-
    ences and index. | Summary: The story of the heroic actions of chaplains George Fox,
    Alexander Goode, John Washington, and Clark Poling of the *Dorchester* and steward's mate
    Charles W. David Jr. of the *Comanche* in the aftermath of a German submarine attack
    during World War II.
Identifiers: LCCN 2021000428 | ISBN 9781629728483 (hardback)
Subjects: LCSH: David, Charles W., Jr. (Charles Walter), 1917–1943. | Fox, George Lansing,
    1900–1943. | Goode, Alexander D. (Alexander David), 1911–1943. | Washington, John
    P. (John Patrick), 1908–1943. | Poling, Clark Vandersall, 1910–1943. | *Dorchester* (Ship) |
    Military chaplains—United States—Biography. | World War, 1939–1945—Chaplains—
    United States—Biography.
Classification: LCC D774.D56 C65 2021 | DDC 940.54/78092273—dc23
LC record available at https://lccn.loc.gov/2021000428

Printed in the United States of America
Publishers Printing, Salt Lake City, UT

10   9   8   7   6   5   4   3   2   1

CONTENTS

PROLOGUE

All around them, in every direction, was dark, frosty water; it was carpeted with constellations of red lights attached to the life jackets of men bobbing in the waves.

It was February 3, 1943, in the middle of the night, in the Atlantic Ocean south of Greenland. Ice coated everything. The wind sliced. Army Chaplains George Fox, Alexander Goode, John Washington, and Clark Poling struggled to stand. They balanced on the jutting stern of the *SS Dorchester,* their massive cruise-ship-turned-troop-transport that had been struck by a Nazi torpedo just a short time before. It had listed first, then begun a nosedive, its propellers rising into the air. Beneath and all around the chaplains, the ocean gurgled and boiled, gobbling up all the decks of the enormous ship foot by foot. In a matter of minutes, the massive maw would swallow them as well.

They had done all they could within the physical constraints of the human body—with their limbs, sinews, muscles, bones, even their vocal cords, they had saved scores of men. They were of different religions, faiths that had clashed—and still warred—with each other over the centuries. But those were other people's battles; they meant nothing in the moment. Each was devoted, to both God and to his fellow human beings. Now, each in his own way, they prayed for help. They needed the interference of the divine for a task that was now beyond their power.

On a nearby ship, a United States Coast Guard cutter called the *Comanche*, Steward's Mate Charles W. David Jr. prepared for whatever order came his way. His primary duties were beneath his abilities, not for any valid reason but due to the color of his skin. He had been a strong swimmer since his youth, a natural leader, a man of both charisma and keen judgment, selfless and dutiful, strong and caring. But because his skin was brown—his family hailed from the Caribbean—he was relegated to the work of a cook and not allowed to advance much in rank. If his ship received orders to go and save the men from the torpedoed *Dorchester,* he would have no obligation to help.

At that precise moment, the men on Charles's ship were scanning the choppy waters, searching desperately for the U-boat that had fired the torpedo at the *Dorchester.* It was still out there, lurking in the depths, like a wolf with blood from a kill on its lips, still hungry for more. If it was like most U-boats, it was not alone, for the Nazis stalked the seas in packs. At the sonar, Charles's friend listened for any sign of the enemy. On deck, other members of the crew searched for the froth and foam of submarines rising from the waves.

What they didn't know: the U-boat had already plunged to the safety of the depths. There it waited in the silent darkness, hidden, but ready to pounce.

The order came to the *Comanche:* it was to rush to the site of the sinking *Dorchester* and search for and attack enemy submarines while other ships looked for survivors. The cutter charged on its course. The ocean heaved and thrashed. The tiny coast guard ship careened into troughs and bounded over waves the size of hills. Charles and the rest of the crew clung to whatever grip they could find.

The chaplains did not know Charles, nor he them. But they had issued a prayer into the frigid skies above the Arctic, and, unbeknownst to either them or Charles, he was coming as part of the answer.

Far below, surrounded by darkness and pressure, *Oberleutnant* Karl-Jurg Wächter, the commander of U-boat 223, was done waiting. He ordered his men to surface.

PART I

PREPARING
FOR BATTLE

★ ★ ★ ★ ★

CHAPTER 1

A DIVIDED COUNTRY

On December 11, 1941, four days after Japan's attack on Pearl Harbor, Adolf Hitler rose to the podium in the Reichstag. Two lengthy microphones and two shorter ones jutted toward his face. Behind him, a massive imperial eagle clutched the now-infamous Nazi swastika in its talons. In chairs both surrounding and in front of Hitler, members of the Reichstag and the Nazi party looked on in anticipation.

"Deputies, men of the German Reichstag!" Hitler said. Light gleamed off the hair greased tightly against his scalp. His double-breasted, military-style suit reflected the crispness of his words. "A year of events of historical significance is drawing to an end. A year of the greatest decisions lies ahead. In these serious times, I speak to you, Deputies of the German Reichstag, as to the representatives of the German nation. Beyond and above that, the whole German people should take note of this glance into the past, as well as of the coming decisions the present and future impose upon us."

With that, the Nazi leader launched into his justifications for declaring war against the United States. It was a lengthy speech, filled with falsehoods and Hitler's perspective of the political rumblings across the world. Amidst all of it, one theme repeated itself: Hitler's belief that a unified, homogeneous Germany would never face defeat.

"In the whole history of the German nation," he roared, "of nearly 2,000 years, it never has been so united as today and, thanks to National Socialism, it will remain united in the future. Probably it has never seen so clearly, and rarely been so conscious of its honor."

His speech charged ahead. At times, thunderous applause interrupted his cadence. Still, he clung to his theme. After declaring war against the United States and England and aligning Germany with Italy and Japan, he boasted: "Today I am at the head of the strongest Army in the world, the most gigantic Air Force and of a proud Navy. Behind and around me stands the Party with which I became great and which has become great through me. The enemies I see before me are the same enemies as 20 years ago, but the path along which I look forward cannot be compared with that on which I look back. The German people recognizes the decisive hour of its existence, millions of soldiers do their duty, millions of German peasants and workers, women and girls, produce bread for the home country and arms for the Front. We are allied with strong peoples, who in the same need are faced with the same enemies."

As he came to a close, he finished where he began—in his belief that the unified Germany he had created through brutality and government oppression was stronger than its adversaries. "Our enemies must not deceive themselves—in the 2,000 years of German history known to us, our people have never been more united than today."

With booming approval, the members of the Reichstag rose and offered Hitler the *Sieg heil* salute. It was surely, in his own mind at least, a glorious moment.[1]

But his speech wasn't just public rhetoric.

Roughly one month later, on January 7, 1942, in his bunker on the eastern front, Hitler held a private conversation with some of his closest confidants. It was evening time. The air outside was crisp. Over coffee and cakes, he mused on a host of topics, as he often did. Nearby, but apart, a discreet, skinny lawyer named Heinrich Heim scribbled shorthand notes, recording everything Hitler said, capturing these private thoughts, believing they would one day prove valuable to the world's posterity.

Hitler blasted Winston Churchill. He discussed the possibility that England might even quit the war. He considered such strategic minutia as America's need for coal.

The night wore on. Hitler droned, expanded, never pausing, it seems, for anyone else in the room to comment. This was a common pattern. Late at night, after dinner, after all the discussions of war that had occupied his day, Hitler would retire for tea and cake, then allow his thoughts to flow freely. Heim's pen scratched nearby.

Finally, Hitler said, "I don't see much future for the Americans. In my view, it's a decayed country. And they have their racial problem, and the problem of social inequalities. Those were what caused the downfall of Rome, and yet Rome was a solid edifice that stood for something. Moreover, the Romans were inspired by great ideas. Nothing of the sort in England today. As for the Americans, that kind of thing is nonexistent."

He discussed the foreign nature of the Japanese, how Germans could never relate to them.

Then his comments returned to the United States: "My feelings against Americanism are feelings of hatred and deep repugnance. I feel myself more akin to any European country, no matter which. Everything about the behavior of American society reveals that it's half Judaised, and the other half negrified. How can one expect a State like that to hold together?"[2]

Despite all the evil and insanity that informed his thinking, in some respects, Hitler was not wrong. The United States is one of the most diverse nations on the planet, and that diversity had already manifested itself by the time the Nazis declared war. That multiplicity—of experience, race, ethnicity, religion, wealth, culture, belief, education—had the potential to tear apart the relatively new nation.

With the country entering two theaters of war simultaneously on opposite sides of the globe, Hitler's theory of the United States' diversity being its greatest weakness would be put to an important test. Although the country's founders had held high aspirations, its history was not always one of helping sheep of a different fold. To put it simply, in the 1930s and early 1940s, American society was—and had been—fractured, like a piece of glass weakened by a thousand cracks. For all of his irrationality, Hitler's assessment that enough pressure might cause the glass to shatter was not outlandish.

Society often makes assumptions about diversity: that it brings better perspective, promotes increased learning, imbues people with tolerance, and forces people to consider viewpoints other than their own. Supreme Court opinions base entire fields of law on those assumptions. Corporations spend millions in the name of achieving them. Universities adjust their admissions standards with those aims in mind. The problem is that the assumptions work only if the people from differing backgrounds, once thrust into a side-by-side existence, come with an attitude of learning and open-mindedness. Too often, they do not. Human history is one of tribalism, of groups oppressing anyone who looks or believes differently from them. Diversity is a strength only in societies whose citizens pass laws and carry attitudes that make it one.

By January 1942, the fissures that weakened America came from a number of sources. A lack of religious and racial tolerance was one of them. Long before the first European colonizers set foot on this continent, human groups showed a tendency to want to protect their own people, but no one else. Legal scholars call this the "Puritan Mistake": we often say that the Puritans came to these shores for religious freedom, which is true. They did, but they were interested in religious freedom only for themselves. As far as they were concerned, any other religious groups—including Native Americans—deserved no religious liberty protections.[3]

But why scholars pick on the poor Puritans when naming this

blunder has always been a mystery. The Puritan Mistake is a near-universal human tendency, stretching back to eons long before the Puritans were even a recognized movement. There is likely no group on earth that has not committed it at some time or another against someone different from them. Christians have committed it against Muslims; Muslims against Jews; atheists against theists and theists against atheists; Orthodox Jews against Reform Jews, who have returned the favor; Muslims against Christians; Jews against Christians and Muslims; Native Americans against each other and Christians; Christians against Native groups; secularists against religionists and vice versa; different racial groups against each other.[4] The list goes on and on, across all continents and all peoples.

Most members of every group believe they are the victims. Most take umbrage at any suggestion that their group could be the oppressors.

But the millennia of human history show that once people gain power, they often use it to oppress those who are ideologically different. This includes political rivals, but also religious and racial ones. Most oppressors believe they are acting in the name of a greater good: promoting truth, protecting the oppressed, enlightening those in darkness, ensuring equality, ridding the world of evil, providing liberty, elevating the good. They also often fear that by protecting those with whom they disagree they are somehow complicit in promoting a wrong. So even if humans don't actively target their enemies, that doesn't mean they are willing to go further and *protect* them from the forces of nature, global enemies, or tyrannical governments. It is one thing to live and let live. It is something else entirely to stand up for those you perceive to be your enemies. Most of humanity simply lacks the conviction or courage to do such a thing.

This phenomenon was certainly potent when it came to the Jews in Europe or Blacks in the southern United States. Prior to World War II, before anyone in the United States knew of the Nazis' plans for genocide, people were already aware of the dark forerunners: the ghettos, *Kristallnacht*, the Star of David as a scarlet letter, invasions, caricatures in newspapers of Jews as rats and cockroaches. And they knew of Jim Crow laws, separate but never equal, roadblocks to prevent an entire people from lifting themselves out of poverty. Yet they did nothing. The prevailing view in far too many countries, and especially the United States, was that oppressed people were on their own.

The Puritan Mistake was raging. It had always been there, of course, but the two decades before the attack on Pearl Harbor saw it as vibrant as ever. The Ku Klux Klan had been reborn. It is known for its violent opposition to the mixing of the races, but it was equally driven to prevent the mixing of religions. Members of the KKK terrorized Jews, Catholics, and Blacks, and its sympathizers attacked anyone who was not a white Protestant. The barbarism that fell upon religious and racial minorities was as cruel as it was intense. The Klan burned crosses in front of homes, terrorized people who attended parochial schools, lynched Black Americans, targeted priests, and paraded on horseback down main streets across the United States.

But Protestants weren't alone in committing the Puritan Mistake. Many of America's religions toiled in isolation. They rarely engaged in interfaith participation, and most eyed each other across religious chasms that, in their minds, seemed too wide to bridge. Jews largely only affiliated with Jews. Catholics knew Catholics. Even among the Protestant sects, there were differences of opinion that prevented widespread cooperation. Latter-day Saints were especially isolated. They lived primarily in the western United States, with just a smattering in communities in the East. Although they shared common theological bonds with Catholics, Jews, and Protestants, they were foreign to all of them. The same was true of Christian Scientists and Jehovah's Witnesses.

And all of this turmoil on the religious side was occurring on top of America's racial divisions. In the military, Black and white soldiers largely could not fight together, since Jim Crow–enforced segregation ruled the day. In the few places where they could, Black soldiers were relegated to minor roles: cooks, mess attendants, labor and supply units, steward's mates. Only in rare circumstances were Black men allowed to serve in more substantive roles. In essence, given the racism of the time, the United States failed to tap into a vast swath of its potential force, thus weakening its position.

Given the near-universal human tendency to commit the Puritan Mistake, Hitler's rhetorical point regarding the United States—"How can one expect a State like that to hold together?"—was as compelling as it was threatening. His vision was as clear as it was diabolical and sinister: a Germany united by Nazi force would crush a fractured United States. The only question was this: when push came to shove, would people in the United States come together despite their differences to defeat a great evil? Or would the Puritan Mistake continue its seemingly unbreakable hold over the hearts and minds of humanity?

CHAPTER 2

TRAINING
FOR THE HUNT

By summer 1942, a world away, just about every German U-boat crew endured deepwater training. When they began the process, many felt confident, given their personalities: wide-eyed, green, and perhaps a little cocksure. When they finished, either they enjoyed a quiet confidence of knowing they could handle anything, or they were broken. And the training threw at them everything the war could.

It was in this uniquely demanding setting that *Oberleutnant* Karl-Jurg Wächter prepared his ship and his men to search out and destroy as many American convoys as possible. As soon as their training ended, their goal would be simple: find American and British ships and send them and their crews to the depths.

As Wächter knew, the drills would push his men to their limits. Near a place called Hela, a narrow peninsular strip jutting into the Baltic Sea, part of a land Germany had conquered in its quest to dominate the earth, the training regime was known as the Agru-Front.[1] The men both feared and respected it. Less than two years old, the regimen aimed to give soldiers harrowing and realistic combat experience. It would test not just their skills but their emotional strength and physical endurance. Seasoned, battle-tested officers hurled every imaginable emergency they could at crewmen. Disabling controls, igniting smoke bombs, forcing full-speed crash dives, simulating power outages, surviving attacks from depth charges—all of it was meant to test the sailor's nerve under fatigue-magnified pressure.

In some respects, Wächter was everything Hitler and the Nazi party prized. He met all the criteria—young, white, deep German roots, pride in his country and his job, ambitious, highly skilled.[2] We don't know how he felt about the Nazi party's evil machinations and genocide, but nothing suggests he had any objections. Just twenty-six, he wore a patchy beard that faded into scruff below his chin line. His eyes portrayed a determined playfulness—perhaps a reflection of both his skill and his youth. Six years earlier, in 1936, he had joined the German navy and became part of the most famous class of cadets the *Kriegsmarine* had ever seen. The vast majority of them took command of their own vessels during the war, and because they had all signed on during the year Germany hosted the Olympics, they called themselves the "Olympia Crew."[3]

In his downtime, Wächter enjoyed a game of dice. The U-boat under his command was U-223. At one point, when Wächter and his men had been playing a game, the dice revealed the numbers two, two, and three. Taking it as a sign of good fortune, they painted three dice on the side of the boat to commemorate the moment.[4]

So he was good-humored, but he was also focused. At a tender age, he had already received a promotion to command his own vessel. He had climbed up six ranks to reach that point, and nothing suggests he intended to slow his ascent. In July and August of 1942, as he watched his men endure the challenges of the Agru-Front, the words of one of his superiors likely rang in his ears. In an essay, one of the highest ranking men in Germany's navy, Karl Dönitz,[5] had described the crew of a U-boat as a "community bound by fate."[6] Dönitz continued, "If one crewman errs, if he fails as a lookout, improperly closes a valve, or forgets a seal, he jeopardizes his boat's success, his life, and the lives of his crewmates." Whether Wächter liked it or not, he and his men were "sworn to one another."[7]

But were these men the type who would hold up under the pressure of warfare? Could Wächter rely on them to keep their composure and their focus when the Americans and British were raining depth charges upon them, or when the seas turned ugly, or when enemy sonar detected them and a quick escape became necessary? Wächter couldn't be sure. They were bound for the Atlantic. And the sea was unforgiving—the enemy even more so.

At the beginning of the war, and even before that, when Wächter had enlisted, U-boat crews were handpicked. People thought of the navy as the elite arm of the German military and the U-boat men as the cream of that cream.[8] But during the first year of naval combat, that changed drastically. The Germans had lost 40 percent of that select group, which meant they had to fill the gaps with men who had only limited naval training and sometimes no U-boat experience at all.[9]

Wächter needed to know how much this patchwork of men could handle. When the lights flickered off and the giant beast was submerged in a cocoon of water, in those claustrophobic confines, would they break? And it wasn't just the crew's survival that mattered. The entire war effort—the survival of Germany and Hitler's grand vision—hinged on the U-boats' ability to choke the American and British supply lines. Starve the beast, and it would die. Control the seaways, and the United States' ability to impact the war would plummet.

To add to the immense pressure and danger of their mission, U-boats were complicated beasts. U-223 was part of a brand-new fleet of Type VIIC boats.[10] In length, it was over two-thirds of a football field, but at its widest point, it spanned barely over twenty feet. Inside, space was scarce. Valves, supplies, gauges, pipes, levers, switches, and control buttons twisted and snaked, leaving little room for anything else—or anyone. Connecting the various compartments of the U-boats were the narrowest of bulkhead doors, just large enough in diameter for a man to squeeze through.[11] The crew would need to maneuver with confidence in those confined spaces without losing their cool. The boat's ability to sink American ships lay mostly in fourteen torpedoes, which it could launch from five tubes: four in the front and one in the rear. On its deck, in addition to a con tower, it carried a quadruple 20-mm gun on a lower platform and a twin 20-mm on an upper platform. When the ship sailed on the surface, the crew could use these to fire at both ships and enemy airplanes, which had become a huge threat.[12]

All of this would have been churning in young Wächter's mind—the glory of success, the thousands of ways he and his men could fail. There was one thing that would have been certain, however: by the end of the training in July 1942, Wächter would have been confident that when his men encountered US ships in the open waters of the Atlantic, they would be ready.

CHAPTER 3

FROM THE RUBBLE

Around the same time *Oberleutnant* Wächter was pushing his sailors to the limit in Germany, a different sort of training was just beginning.[1] In Cambridge, Massachusetts, men arrived from all over, separate dots on the United States map coalescing to a single point. They came by train and car and bus. They arrived from the Northeast and the deep South, the heartland and the Pacific West. They carried Bibles and Tanakh, crosses and rosaries. They brought not a desire for battle but a hope to lift weary arms, comfort those in need of comfort, calm emotional storms, and bring compassion to settings where it was most often forgotten. This was the Army Chaplain School, which had just relocated to the campus of Harvard University from Fort Benjamin Harrison, Indiana.* Here, the men would learn their duties and the ways of the military.

Among those arriving was George Lansing Fox. He likely drew little attention the day he arrived on campus. He would have blended into the crowd the way a humble and penitent parishioner might meld into a congregation during church services. He was average height and build and, according to his wife, *just* on the cusp of being handsome.[2]

---

* Harvard, as an institution, played little role in the instruction of chaplains, other than providing the location and dormitories. Over the decades, the chaplain school has been located at a variety of locations and states, often chosen for reasons of convenience and strategy.

He dressed neatly and modestly. Nothing about him hinted of money or extravagance, which was appropriate, because he and his family had none.[3] In the previous nineteen years, he and his bride and children had lived in humble homes, driven barely functional cars, slept on mattresses infested with bedbugs, spent nights outside next to a literal pigsty, and endured trousers and dresses riddled with holes. But in the summer of 1942, he carried a quiet confidence that can come only from knowing one's purpose in life. His square chin, flared nostrils, constant hint of a smile, piercing gaze, and the somewhat unruly eyebrows that he refused to trim added to the general air that George L. Fox was a man who knew who he was.[4]

George L. Fox

Consistent with his orders from the army, he arrived in Cambridge around August 4, 1942. The temperature was pleasant but would climb to the mid-80s as the day wore on.[5] Like almost all of the new chaplains, George would have registered and received directions to head to Perkins Hall, a late-nineteenth-century Georgian Revival style dormitory. Like so much of Harvard's campus, its exterior and corridors were brick. Wide, iron staircases led to the chaplains' rooms. A pay phone booth hid near the building's entrance. In dorm rooms meant for one or two college students, the army had crammed three bunk beds.[6] He would house there with five other chaplains, all potentially from faiths other than his own.

Because the Army Chaplain School was still in a bit of disarray from having recently relocated, the first couple of days, George found himself sweating in a field under the hot sun while a drill sergeant by the name of Harris forced the chaplains to learn marching drills. There were no classes, no trainings, no inspiring speeches—just sheer military discipline, enough to take a ragtag group of men who hadn't marched in years, if ever, and give them a sip of what the regular men endured.

"Right," Sergeant Harris barked. "Left."[7]

The goal of the drills was to put the chaplains in a place where they could survive on the front lines alongside the enlisted men. Strength was critical. Physical and emotional endurance mattered. Spirituality was important, but if the body and mind were neglected, the chaplains would never be in a position to impart transcendent truths to the soldiers. Most of the chaplains carried the rank of first lieutenant, which meant they outranked their drill sergeants. The latter were not impressed. One chaplain recalled his first day enduring the drills George was now going through:

"I don't care what kind of rank you guys have got," the drill sergeant barked. "During drill, you are under my command. I'm the commanding officer, and you'll do everything I say. Is that clear?"

None of the chaplains replied—most likely because they were confused.

The silence lingered for a moment, then the sergeant shouted, "Gentlemen, I don't hear you."

The chaplains barked back in unison, "Yes, sir."

"If I order you to march into some strange places, you follow orders. Is that understood?"

"Yes, sir."

After instructing the men on various techniques, the drill sergeant marched them through campus, past the red brick buildings and the majestic old churches, through the towering maples, and onward toward the Charles River and its inspiring stone bridges. It took the men ten minutes. When they reached the grass next to the river, the drill sergeant ordered the chaplains to stop. They did. The scene was likely beautiful. The river flowed to their left. The sycamores, in all their summer glory, looked down on Memorial Drive.

"Left face," the sergeant commanded.

The men obeyed, now facing the river. The water was about forty feet away.

"Forward march."

The men stepped forward, unified. With each step, the river drew closer. At least some of the men were waiting for an order to change directions—to turn right, left, to halt. Instead, the sergeant maintained his normal marching cadence: "hup two, hup four." At least some of the chaplains wanted to break ranks, but lingering in their minds were the sergeant's earlier orders. Then, without pause, the lower-ranked sergeant marched hundreds of his superiors straight into the Charles River until all of them were standing with water up to their knees. At least one of the chaplains thought the man was out of his mind.

After the men had stood for several moments in the water, the sergeant yelled, "about face." The men spun 180 degrees. He then marched them out of the river and onto the grass.

They looked at him.

He met their gaze, looking amused. "Now, gentlemen," he said, "we will walk until those shoes are dry, and if any of you get corns or blisters, you can sue me."[8] As one chaplain reported, they never did.

Still, just as with many of these new recruits, it's highly likely George's feet ached. So did his back. By the time he began marching on that grassy field in Massachusetts, he was determined, confident, disciplined, exuberant, and utterly out of place. No rational person would have expected him to be there. He was forty-two—decades older than some of the men he would be called to serve and years older than many of the other chaplains.

The life he had led to that point had been that paradoxical cup of sacrifice mixed with physical and worldly pain, which somehow leads to joy and contentment. He had been raised Catholic, but at seventeen, he rebelled against his family and snuck off in search of adventure, in the form of enlisting to fight in World War I. By 1918, twenty-four years before he arrived at Harvard, George had found himself as a first-aid man on the front lines in Europe. He was, quite literally, in the trenches of the western front.

At least two times, he went onto the battlefield to save wounded soldiers. In one case, following a mustard gas attack, he took off his gas mask and gave it to a wounded soldier, suffering damage to his own lungs in the process.[9]

Days before the Great War ended, he hunkered in a stone building in France, struggling to transform it into a makeshift emergency hospital. His focus would have been to care for the men pummeled and choked by German shells and gas. Instead, those shells dropped on the roof over George's head. The blasts rocked the structure to its foundation. And the stones, a building's worth of them, collapsed on top of him. They broke his back. There, in the rubble, he lay unconscious. Later, when he woke in a hospital, aching and confused, the war was over and George had been partially disabled—an injury that would affect him the rest of his life.

He eventually returned to the United States, partially broken in body, plagued by nightmarish dreams, but eager in spirit. Something in the war had planted in him a yearning to serve others. It was an itch he would spend the rest of his life trying to scratch. His purpose was clear: he would attend the Moody Bible Institute in Chicago, get his degree to be a minister, then travel to Africa as a missionary. Nothing would get in his way.[10]

Of course, life often redirects people down unexpected paths. For George, the redirection came in the form of a beautiful young student named Isadore Hurlbut, who had just enrolled at Moody from Vermont. When they first met, neither George nor Isadore wanted to date. Both wanted to focus on their studies and their goals. But she heard his "beautiful tenor voice" one evening early in the school year, and he couldn't keep his eyes off her as they scrubbed dishes together in the college kitchen to pay tuition. Soon he was leaving her small gifts—bunches of grapes, a red apple, a pear, roses—and they walked to class together or along the windswept shores of Lake Michigan.[11]

Both felt the rush that comes with falling in love. They found ex-cuses to be together, experiencing a thrill every time they saw one an-other. Isadore's sister tried to plant seeds of doubt in Isadore, suggesting it would be an impossible challenge to marry a disabled veteran. Isadore allowed those seeds to grow for a short period, but the mere thought of being without George left her in a cloud of anxiety. After Bible study and prayer, Isadore knew: she would spend the rest of her life "trying to help him forget the memories of eighteen months in the front-line trenches in World War I."[12]

They embarked on the path of life together, and their journey was something to behold. One word captures George and Isadore Fox's marriage: *sacrifice*. It was the defining theme of their relationship and their life, and it manifested itself at the very beginning. On their ear-liest dates and even as they drew closer and closer, whatever physical desires they had for one another they set aside until they were married. Even then, on the night of their wedding, Isadore fell terribly ill. It was the belief—at least among some ill-informed men, then and now—that for a marriage to start successfully, the relationship needed to be con-summated on the wedding night, if not much sooner. But when their wedding was over, Isadore lay in bed, with no desire to be touched. George didn't try to wake her. Instead, when she finally stirred the next morning, she found him in a chair by her bed. "I sat here and looked at you all night," he said, "and asked myself over and over, 'Did it really happen? Is she really mine? Or will I awaken to find it all a dream, like many other dreams of recent months?'"[13]

That pattern—George sacrificing for Isadore, she for him, both for their kids, all of them for the parishioners they served—drew them closer together in a fairy-tale romance. Setting aside the allure of money, George and Isadore sought spiritual pursuits immediately and continuously. This was no minor inconvenience. Ministers of the day—and almost all today—received only a pittance on which to survive. So, early in their marriage, when George was working in various jobs to put food on the table and received numerous offers for promotions or to progress in a career in finance, there must have been a temptation to accept. Yet some deep part of them always returned to the ministry. That meant a life of poverty. It resulted in student loans George and Isadore could never repay, driving a used car with no doors and nothing but curtains hanging from the roof to protect them and their children from the elements and the road, evenings when their children moaned from empty stomachs, and living in whatever meager housing the various congregations George served could provide, including basements, infested shacks, and homes without heat or water.[14] But it also meant levels of service, caring, purpose, and tenderness most people aspire to but never achieve. George and Isadore spent their days losing themselves in uplifting others. Week after week, year after year, George trudged in worn shoes to the homes of sick parishioners, prepared sermons, officiated at funerals, tended to widows and widowers, listened to stories from the elderly, raised money for the poor, performed skits to entertain the youth, and counseled people through difficult times. Along the way, he and Isadore welcomed two children into the world. Soon, the entire family was by George's side in his ministry.

Sometimes, the children didn't understand their parents' sacrifice. On one occasion, their son, after he had reached his teenage years, commented that he would never be a minister: "I would not put my family through what we have to go through." But even those times of discontentment almost always yielded to respect. In service, the Foxes found purpose behind their poverty. Others may not have understood it, but when someone once asked George why he had turned down so many lucrative offers from private business, he said simply, "I am paying a small price for my Christian ministry."[15]

Few men have demonstrated more exuberance and enthusiasm in the face of adversity than George. When the Japanese attacked Pearl Harbor on December 7, 1941, he paced the living room. "Now we will go after them!" he said, pounding his fist into an open hand. Almost immediately, he discussed the possibility of signing on as a chaplain.

"I've got to go back," he told Isadore. "I know what these boys will go through."[16]

No rational person would have expected George to enlist. He was already receiving a disability check for his broken back, and the nightmares of toxic German gas choking his lungs still lingered as a driving force in his life—he couldn't swim because something about the gas the Germans used in World War I had instilled in him a debilitating fear of water. In one story, George was visiting a lake with his wife and her family. They all pressured him to get into the water. He refused but eventually relented. After a time, his wife scanned the water and couldn't find George anywhere. Then she noticed a hand, a single fist protruding from the lake's surface. She screamed. Her father dove into the water and pulled him to the surface. When they reached the shore of the lake, George apologized, explaining that it had something to do with the gas attacks.[17] For what he had endured, he had already received the Purple Heart, the Silver Star, and the French Croix de Guerre.* He could have easily faded back and let younger men sign up. By instinct or out of a love for country, he did the opposite. In the months following the United States' entry into World War II, George Fox worked to receive his commission in the Chaplain Corps.

The months before he finally reported to the Army Chaplain School were emotional ones for the Fox family. His and Isadore's son, Wyatt, was a senior in high school and decided to enlist immediately after graduation.[18] Easter Sunday rolled around. It was a pleasant spring day, four months after Pearl Harbor and four months before George would leave for Cambridge. Isadore was in the kitchen preparing dinner. Earlier in the day, George had given a rousing sermon that would have resonated in the grandest halls on earth. As she worked, Isadore heard what sounded like sobbing coming from somewhere in the

---

* The Purple Heart is awarded in the name of the president of the United States to those wounded or killed while serving. The Silver Star is the military's third-highest individual decoration, awarded for valor in combat. The Croix de Guerre can be awarded to either a unit or an individual to recognize heroic deeds in combat.

house. She climbed the stairs and found Wyatt in his room, weeping. Teardrops had spotted the floor. She asked him what was wrong. "That may be the last Easter sermon I may ever hear Dad preach," Wyatt said. On a day of extreme religious significance to a Christian minister and his family, when they celebrated the miracle of the Resurrection, they all knew that, in the years ahead, it was possible that neither Wyatt nor George would ever return home.

In a prophetic moment just a short time later, perhaps with the same sense of wistfulness that had brought Wyatt to tears, Isadore stood in her sister's kitchen, wiping dishes. Through the window, she watched George in the yard, joking with family. "Somehow, I can't see George growing old," she said.

And in June of 1942, the entire family stood on a train platform in Albany, New York. For Wyatt, graduation had come and gone, and now he was headed to war. At a time in life when many in future generations would think of nothing but parties and college and self-interest, Wyatt was hurling himself into battle. Other recruits and their families milled about them. Wyatt reached out to shake George's hand. In that precise moment, the conductor hollered, "All aboard!" The emotion overcame the seventeen-year-old boy, and he sprung into George's arms and kissed him.

With that, father, son, mother, and daughter started down very different and diverging paths. Two months after Wyatt disappeared on that train, George said goodbye to Isadore and their daughter, Mary, and set off for chaplain training.

There in the baking sun on the Harvard campus, George's family likely lingered in his mind. He had given up so much to be here. Would it be worth it?

"Forward march," Sergeant Harris said again.

George didn't hesitate.

CHAPTER 4

A NEW ERA OF HUMANITY

W hile George marched, sweating under the August sun and probably wondering when his training to be an actual military minister would begin, a chaplain with a round face, blue eyes, and dimpled chin struggled somewhere alongside him. He was ten years younger than George, a confident young man with a cocksure smile that left the impression he was always in control of the situation. His name was Alexander Goode, and he was a Jewish rabbi. His history—and that of his people—was decidedly different from George's. If there was a theme to Alex's life, it was independence: of thought, action, and spirit. And that didn't change when he arrived at Army Chaplain School. Looking out at the other chaplains, hundreds of them, he realized he was one of only two Jews.[1] Alex was

Alexander Goode

independent, but it was a trait developed through isolation—years of it.

It began when he was young. Born in Brooklyn, New York, in 1911, Alex never showed any fear of going against the crowd. Some of that undoubtedly stemmed from his lineage. From the day of his birth, his people were different. As a Jewish family in the United States, they represented just a tiny sliver of the overall population. As a devout Jewish family—his father was a faithful rabbi—the Goodes stood apart from everyone outside their immediate family. Their practices, their customs, their beliefs, their sabbath, even their clothes—all of it set them apart from the broader culture in which they lived. And it meant that, often, to stand as a member of the Goode family meant to stand alone.

From the start, this never appeared to bother Alex. He was comfortable going his own way, down new paths, even if they might have been forbidden. One evening, when he was a little boy, his father walked into their house on Myrtle Avenue in Brooklyn, something in his hand. "This year I'm going to have a real garden," he said. Gathering the family around the dining-room table, he showed what he had carried home: little packets of seeds for red cabbage, onions, radishes, leeks, and asparagus. For a family without much money, living in early twentieth-century Brooklyn, this was an exciting prospect.

The next day, after he had finished his work, Rabbi Goode came home ready to garden. He walked to the mantel where he had laid the seeds. Nothing. Curious, he wandered the house. He looked in the cupboards. He searched in the sideboard. They had vanished. "My seeds," he finally announced out loud. "Where are my seeds?"

Alex bounded into the room, a look of enthusiasm on his face. He snagged his dad's hand. "Come with me, Papa. I'll show you." He dragged his father out of the house. There was a narrow path that led to a shed near the edge of their backyard. Right next to it, Alex proudly showed his father a patch of freshly turned dirt. "Your seeds are here,"

Alex said, pointing to the small hole in the ground. "I planted for you so you won't have to work so hard."

The rabbi simply stared, unsure of whether he should punish his son or thank him.

Again and again, Alex showed signs of becoming a man who could stand on his own feet. When he was just a boy, his mother lost him while on a trip to Coney Island. As a large storm approached, she tried to rush the family to the subway. Somehow, Alex got separated. His mother didn't realize it until the train was already underway. Thunderstorms swept in off the Atlantic, pummeling the entire area with lightning, thunder, and an intense downpour. She worried into the evening about her boy, who couldn't have been more than ten years old. Finally, at seven o'clock, he walked into the house, as proud as could be at having navigated the way home all by himself. When the storm had hit, he had simply ducked into a nickelodeon and waited it out.

In time, rather than being a stress to his mother, Alex became a source of relief. He helped prepare the home for the Hanukkah celebrations, earned good grades in school, polished candles, dusted the house, set the table, and contributed each week to the family's celebration of their sabbath.

Change hit suddenly and impactfully. When Alex was a preteen, his father came home one night with an announcement. He had just accepted the invitation to be the rabbi of the synagogue in Georgetown, Washington, DC. The family was moving. For Alex, the shift was of eternal consequence. Away from the confines of a mostly Jewish neighborhood in Brooklyn, he experienced just how unforgiving the United States could be of anyone different. On multiple occasions, he and his brother were robbed or assaulted on their morning walk to school.[2] At school, other boys swore at him. Often, they referred to him only as "Jew Boy." They mocked his kosher food. They invented insulting rhymes about Jews and chanted them to him and his brother.

But Alex found myriad paths to distract himself from his family's isolation. He had the rare gift of being both lighthearted and serious about life. He was drawn to humor and scholarship, but he also found allure in spirituality. When he was eleven years old, on November 11, 1921, three years after the end of World War I, body bearers from the army, navy, and marine corps lifted a casket from the center of the Capitol rotunda in Washington, DC. The identity of the body inside was unknown to all—and the military had taken painstaking efforts to keep it that way. The soldier was to be a symbol, forever, of all those lost in war who could never be identified. In the days leading up to the ceremony, Alex's father had read news stories to the family about it. It was as if a small spark had ignited something in Alex. He needed to see this event.

On the day of the ceremony, soldiers began a procession that would carry the casket from the Capitol to Arlington Cemetery, where the president would then dedicate the Tomb of the Unknown Soldier. Alex's family attended the ceremony at the Capitol. Once the procession left, his family and most spectators returned home.[3] Something in Alex would not let him leave. There was a solemnity to the occasion, a deeper meaning he couldn't escape. He followed on foot, transfixed by what he was witnessing, mesmerized by the sacrifice of this unknown man for his and others' countries. A procession began toward Arlington. It included the Supreme Court, members of both houses of Congress, veterans from the Great War and the Civil War, and the president's cabinet. Alex followed. He trudged along cobblestone streets near downtown DC, then slogged through muddy paths as the procession reached the countryside and the cemetery. For two and a half hours, Alex walked. At Arlington, leaves still clung to the trees, though many were already falling. A blue-silver mist hung in the air, giving everything the sensation of a dream beneath a bright blue sky.[4]

Alex found a patch of grass where he could watch the funeral. The stars and stripes of the American flag seemed ubiquitous, fluttering at every turn, draped over the coffin of the honored soldier. President Harding, joined by General Pershing and dozens of other dignitaries and spectators, streamed into the marble amphitheater. After the ceremony began, for two minutes, they all sat in silence, as did others across the country listening by radio. Silence to honor the unknown soldier. Quiet to ponder the lives lost in war. Stillness to consider how to avoid warfare in the future. The primary message from the ceremony was straightforward: humanity needed to find a way to end warfare forever. The sentiment etched itself into young Alex's heart. Neither he nor anyone else knew what was already brewing in both Germany and Japan, but he walked from that ceremony touched. His parents, too, were in awe that their eleven-year-old boy had been so moved by the ceremony.[5]

Alex's intellectual independence also set him apart. What people often thought about him was that they couldn't keep up with his thoughts. He dominated his father in checkers and found solace in logical, concise thinking.[6] Whenever he had free time, his face was buried in a book. He loved learning as much as he loved boxing and running—and he excelled at all of it. If anyone mocked him for studying so much, he shrugged it off: "How can I know if I don't find out for myself?"[7] He was so good at mathematics and machinery that he would develop his own formulae for solving math problems. Though he hailed from a long line of rabbis, his parents dreamed of him becoming an engineer. It was a fantasy his father projected on him the day he was born.[8] For some reason, building bridges and designing skyscrapers seemed more important to his father than serving a rabbi.

The only problem with his parents' well-laid plans: science and mathematics weren't Alex's only talents. His mind was so fast that perhaps his greatest blessing was that his oratorical skills were just as powerful—he could express complex ideas simply, and with force. This became more and more evident as he moved into his teenage years in DC. And he showed the work ethic to develop those skills. He would spend hours in front of the mirror reciting passages from *Macbeth* and *Hamlet,* developing his intonation, tone, satire, volume, and humor. As a result, he could have excelled at any profession he chose. Years earlier, when his father had announced his new position at Georgetown, he had said, with a smile, "Now Alex can be a senator." It wasn't a crazy dream, given Alex's seemingly unparalleled skill set.

In high school, when he won multiple DC–wide speech contests on democracy and government, Alex likely seemed a perfect candidate for politics, or even law. When he laughed, he filled whatever room he was in with a roar, a talent he inherited from his father, who gained it from his father before him. Raised in a stable home, taught the value of hard work and scholarship, blessed with the gifts of a bright mind and an articulate voice, proud of his family and his heritage, confident about what life offered him—Alexander could have followed almost any number of lucrative paths.

But always he was drawn to deep thinking. It made him different, perhaps from every other boy in his high school. At least, that was how a young girl named Theresa Flax felt. He had spied her in his neighborhood, on walks to school each day, but they met in French class. Whenever he forgot his book, the teacher would suggest he look on with his neighbor. He made sure that neighbor was always Theresa.

She had the kind of smile that made every boy in the school want her but the kind of intellect and high morality that signaled none of them had a chance. Any boy in her circle was there only because she allowed it. Her standards were high, and few could meet them.

Alex was smitten almost immediately. The more time he spent with Theresa, the more he knew she was the woman for him, even in high school. To one of his friends, he said, "That's the girl I'm going to marry."

And the more he mooched off her French book, the more she realized, he might actually rise to the level of someone she would want to share her life. At first, when he asked her on a date, she told him no. But the next day, she gave him a little hope, telling him she was sorry it hadn't worked out.

He tried again, she said yes, and soon they realized they were kindred spirits. Both were popular. Many likely assumed they were obsessed with all the superficial things teenagers care about—he with athletics, she with being social—but the truth soon became clear to each of them. The world around them was deep, like a vast ocean just begging to be explored. And it was worth pondering, it deserved serious study, even while they were having fun. So, as he taught her tennis and she tutored him in dance, they fell in love. Each could have gotten lost forever in the universe of the other's mind. That was where they preferred to linger.

In those intellectual journeys together, Theresa developed into one of several guides for Alex. She helped him realize that his oratorical skills and academic curiosity made him a natural and gifted teacher. She also introduced him to other influential rabbis in the DC area. His interest in spirituality suggested that being a rabbi and a scholar, in the footsteps of his father, made imminent sense. It wasn't his parents' dream, but it was most certainly the right road for Alex. While his father imagined a boy who could play an influential role in building the physical world, Alex had become consumed with the development of people and societies. He would study not engineering but scripture; he would construct not bridges but individuals.

It was a rough time to start a career. By 1930, Alex's boyhood was over. He graduated high school that spring. The world's economies began to collapse a few months later. In some of the Jewish circles in DC, there were various women's groups who would, at times, take an interest in helping the youth in their temples. One group came together to provide Alex a meager scholarship. That, combined with whatever jobs he could scrounge, would allow him to pay for his schooling. He said goodbye to Theresa, fearful someone else would steal away her heart. And with little in his pocket, the Great Depression bearing down, he hitchhiked his way from DC to Cincinnati, Ohio, home of Hebrew Union College and the University of Cincinnati, which are within walking distance of each other.

★ ★ ★

Alex stretched his money, held his own intellectually, worked his way through school, and learned a lot. He developed a love for history, found mentors in his professors at both Hebrew Union and Cincinnati, and thought constantly of Theresa. Every time he returned to DC, he raised the prospect of their marrying. Her answer was always some variation of her first response: "It is too soon to decide these things. Besides, who but a fool would make plans in this time of growing depression?"

Each fall, Alex returned to Cincinnati more determined than ever to marry Theresa. He knew she was right. These were hard times. And, given the daily news of soup lines and suicides, the possibility of losing his scholarship meant he might not be able to provide for her if they did get married.[9] "Still," he told her, "it is a time for trust in God and trust in the nation."[10]

While he studied, he wrote letters to his love. They showed his devotion and his prescience. "Darling," he wrote in 1933, "why don't you write me sometime more intimately about yourself, what your opinion on things is, what you think about, what your interests are, anything at all so that I can feel I am closer to you when I read your letters, something that will reveal you yourself, in all your charm and sweetness, just say anything at all as long as it concerns you and I will love it." He also predicted that the rumblings in Europe and Hitler's rise to power would spell disaster for the Jewish people and, perhaps, for the world.

Remarkably, he wrote it eight years before the United States went to war with Germany, and many years before anyone else was even paying Adolf Hitler much attention. Still, as he looked across the Atlantic to the dangers brewing in Hitler's rhetoric just after he became chancellor of Germany, Alexander saw something disheartening for his fellow Jews: "Perhaps if Hitler read some of [the Bible's] valuable sayings he would be a wiser ruler than he is destined to become. His policy now means utter ruin, not only to the Jews, but to the whole of Germany itself. . . . I see no hope for our kinsmen abroad."[11]

The summer of 1935, Alex returned to Washington. He had

waited long enough. It had been five years—five summers of trying to get Theresa to fall in love with him. The economy was gaining steam. He was finding success in his schooling. Through writing contests and odd jobs, he had purchased an old Oldsmobile. All of Theresa's excuses—they were too young, the Depression was raging, they didn't have enough money, she didn't want to stand in his way—rang hollow to him. "I want you to be a great man," she had told him. "You will be, I'm sure."

"Not without you I won't," Alex said.

At some point over that summer, her sensible side yielded to her feelings for him. She said yes. The wedding followed a few months later, in October. It was a simple affair. In reality, neither Alex nor Theresa wanted a wedding at all. They would have been happy simply eloping and moving on with their lives, but they knew too many people would be disappointed. So, in a modest wedding dress in her family's living room, Theresa wed Alex, her grandfather acting as officiant. Alex's hands shook. Theresa was so excited, she later wouldn't remember a thing her grandfather said. At long last, Alex felt complete.

The next few years were a whirlwind. Alex finished school, rising in scholarly and rabbinical circles. He was offered the rabbinate at Temple Beth Israel in York, Pennsylvania, and at the same time worked on his PhD from Johns Hopkins University in Baltimore. How he and Theresa did it all at once is a testament to their intellect and stamina, but also to their dedication to what they were building. In a short time, they were involved in nearly every civic group imaginable: the Elks Club, Rotary Club, YMCA, Boy Scouts, Social Service Club, University Club, Jewish Organized Charities, United Jewish Appeal, United Jewish Council, B'nai B'rith, and the Board of the Jewish Community Center.[12] Along the way, he developed a sense of the importance of people living alongside one another in peace. He wrote of democracy, he preached of tolerance, he decried the horrors coming out of Europe and the decimation of war.

In December 1939, Alex and Theresa welcomed a little girl into the world. They named her Rosalie. In 1940, he finished his PhD. His congregation was humming. Their future seemed bright. But, in other places around the world, the lights were dimming on the Jewish people. From a distance, Alex looked on with concern.

The United States was amassing an army. This was even before Pearl Harbor. Shadows were forming in the East and the West, a brewing conflict, and President Roosevelt and Congress felt the need to be ready. Serious recruiting and drafting began in September 1940. Watching the threats to his people in Europe, Alex wanted to be a part of it. In January 1941, he applied to be a navy chaplain. Not yet seeing the need, the navy rejected him. A year later, after Pearl Harbor, he received his assignment as a chaplain in the army. His first task: attend Army Chaplain School at Harvard.

CHAPTER 5

NEVER SEEN A JEW

The unconnected paths of George Fox and Alexander Goode now pointed to the same destination on the map. Their shared date with history had begun. But like all the chaplains arriving at Harvard, they needed to overcome the bigotry and turmoil of their fractured country. It would not be easy.

Alexander learned that lesson immediately. When he arrived at Harvard's campus, the red brick buildings contrasting against the luscious trees, he would have noticed one indelible fact: there were almost no other Jews. At Perkins Hall, during the short walk to the divinity school, in their assemblies, on the lawn where they did their drills— Alexander would have observed that, with one exception, he was alone in representing his faith and his people.[1]

For many Jews at the time, the only thing more dangerous than being a minority was being one surrounded by ignorance. The other rabbi, a man named Isaac Klein, noted almost immediately how little the Christian chaplains knew of Judaism.[2] No doubt Alexander felt it as well. Some chaplains tried to show off their "knowledge of Hebrew" by reciting "the first verse of Genesis" in the language. All it showed was how little they actually knew. And that ignorance spread to many other areas regarding the Jewish faith and people. This left Rabbi Klein with a sense of dread. "A void like this can easily be filled with wrong information," he wrote much later. "There was the ever-present danger," he thought during those early days of the Chaplain School, "that people like these, with all the good will in the world, will be ready to believe the wildest notions about the Jews, and would be potential candidates for the ranks of those who considered the Jews the root of all evil."[3]

The unfamiliarity was shocking but perhaps, in some instances, forgivable. One chaplain would have stood out to Alexander at the outset. A hulking man, nearly three hundred pounds and equally tall, Taylor Herbert Minga hailed from Honey Grove, Texas—a small farming town surrounded by miles and miles of nothing. In another life, Minga could have been a football player or a professional wrestler or a bodyguard for the president. But his soul was as gentle as he was large. One day, he approached Alexander and Rabbi Klein and asked in all seriousness if they would be willing to pose in a picture with him.

They agreed.

He intended to send it to the folks back home, he said. It would hang in the hall in his church. "Many of his parishioners had never seen" a Jew.[4]

One relative certainty is that the two rabbis weren't alone in feeling isolated and misunderstood. Nearly every religious belief or practice is difficult for outsiders to comprehend. They come with an elusive depth—eternally significant to the devotee but comically meaningless to the critic. This includes atheism and agnosticism. At the end of the day, nearly everyone there represented differing denominations, unique shades of Protestantism, the individual culture of a particular diocese, the nuanced differences between the various forms of Judaism, not to mention the own complexities of their personal faith.

The bottom line was this: every single one of those men had traveled to Cambridge from a culture that was uniquely his own. And if they were going to buoy the spirits of the men they served, they would need to find a way to connect with each other.

The drills of the first few days helped. Bound by pain, the

discomfort of having to drill together, the chaplains found a common enemy: and it was largely the comfort of the lives they had lived previously. Most of the chaplains were older than the regular soldiers they would serve. One chaplain was even fifty-six. As with so many of the other men there, Rabbi Klein's feet needed regular care. And he spent plenty of time bandaging them after every long march.[5]

But it wasn't just the hard drills under the August sun that would help these men become united in a common cause. The military had been working for decades to try to find chaplains who had a sense of ecumenism. Since World War I, the powers that be had realized that the armed forces were a testing ground for how people of very different faiths could live side by side without tearing each other apart.[6] Across the broader United States, the fact that people of so many different religions had survived without war was as much a product of space as it was of tolerance. The country is big. Before the twentieth century, if one religious group didn't like their neighbors, either they or the other group could move—and they often did, sometimes with the barrel of a gun pointing at their backsides. So the Puritans controlled Massachusetts, Jews found early havens in Rhode Island and Ohio, Catholics in Maryland, Latter-day Saints in the West, the Greek Orthodox in New York City, Native Americans on traditional tribal lands, and other groups in various locales across the country.

Military men, however, did not have the luxury of space. In a trench in France, in bunk beds in the holds of ships on the way to the front, in dormitories during training, in military prisons, as prisoners of war, even in Civilian Public Service camps for conscientious objectors—soldiers faced the daunting task of surviving, even achieving military victory, alongside men of different faiths and levels of devotion.

It was a problem the American military needed to solve, or Hitler's prediction about the United States tearing itself apart from the inside would prove disastrously true. If a soldier was huddled in a bunker in the middle of the night, death imminent, chaplains needed to be able to provide comfort and peace, regardless of the soldier's religious

background. The socialist solution of the Nazis was to murder any dissenters. The same was true of Lenin, Stalin, and the Communists.[7]
If the United States was truly going to fight against that tyranny, it
needed to find a better way.

The military found that better path in recruiting. Converting in-
tolerant people into charitable shepherds was far more difficult than
molding the already tolerant pastor into an effective chaplain. To be
sure, the military needed men so devout they would put their own faith
above even their own lives, men who could speak with the power of an-
gels, who possessed courage under fire but calm in chaos, who reflected
both strength and selflessness. But it also wanted men who were willing
to allow other people to live out their convictions in whatever way
would make them the most effective soldiers. Not surprisingly, then, as
now, such men were few and far between.

Yet they did exist. Hidden away in the churches and synagogues
and cathedrals across the United States were spiritual leaders who
placed the siblinghood of humanity above sectarian differences. The
challenge was separating the wheat from the tares. At first, it wasn't
obvious how to do that. Every denomination offered its own men
as chaplains, which meant if the denomination picked someone
who was incapable of playing well with others, the military would
be stuck with him. To overcome this obstacle, military officials put
together a robust application process. It also allowed interfaith third-
party groups the chance to vet candidates. Chaplains needed to fill
out forms, supply letters of endorsement, and write personal essays on
topics designed to ensure how "fair-minded" they were.[8] The forms,
in particular, were grueling. They ferreted out the potential chaplains'
views on "a) democracy, b) interdenominational cooperation, c) social
problems, d) economic order, e) people of different racial or religious
background, f) pacifism and militarism."[9] A common practice was
to force the would-be chaplains through demanding interviews.[10] It
wasn't enough to be a good preacher or to show devotion only to
those soldiers with which the chaplains agreed. Almost any religious

leader could do that. The United States needed men who could minister even to those soldiers with whom, in another setting, they might
vehemently disagree. For the Christians, this meant men who took
seriously Jesus's admonition in Matthew 5:43–47:

> Ye have heard that it hath been said, Thou shalt love thy
> neighbour, and hate thine enemy.
>
> But I say unto you, Love your enemies, bless them that curse
> you, do good to them that hate you, and pray for them which
> despitefully use you, and persecute you;
>
> That ye may be the children of your Father which is in
> heaven: for he maketh his sun to rise on the evil and on the good,
> and sendeth rain on the just and on the unjust.
>
> For if ye love them which love you, what reward have ye? do
> not even the publicans the same?
>
> And if ye salute your brethren only, what do ye more than
> others? do not even the publicans so?

That the country required such open-mindedness from its chaplains might lead many to think the United States had achieved its
goals to perfection. Unfortunately, this was not so. The multitude of
faith groups that were excluded or shoehorned into religious categories
where they didn't belong was disheartening. In its efforts to create a
fighting machine open to all, the military had targeted America's three
largest faith groups: Protestants, Catholics, and Jews.[11] This was done
in the name of promoting and embracing religious diversity in the
ranks. And for Jews, Catholics, and Protestants, it worked relatively
well. But every other chaplain chosen to serve needed to fit into one
of these categories or could not serve at all. Christian Scientists, for
example, found no true space in the military's tri-faith tent, so they
were labeled as "Protestants," which completely ignored the important theological differences between the two groups. The same was true
of Latter-day Saints and the Eastern Orthodox.[12] Japanese American
Buddhists, meanwhile, were banned altogether.[13] The best champions of American spiritual life—women, who dominated church pews

in most faiths and promoted spirituality in homes across the United States[14]—couldn't serve as chaplains even if they craved the opportunity.[15] And some did.[16] Muslims, Native Americans, Filipino Catholics, atheists—all lacked any formal representation among the chaplain corps.

The United States has always been two countries: its ideal and its reality. Both exist side by side, never fully aligned, one always tailing the other. Still, in the Army Chaplain Corps during and building up to World War II, we see men pressing toward a reality that would be far better than the past, even if it was not yet perfect.

George and Alexander took their seats in the Harvard stadium. Like the other chaplains, they didn't know each other yet, except what they had gleaned in the first few days of marching. The commandant of the chaplain school, Colonel William D. Cleary, who was also a Catholic priest, stood in front of the group. An Irishman from Brooklyn, brilliant, with keen powers of judgment, he would command the chaplains' admiration and respect. His face was long, his eyes kind. In another life, he could have passed for a rural yokel, the kind who sipped lemonade on the porch at sunset and told stories to anyone who would listen. But dressed in his finest military service uniform, he instead carried an air of intimidation. You couldn't help but want to hear what he had to say.

In a powerful tone, he welcomed the chaplains to their training. The initial days of doing nothing but drilling were over. It was time now for the training for which they had actually come. Cleary spoke boldly and directly. His message was straightforward and powerful: the chaplains were headed into war, or, at a minimum, they would be ministering to men headed to battle. The soldiers' needs would be far more serious than anything the chaplains had dealt with among their parishioners. Men would be dying. They would see their brethren die. They would kill others. They would suffer wounds, spiritual and physical and emotional. The chaplains needed to be ready to take care of all those transcendent needs and more. This was a message the chaplains would hear often. On another occasion, a medical officer would instruct a group of chaplains:

> I knew a chaplain once, who, when he went on maneuvews [sic] always dropped back in the line towards the close of the day and somewhere he would find a young soldier who would be having trouble carrying his rifle along with his pack so the chaplain would carry his rifle for him. That, Chaplains, is your job—to carry rifles for the boys and they will not always be of wood and steel but burdens, problems, sins and sorrows.[17]

The chaplains listened intently. This was their moment. If the fatigue of learning how to drill like soldiers had burdened them, it was likely gone now. They were young again; their roads lay before them with the clarity of the path to Egypt Moses saw after he returned from the burning bush. Even the seemingly mindless drills revealed their purpose: through them, the chaplains would come to understand what the regular soldiers endured; by participating in them, they would earn their soldiers' respect.[18]

Cleary continued. His message was as crisp as his hair and uniform. He spoke of the need for devotion. If any message would help the chaplains overcome their religious differences, it was this. He did not direct them to forget their religious variances. That was a path the military could have followed, a demand that the chaplains follow a watered-down version of their faith, embracing only universal messages of kindness and service and charity that nearly all religions and philosophies shared. He could have forbade them from delving deep into the cherished spiritual and theological bases that led each religion, in its unique way, to those endearing common principles. It would have been an easy command, given in the name of unity for the troops.

Instead, he urged the chaplains in the opposite direction. What the troops needed, said Cleary, were men whose own faith and religious commitment were so strong they could share them with others, so strong, the ravages of war would not shatter them. The message resonated.

"*Nemo potest dare quid non habet,*" Cleary said. It was a Latin phrase. "No one can give that which he does not have." If the military's search for "fair-minded" men had left any of the chaplains with doubts about whether they could fully live their religion while serving the army, Cleary's speech erased it. As his comments made clear, in the days that would come, what the world would need were not men who sacrificed the core of who they were just to get along with others. It would need men whose foundation was so solid, they did not feel the need to oppress others.

While Alexander and George listened to the speech, Rabbi Klein, also in the audience, pondered Cleary's words. "It made me think," he later wrote, "of how many of us are purveyors of a religion which we neither practice nor believe in."[19] Going forward, those types of people would not save the world from totalitarianism. What the moment called for were men who could remain absolutely true to themselves while allowing others to do the same. With that message on their minds, the chaplains set into their training with renewed vigor.

But the divisions in society were so severe that inspirational talks weren't enough. The remaining cultural divides and bitterness had to be eliminated with action. Many chaplains took that task upon their own shoulders.

From the beginning, Alexander Goode found himself housed in a room with Rabbi Klein, so the only two Jewish chaplains in a class of one hundred and seventy were housed together. The situation was tight. The rooms were designed to house one or two college students, not six grown men. Along with an Episcopalian, a Presbyterian, a Christian Disciple, and a Baptist, Goode and Klein crammed into three double-decker bunk beds.[20] On the first morning, each man climbed from his bed, shook off the grogginess of sleep, and began his morning devotions. They eyed each other warily, as if they had one eye on their task and one on the men around them.

Finally, Rabbi Klein broke the silence with a suggestion. Rather than "each of us eyeing the other with curiosity," he said, "we should . . . explain to each other what we" are doing.[21]

Everyone else agreed. Within minutes, each was explaining his own religious tradition. The men quickly became friends. For Alexander, the education he received during the day—military law, map reading, defense against chemical warfare, drills and physical exercise, military custom, first aid, proper bed making, army organization, hygiene in the field, ministering to servicemen not of his faith—was surpassed perhaps only by what he learned in his own dorm room. In the evenings, he and his roommates joked and laughed and taught each other about their various religious traditions.

One night, as the six of them shared their time together, a knock rasped at the door. They opened it to see nearly the entire rest of the class lined up outside, a queue of men stretching the length of the hall and beyond. Both Alexander and Rabbi Klein looked on curiously.

The man at the front of the line asked if he could speak to the two rabbis.

Perhaps with some trepidation, Alexander and Klein asked why.

Earlier in the day, the man explained, one of their instructors had given them a difficult assignment. After impressing upon them that a Protestant chaplain was responsible for every man in his unit, despite their religious affiliation, the teacher provided a hypothetical: they were deep in a war zone; there were no rabbis in the ranks. The nearest community with a rabbi was over two hundred miles away. How would they provide religious services to the Jewish soldiers?

Every single chaplain was stumped. They needed to find the answer, so they had come to Alexander and Rabbi Klein for help. The two men met with their classmates, explained some of the basic principles of Judaism, and helped them understand that a rabbi was not necessary to hold services—all they would need to do is find a Jewish soldier among their men who had received an education on what to do, and he could take care of it.[22]

Distrust and curiosity melted into true camaraderie. The men came together. It was a unique time, unprecedented and perhaps never repeated. The men found common ground in a common purpose. Though the days were long and hard, filled with drilling and a return to studiousness, they were never to be forgotten. Decades later, Rabbi Klein would look back on this time with longing. "During the postwar years," he wrote, "I often looked with nostalgia to those days of genuine brotherhood when I compared it with the artificial efforts of cooperation of the interfaith activities that became popular in the later years. Our minds gave compelling reasons for those interfaith projects, but our hearts were not in them. During the war years our hearts and souls were in the common effort to serve the soldiers, all soldiers. The Chaplains' Corps wrote an inspiring chapter in the history of understanding, cooperation and appreciation between the clergy of all faiths."

Perhaps the most important friendship forged for Alexander and George was with each other. How they met at the Army Chaplain School and how much time they spent together are unknown, but it's not surprising they became fast friends. Both shared a kindness and devotion they would have recognized in a kindred spirit. Both longed to serve and comfort soldiers on the front lines. Though their differences in theology were vast, their commonalities bridged that divide. And it was on that bridge where, in the months ahead, they would leave this world together.

There, in the very land where the Puritans were all too quick to banish anyone different from themselves, having overcome the temptation to commit the Puritan Mistake during their training, the chaplains rejoiced. Graduation day arrived. It was September 5, 1942.[23] With some families present, a military band accompanying their gait, the chaplains marched as one into the ceremony. After all the hours and hours of drilling in the hot sun to nothing but the orders of their sergeant, this was a unique opportunity. Their boots rose and fell to the earth with extra zeal, spurred on by the cadence of drum and trumpet. Sergeant Harris looked on with pride. There were speeches, the chaplains received diplomas, but what they really wanted came last: their first assignments.

They arrived in the form of sealed envelopes. Each chaplain received his own.[24] Some tore them open with gusto. Others already seemed to know where they would be going and so were less hurried. All wanted, at long last, to head to the front where they could serve the soldiers. Both George Fox and Alexander Goode received orders to head to North Carolina, Fox to the 411th Coast Artillery Battalion at Camp Davis and Goode to the Army Air Force base at Seymour Johnson Field in Goldsboro.

When the time for departure came, they likely shook hands, perhaps exchanged hugs, and promised they would see each other again, if not after the war, then on the front in Europe or the Pacific. It was a promise that was surprisingly prescient.

After training, reality set in quickly for Alex and Theresa Goode. And it was not pretty—the challenge he would face as a chaplain, bringing people of different faiths together, seemed an impossible task. When Alex arrived for his assignment in Goldsboro, he hunted everywhere for housing that would work for his little family. Theresa and Rosalie would be joining him soon. He couldn't afford a hotel, so he wandered the street grid, knocking on doors.

Nothing was available. With the influx of military personnel at the airfield, Goldsboro didn't have the supply of vacant rooms necessary to house everyone.

Dressed in his army uniform, Alex pressed on. He had no choice. Then he finally saw an opening. He spied a man leaving a house with a suitcase. There was his chance. He marched over, knocked on the door, and waited.

The door opened. A woman stood there, a little girl by her side.

Alex asked if she had a room.

She did, and she would be glad to rent it to him, she said.

"I have a child," Alex said. "A wife and a child." He fumbled for a five-dollar bill he could give her for the deposit.

"That's fine," the woman said.

A surge of relief must have washed over Alex. He handed over the deposit.

Then the little girl noticed something different about Alex's uniform. "What's that?" She pointed to his chaplain's insignia. As part of its efforts to allow Jewish chaplains the ability to serve consistent with their faith, the military had, in 1917, changed its policy. Prior to that, all chaplains wore a cross pin on their lapel to signify their status. But after World War I, Jewish chaplains were authorized to wear a pin of the Ten Commandments under a Star of David.

"I'm a chaplain," Alex said.

"I've never seen that before," the little girl said. "I've always seen a cross."

"Well," Alex said, "I'm a Jewish chaplain."

There was an awkward pause. The woman reached the money back to Alex. She wasn't comfortable renting to Jews.

After his month at Army Chaplain School, where the spirit of ecumenism thrived, Alex must have felt crushed. He was living a stark reminder of the barriers the United States faced in the war. How could a country save the Jews of Europe when it couldn't put its differences aside long enough to ensure people had roofs over their heads? How could Alex be expected to serve soldiers who came from and tolerated a place like Goldsboro? He would have been justified in storming away in a maelstrom of curse words. Instead, he stood there a moment longer. Alex was a thoughtful man; he knew that what likely drove this woman was ignorance and rumor—nothing based in reality. It was unlikely she was driven by any rational hatred . . . just hundreds of years of misinformation and stereotypes and caricatures, the kind people the world over apply when they want to oppress someone.

It's hard to say if it was the look on his face, or something about the spirit he carried with him; perhaps it was just his general reaction, but the woman softened. Without explanation, she said he looked like a nice man, and she should be kind to his wife and child. She let him in. The space was his.[25]

When Alex entered the room, he sat. The ghosts of humanity's past lingered beside him; he drifted with them in the current of thousands of years of history of people refusing to show basic kindness to people with whom they disagreed. The voices of millions, including the Jews across the ocean, were a part of whatever he was feeling in that moment. He likely experienced a vast range of emotions in an instant, but one thing he knew for certain was that his mission was going to be far more difficult than he imagined.

CHAPTER 6

TIDINGS OF
DAYS TO COME

A round the time George and Alex were finishing up their training at Harvard, not too far to the north, in the Strait of Belle Isle, the steamship USAT *Chatham* puffed toward the Atlantic. Its destination: Greenland. It was just after breakfast on August 27, 1942.

The *Chatham* was never supposed to be here. Because of a shortage of military vessels, the United States War Shipping Administration had chartered a number of ships from the Merchants and Miners Transportation Company.[1] Two were sister ships: the *Chatham* and the *Dorchester*. Built just two months apart, they were, for all intents and purposes, identical: same passenger capacity, could haul the same gross tonnage, constructed from the same materials, the exact same dimensions at 350 feet long and 52 feet wide, and traveled at the same snail's pace of just thirteen knots.[2]

For reasons perhaps only providence can provide, the two ships' destinies were linked. The *Chatham* would meet that destiny first.

The passage the vessel navigated was narrow enough that land would have been visible from the ship's deck. On board, 428 civilian passengers, mostly construction workers, joined 10 officers and 96 crewmen. Twenty-eight armed guards manned the ship's multiple

46

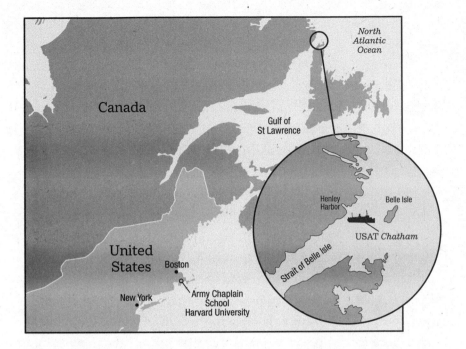

guns,[3] but these were meager protections—she was not designed to be a warship. She was originally an ocean liner, with multiple decks of sea-view cabins and a great black smokestack jutting from her center like a bulky cigar. The War Shipping Administration had chartered her to carry supplies and men—both soldiers and civilian workers—to the front. Hulking, slow, and stuffed with more than twice the number of men she was built for, the *Chatham* was an obese, clunky transport. This would not have been comforting to the men on board. These were troubled waters. And a ship with little protection was as vulnerable as a bleeding sailor swimming through sharks with nothing but a knife.

Ahead of the *Chatham,* the U.S. Coast Guard cutter *Mojave* led the way through the strait. At 240 feet, it was a small ship, far more nimble than the large troop carrier. Its job was to protect the *Chatham* and its passengers—it boasted multiple guns, as well as depth-charge projectors and tracks. If an enemy appeared, the *Mojave* would be ready.

But that was the dilemma: the enemy often didn't appear until it was too late.

Strategically, in 1942, the sea lanes of the North Atlantic became one of the most important parts of the war. As soon as Germany realized the United States intended to intervene following the attack on Pearl Harbor, Reich leaders shifted their sights to the oceans. They knew one thing for certain: Britain's hope stemmed from North America.[4] If they could cut that hope off, they would be able to defeat the Brits, then turn their sights on defeating Russia in the east. The head of the German U-boat fleet, Admiral Karl Dönitz, ordered some of his fleet of U-boats to enter American waters for the first time.[5] He referred to his attack plan as "Operation Drumbeat"—the idea being that the attacks on US interests would be as steadily deadly as the consistent beat of a drum.[6] Like unseen monsters lurking in the depths, the U-boats fanned across the Atlantic Ocean in search of prey. The first official attacks began in January of 1942 across the waters of the Atlantic. The United States was ill-prepared.[7] As it attempted to ship soldiers, workers, and supplies across the ocean to Europe, its vessels fell one by one, victims in a classic horror tale. Too often, many didn't even know their attackers were close until it was too late.

As ships sunk, so did their men. By the time the *Chatham* sailed into the Atlantic on that warm day in August, just seven months after the attacks began, the Germans had destroyed 22 percent of the United States' tanker fleet and had sunk 400 ships in both the Atlantic and the Gulf of Mexico. Over five thousand seamen and passengers had perished—more than double the number of deaths at Pearl Harbor.[8] In the previous few months alone, at least six other ships in the Gulf of St. Lawrence had suffered devastating attacks from unseen U-boats. The North American Allies, to put it simply, were overmatched. Meanwhile, German submarine captains had taken to calling Operation Drumbeat the "Second Happy Time" or the "American Shooting Season."[9]

The men aboard the *Chatham* would have known that beneath them, hidden under the blue and gray sloshing surface of the ocean, the remains of thousands of men just like them scattered the seabed. More important, the enemies who had put them there were still on the hunt, unseen and silent. The surprise of the staggering losses the United States had suffered to that point is that so many of them may have been preventable. As soon as the U-boats picked off the first US ships, Britain offered advice, learned from sad experience: Americans needed their ships to travel in convoys with smaller vessels to protect the larger, slower ones—this had proven to be the most effective way to prevent U-boat attacks. US Navy leaders, however, were slow to accept that, in part out of stubbornness and in part because they simply did not have enough smaller ships to escort the larger vessels.

By the time the *Chatham* churned for Greenland, its men could at least take comfort that the navy was beginning to learn its lessons. With the *Mojave* forging the path ahead, they were not alone. Even if they had only one cutter—not nearly enough—to protect them, it was something. The journey from Newfoundland to Greenland is not a long one, as sea voyages go, but to the men aboard both ships, it could have felt like an eternity.

The morning of August 27, at approximately 8:45 a.m., the two ships neared the end of the strait. The *Chatham* trailed about 1,200 yards behind its escort. Many on board would have eyed the water warily. The weather was warm. Though they were relatively close to land, the ocean here was still deep, and cold, as if it had never really forgiven the winter for its brutality.

These could be lonely moments for crew and passengers on these ships. The sea can be silent beyond the sounds of the ship ploughing through the waves. Other convoys were sailing along a similar route that day, but they were miles behind the *Chatham*. One even had a bomber escort to spy for surfacing U-boats, but the men of the *Chatham* didn't enjoy that luxury. For any on the wooden deck,[10] the vast expanse of the Atlantic Ocean would have come into view. They were heading into its void, hopeful the silence would last.

And then, chaos. The ship transformed into a frenzy of stench, instability, heat, color, and noise. A torpedo struck the starboard side,* just forward of amidships. It punctured the hull and blasted into the engine room with a release of energy roughly equivalent to a crash of a car filled with TNT, a maelstrom of fire and twisted metal. Cold seawater flooded into the space. As soon as it touched the boilers, each larger than a car, their metal ruptured. They belched a mixture of steam and water so hot, it might as well have been fire. Anyone in the room would have been killed instantly. With nowhere else to go, the release of energy hurled the ruptured boilers upward through the interior decks of the ship.[11]

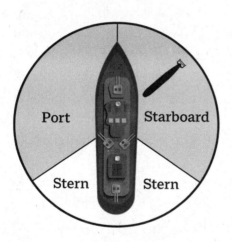

Topside, the entire vessel lurched the moment the torpedo struck. Sailors lunged for any hand- or foothold they could find. Then, metal, smoke, steam, and fire raged from the bowels of the lower decks, snapping through the wood of the upper platform as if it were no more than paper. The *Chatham* immediately listed about twenty-five degrees toward the torpedoed side, while water flooded through the gaping hole. All but two of the lifeboats on the starboard side were destroyed.

Ahead, the *Mojave* immediately changed course. Its men would have kept their focus on first finding the submarine that had fired the torpedo and, second, searching for survivors. In the sea, they looked for the telltale signs of U-boats: a periscope jutting through the waves, an antenna poking from the gray surface, or a wake of any sort. They saw

---

* Because the words *right* and *left* can be confusing and shift depending on which way someone is facing, over time, mariners developed their own terms to avoid any ambiguity when communicating in tense situations. *Starboard* always refers to the front right third of the ship, *port* always refers to the front left third, and *stern* always refers to the rear third.

nothing. Unbeknownst to them, U-517 had immediately plummeted after firing its torpedo. Lost in the darkness of the depths, it would not emerge again until ready for its next hunt.

On board the *Chatham,* word spread among the men that they were to abandon ship.[12] She was sinking. The guns were inoperative. The steering mechanisms had failed. They could not save the ship or its 150 tons of food and supplies, but they could save anyone who hadn't already died from the initial attack. Men scrambled to escape. Luckily, just two days earlier, the captain had run a drill, ordering all men to practice abandoning ship. Each man knew precisely which lifeboat was his.[13] In all, they filled twelve boats and nine rafts. Once in them, all they could do was watch as the sea swallowed the *Chatham* whole. It took only thirty minutes, and the entire vessel was gone, as if it had never existed.

Some of the men in the boats rowed their way to shore. The *Mojave* picked up others. As the day waned on, other ships arrived and helped rescue even more. Airplanes circled over them. They sent signals to rescue ships. All in all, only fourteen men died in the attack—seven crewmen and seven passengers.[14]

But this was no time for celebration. The survivors' crewmates were dead. More important, the German onslaught was showing no signs of slowing. The passage across the North Atlantic to Greenland, the British Isles, and the front in Europe was as treacherous as it had ever been. Deep beneath them, U-boats were still circling, lurking in the depths for their next target. The German drum was still beating, thrumming and thrumming, a constant threat.

CHAPTER 7

PREPARATION OF AN ANSWER TO PRAYERS

When news of the *Chatham*'s sinking reached the ears of Petty Officer First Class Charles Walter David Jr., it would not have been surprising. Another day, another ship torpedoed by the Nazis. That had become the norm of the war. Charles was on board a different coast guard cutter, known as the *Comanche*. Almost identical to the *Mojave,* it was stationed off the coast of Greenland, churning through icy waters, preparing for the *Chatham* and its men, who would never make it.

Charles could have been in any of a number of places at the precise moment he heard the news. As a petty officer, he may have been serving meals to the *Comanche*'s officers. Or he may have been in the kitchen, getting food ready. He was a tall man, with an uncanny strength, but his roles were limited. Charles stood out for a number of reasons: his height, his love of music, his ability to play the harmonica, the way he smiled and put people at ease almost the second they met him, his family's unique heritage in the Caribbean, his natural leadership abilities and charisma. But of the thousands of little traits and characteristics that made him who he was, at that time, as far as the military was concerned, *one* affected his responsibilities more than anything else: his brown skin.

Charles entered the world in New York City on June 20, 1918, the first in his family to be born in the United States. His father, Charles Sr., had been a carpenter in Antigua, a dot on the Caribbean map east of Puerto Rico and just fifty-four miles in circumference. His mother, Elizabeth, was likely a housewife, and may have been pregnant with Charles Jr. when she and her husband made the journey from Antigua to the United States.

Wedding day photo of
Charles W. David Jr.

The tiny island may have been a pinprick on a map, but it was an important one—some might argue the most important island in the British empire during the colonial period. It was Antigua that had become, on the backs of African slaves, the cornerstone of Britain's sugar industry, and it was on that tiny island that Admiral Horatio Nelson established England's temporary dominance of the Caribbean Sea.[1]

Like many from those island nations who immigrated to New York's shores in those days, Charles Sr. was a skilled man with a marketable talent.[2] He had developed a gift for carpentry. Husky, thick, and muscular, with a booming voice and melodic accent, he carried the type of presence that demanded respect.[3] We don't know why he moved his family to New York, but if broader history is any guide, there were several motivations: by the early 1900s, the Antiguan sugar industry had collapsed, the population in the country had soared after the abolition of slavery seventy years earlier, and many who had left to Central America to work on jobs like the Panama Canal had returned home.[4] In short, by the 1910s, jobs were scarce but demand for them was high. Those like Charles Sr., who had the talent, took control of their destinies and traveled abroad in search of a place where they could build a better life. The myth of New York City beckoned to them the same way it called to immigrants from various countries in Europe.

They set sail, left their families and the heat of the Caribbean behind, floated past the determined visage of the Statue of Liberty, walked through the lines on Ellis Island, and began to build their lives.* It appears Charles Sr. and Elizabeth lived in East Harlem for a time,[5] but they eventually settled into a neighborhood in the Northeast Bronx, which so many other people from the Caribbean called home.[6]

There, they raised Charles Jr. Though they had thick Antiguan accents and likely felt out of place in the cold and culture of the Northeast, Charles Jr.'s childhood reflected what was quickly becoming the quintessential experience of American youth: he attended Cooper Junior High School, Benjamin Franklin Junior High School, and the Gompers Industrial High School. His mother and father instilled in him a sense of responsibility, and in high school, he learned both carpentry and cabinetmaking. He loved basketball and swimming, although his talent and prowess in the latter came almost by accident— when he was just a little boy, he and some friends were playing on a pier. One of the other boys pushed him off as a joke. When he hit the water, he realized he had one choice: swim or die. Rather than panic, he figured out how to keep himself afloat.[7]

From that point on, his strength as a swimmer was unquestioned. And the traits he inherited from his parents—determination to thrive despite hardship, to achieve self-reliance no matter the circumstances— shaped who he would become in adulthood. When world events would later drag him into the largest war in human history, that irrepressible determination would define him.

★ ★ ★

---

* There is also some evidence that the Davids may have traveled north to Canada first, then moved south into the United States immediately after.

During Charles's youth, the family was involved in the community, especially St. David's Episcopal Church, where Charles Sr. put his carpentry skills to work and built the pews for the entire congregation.[8] They met and connected with other families from various parts of the Caribbean and slowly but surely melted into the pot the United States was becoming. In time, they welcomed another boy into the family, then a little girl. Back in Antigua, two of Charles Sr.'s sisters had established themselves as influential educators, but his brother and family, along with another sister, had also made the arduous journey to the Bronx. The family was expanding. The future looked bright.

Then, tragedy struck. Not much is known about Charles Jr.'s mother, Elizabeth. Records suggest she had always stayed home as a housewife to care for Charles, his two siblings, and some of his cousins. For reasons that are unclear, she passed away suddenly not too long after the birth of their daughter. Sometime during or immediately before the Great Depression, with her husband trying to establish himself in a foreign land, she slipped out of this world, leaving behind three children and the entire David family without its matriarch.

This must have been devastating for both Charles and his father. But his mother's passing would have taught Charles early in life the necessity of perseverance through even the darkest tragedies. The family survived. Charles's aunt and uncle and cousins were still there, providing Charles the community he needed. Aunt Rhoda became a beacon of strength and would later become an influential matriarch to many. Young Charles developed his cabinetmaking and carpentry skills, no doubt apprenticing under his dad. He fell in love with music, both singing and playing the harmonica. He honed his swimming strengths. And by the time he graduated from high school, he had a means of taking care of himself and his future family.

★ ★ ★

That family came into reality in an unexpected way.

In the same community with Charles was a young woman named

Kathleen Wiggins. She was three years his junior, the second of five children. Her father had come from Barbados, her mother from the Guianas region of South America. In so many ways, her life mirrored Charles's. Like his parents, hers were the ancestors of slaves torn from Africa who had achieved freedom in the Caribbean. Like the Davids, they chose to immigrate to the United States in search of a better life for themselves and their posterity. As with Charles, Kathleen's mother passed away unexpectedly, when Kathleen was just sixteen years old.

With the economy still hobbled by the Great Depression, times were tough. Jobs, if people could find them, were unstable. Kathleen's father wasn't in a position to provide for Kathleen and all of her siblings, so she and her older sister needed to find a way to survive. Their aunt helped for a season but could only do so much. This was an era when many men couldn't find paying work; most women weren't even considered. Kathleen and her older sister, who was seventeen, lived together, but in one of the largest cities in the world, they seemed alone, and every possible door seemed closed.

Kathleen was a determined woman with a fighter's spirit, as thoughtful as she was beautiful. She would sometimes pause before speaking, long enough to give a conscientious and nuanced answer.[9] And she joined the Harlem Labor Union at the age of sixteen, believing they could help her people. Intelligent and capable, in a different time and place, she could have achieved anything. But there, at that time, she needed help.

The lifeline came from an unexpected source: Charles W. David Jr. Their families knew each other. The Northeast Bronx was close-knit, a tapestry of families from various island nations who lifted and helped each other when needs arose. Someone suggested that Charles and Kathleen should marry—that would give her some stability, someone to protect and care for her.

Years later, she would reminisce that she wasn't happy about this idea, that it felt more like an arranged marriage than anything else, but it was her only option. Charles may have had the same hesitancy—out of nowhere, he suddenly faced having someone else to provide for. Despite the worries, they wed in 1939. She was only nineteen, he twenty-two.

Almost immediately, she was expecting, something she never expected. And in 1940, she gave birth to a little boy, whom she and Charles named Neil Adrian.

The couple moved to Harlem, to a brownstone in a row of similar-looking buildings. In a small rented room at the top of a narrow staircase, where they had a bed, a bureau with drawers, a small refrigerator, and a few other odds and ends, they started the process of building a life.[10] The situation wasn't ideal, but it was the hand they had been dealt. It turned out that Kathleen had an innate love for music as well, and some talent as a singer and dancer to go with it. Whether she and Charles discovered that shared love during their time together is unclear. Perhaps, but perhaps not, since they dedicated so much energy just to survival. They raised Neil together, while Charles did his best to provide for the family.

The country had yet to recover from the Depression. Though their marriage wasn't born out of the traditional romance that luxury allows, Charles knew he needed to provide for his wife and son. It was a responsibility ingrained in him by his father, by a family and cultural heritage of self-reliance and can-do toughness.

To that end, he turned to the military. In most respects, it was still segregated. Only a few of the branches allowed white and Black soldiers to serve together. The coast guard was one of them. Even then, it placed restrictions on Black men, refusing to grant them positions that would allow them to rise in the ranks. Charles was undeterred; paying work was paying work. On March 6, 1941, in New York, he enlisted.[11] Though it would take him away, the job would give him the money he needed to provide for Kathleen and Neil.

While Charles was taking on the world, Kathleen took on the battles of New York City. She joined in a boycott against two major private bus lines that refused to hire Black bus drivers. With Neil by her side, she settled into life on her own.

After the attack on Pearl Harbor later that year, Charles was assigned to the United States Coast Guard cutter *Comanche*. The possibility of death loomed large. Charles embraced this. One time, perhaps when he was in port on leave, he told his wife and son, "I have to die someday, and I can't think of a better way."[12]

The *Comanche* had barely entered the war before Charles made an unlikely friend. Wearing a white waiter's shirt with a banded collar, he cooked and prepared food for the other men. It was beneath his natural skills—as future events would prove—but it placed him in a room across from one of the sonar stations.

One day, he heard a sound, a sweet sensation that invoked memories of home: a saxophone. He followed the notes the way someone might follow the scent of a lovely meal floating on the air.

Out his door and across the hall, he found twenty-year-old guardsman Dick Swanson sitting in the sonar room and belting out the tunes on a saxophone. A saxophone—it would have caused Charles to do a double take; it didn't belong here any more than a pool table would have. Coast guard cutters were not large, but somehow this boy had smuggled it on. And he was a boy—he looked as handsome as he did innocent, reflecting precisely what he was: a recent high school graduate with almost no real-world experience. His smile was as charming and disarming as Charles's own.

Charles introduced himself, perhaps a little wary. Not everyone in the coast guard was friendly to him, especially some of the enlisted men from the Southern states.

Swanson was thrilled Charles had come in. The conversation came easily, mostly about music. Turned out that Swanson was from Nebraska and loved playing his saxophone so much, he couldn't go without it. Anytime he wasn't on duty, he would sit in his office and belt out whatever tunes came to mind.

Charles flashed both his smile and his harmonica.

Swanson was thrilled to have a playing buddy. Soon, whenever they were both off duty, Charles was in Swanson's office, where they made music together, Swanson on the sax, Charles on the harmonica or vocals. Others on board would stand outside and line the hall, enjoying the music, which they eventually called the "*Comanche* Blues."[13]

In time, the two men were nearly inseparable. For all of 1942 and into 1943, their friendship sustained them. When they pulled into most ports, they would do their best to eat together. When they encountered restaurants that wouldn't serve men with brown skin, Swanson refused to leave his friend's side. They would hunt until they found someplace that would, always determined to make it work. Charles returned the favor. When they had ported in New York, Swanson one time suggested they head up to Harlem, where they could hopefully hear some real blues musicians perform. Charles told him it wasn't a good idea—Swanson might not be welcome in certain places.[14] Still, they were partners as much as they could be.

But restaurants weren't the only places Charles met resistance. He rose from being a cook to a steward's mate to a petty officer, where his duty was to serve the captain and other officers on the ship rather than the enlisted men. This wasn't a bad job—he spent time in the officers' dining room rather than the mess hall; the plates were glass, silverware clinked against fine glasses, and wooden chairs eased up against a cloth-covered table. Although there was no escaping they were on board a very small, metal ship with its pipes and HVAC and fluorescent bulbs, there were even paintings on the walls of various ships and cutters. As far as assignments went, it was a cushy one. But the coast guard still would not let him progress beyond being the fifth-lowest-ranking person on board.

Charles also met defiance from some of the white crew, mostly those from the Southern United States. They often gave him a hard time. More than once, they hurled racial epithets at him, including the most offensive word of all. Their attitudes were "hateful," according to Swanson.[15] To him, the use of the N-word, as well as their overall attitude, was a shock. Having come from the Midwest, he hadn't heard it, had never experienced the explicit racism still so rampant in the states that made up the defeated Confederacy. This was, in the racial sphere, the Puritan Mistake refusing to die.

But the insults seemed to bounce off Charles like bullets off steel. Perhaps it was from having lived in the city all his life, or just his generally upbeat disposition, or a determination not to allow the ignorance of others or the ghosts of the past to control his future; whatever it was, Charles regularly bounded into Swanson's office, harmonica in hand, ready to play. "But he'd always come in with a big smile," Swanson would later remember. "Big grin. We became real good friends."[16]

Charles was as determined as he was friendly, with a smile that suggested an easy laugh. Crewmates would later recall him as a giant, some Herculean figure, almost mythically large. And later articles would describe him as over six feet tall and weighing nearly 220 pounds. It was all legend—created, perhaps, by memories of the acts he would later perform. In reality, he stood just around six feet and didn't weigh more than 175 pounds.[17] He seemed to have inherited his father's height, but not his muscular build. On his wedding day, he looked as skinny as the young swimmer he was.

But what he did boast would prove more crucial in the days ahead: a strength of character few could match.

CHAPTER 8

LOST ON A MOUNTAINTOP

Thousands of miles to the south, just after Alexander and George had forged their friendship at Harvard and a week or two after the ocean had swallowed the *Chatham,* Clark Vandersall Poling stood in the sweltering humidity and heat of Camp Shelby, Mississippi, and seethed. He was frustrated. He had been waiting with anxious anticipation for a moment that was seemingly never going to come. Whether he liked it or not, he would have been sweating. That's just what a Yankee like Clark did in Mississippi that time of year, when the average temperatures rose into the nineties. The moment he had been hoping for—an assignment to go overseas with the men he had been serving the past couple of months—had just evaporated like a dream. He had expected an order to go with them. Off to the front. He had been their chaplain now for two months—the only one any of the young boys had ever known.

Instead, when the 131st received their assignment to move out, Clark was ordered to stay behind. He would be transferred to a different unit.

He went back to his apartment. Unlike many chaplains, he was fortunate to have his wife and child with him, at least until he was finally ordered to the front. He shared the news. His bride, Betty, was sad for

61

her husband but secretly glad. This was more time they would get to spend together, cherished moments before a separation that seemed as inevitable as the Southern humidity. Looking at Clark—his warm smile, his handsome features—Betty could feel his disappointment. He so badly wanted to serve. It was who he was.[1]

How he came to be that way began thirty-two years earlier. Clark Poling entered the world at home in Columbus, Ohio, on August 7, 1910, a bright red storm of coughing and hacking.[2] His father, Daniel, who would one day become a famed minister and writer, was studying for a PhD at Ohio State University. His mother, Susan, had contracted whooping cough just before his birth, and it left her lungs permanently damaged. It also spread to her baby. In those early days, before the vaccines were developed, no one knew if Clark would survive the cough. Prior to 1940, roughly 200,000 children in the United States contracted the disease every year. Of those, nearly 9,000 died.[3]

Little and chubby, Clark spasmed from the phlegm in his lungs, struggling so much to breathe that sometimes his face turned purple. Again and again, his parents wrapped him in cotton and soft bandages from his neck to his waist, hoping it might have some positive effect. They even tried treatments that today might seem insane: hanging him by his toes so the phlegm could clear from his throat. During those long nights and days, with both mother and child ill, parents desperate and trying anything, science decades behind any sort of treatment or vaccine, the question of whether Clark would survive into boyhood rested on the edge of a knife.

But survive he did. Even as his mother continued to deal with the disease's lingering aftereffects, Clark progressed from baby to boy. By the time he was two, the family felt secure enough to move to a different house in Columbus, where Susan gave birth to another child, Clark's sister Mary.

From almost the moment he could talk, Clark was arguing with someone. His father recalls the boy bouncing about, debating father, mother, and older brother—anyone who would take him on. This, coupled with an unyielding independence, seemed to be his defining trait. As the family moved from city to city, following Minister Poling's ever-changing assignments, Clark spent his days hunting for the last word in every conversation. Nothing stopped him. Where spanking seemed to correct his older brother Daniel's course, it merely encouraged Clark to be more obstinate. Even sleep had no effect. As his father recalled, "He never lost a debate; that is, he never acknowledged defeat and when *you* went to sleep *he* was still talking."[4]

When he was just eight, tragedy struck. The family had moved to the Boston suburbs of Brookline and Auburndale, where his father had taken positions as a minister. Then, war. Before it became known as World War I, it knew many other names: the Great War, the War of the Nations, and the War to End All Wars. Clark's father was called to duty and shipped off to France. In an old white house in Auburndale, Clark stayed behind with Daniel, his little sisters Mary and Jane, and his ailing mother. No one knew she was sick. She had kept her pain a secret. But the whooping cough that had plagued her at the time of Clark's birth had left lasting damage to her lungs.

Clark's father survived the war. His mother lasted only a short time longer. In 1918, with her husband home and excited to resume their life together, she passed away. These were dark days for the Poling family. To have survived the deadliest war humanity had ever known to that point, only to come home to a sick wife who died within the year, must have torn Daniel's heart from him. For Clark, the memory of his sweet mother never diminished. Years later, he penned this poem, a part of which reads:

LITTLE MOTHER

Here, my mother,
"Pretty Head,"
Is a rose
A deep dark red.
You are white.

Look, dear Mother,
At the cloud,
It would make
A ghostly shroud
Soft and white.

Gentle Mother,
May I ask
Why your face
Is like a mask,
Still and white . . .

Dearest Mother,
Can't you hear,
Don't you see
That I am near?
You're so white.

Oh! My mother,
You are dead;
Lying there
Upon your bed,
Cold and white!

Mother! Mother!
Lift your head;
Rise again
From your bed,
White, all white.

Gently falling
Comes the snow;
All is still,

The clouds are low,
Cold and white.

Weeping, weeping,
Soft I tread
On the snow
By Mother's bed,
Cold and white.[5]

For a time, the Poling family descended into darkness. Family members and relatives nurtured them. Clark no doubt grappled with the meaning of death, with questions that torment every human being at some point: where do we go when we die? Is there life after this one? Would he ever see his mother again? How could he remember her and keep her memory vibrant? Those questions were thrust upon him at a much earlier age than many, yet, at eight years old, his brain was just developing the sophistication to think about them, perhaps for the first time.

The sun eventually penetrated the Poling family's mists of darkness. The family moved several more times in Massachusetts and New York, Clark's father fell in love again and remarried, and Clark started prep school. Clark's world was changing.

One thing never shifted: Clark's insatiable appetite for debate. He was a one-kid controversy. If he didn't have a person to argue with, he would go out and find someone. It drove his family to exhaustion. On one occasion, a preadolescent Clark argued with his stepmother about a topic now long forgotten. They were in a white house in Hastings-on-Hudson, a village in Westchester County that overlooked the Hudson River, just north of New York City.[6]

Late into the night they debated, back and forth, like boxers exchanging verbal jabs. Though she was decades older, Clark's mind was so versatile, he always had another point to make. Finally, after he had driven the poor woman to the brink of collapse, he said, "All right, Mother, you win!"

This had never happened before. His stepmom was so fatigued, she didn't even process the miraculous nature of what had just occurred. She went to bed, content she had finally changed the boy's mind about something.

The next morning, the family gathered around the breakfast table. Clark's first words were: "Mother, I've got to be honest with you. You didn't get anywhere with that proposition last night. But I just got so sorry for you I had to let you go to bed—now, it's like this . . ."

And he pushed the argument forward.

On another occasion, he strutted up to his dad and said, "Daddy, when I become a father, I'll show you how it should be done."

His dad, who was as handsome as he was intelligent, looked on in amusement.

"I've been observing," Clark continued. "I wish I could do something to show you right now, but you won't listen to me."

His dad perceived immediately what was happening. Clark wanted to debate, to argue, to feed that insatiable beast inside him. Too busy with his own work, the elder Poling leaned in and said, "Listen, man, I have to earn a salary to put coal into your furnace and shoes on your feet, and you'd keep me here talking until next Christmas."

An embarrassed grin cracked Clark's face. He shook his head. "Well, it might be worth your while—you'd learn a lot!"

It seemed that, more than anything else, Clark Poling as a boy needed stimuli—lots. He found them in intense debate, but he sought them in other places as well, and the outcomes were rarely positive. After his father had wallpapered and painted a room, Clark colored the entire space with crayons, forcing his dad to redo the work. When his dad chastised him about it, he hid his head under his blankets, only to peek out long enough to wink, which resulted in a much sterner punishment. To stay up late, Clark offered bedtime prayers that listed every person the family knew (and some they didn't, including Santa Claus) just so he wouldn't have to crawl into bed. He regularly got into mischief and fought with his brother Daniel. In church, with their father leading the congregation from the altar, the two boys egged each other on in gymnastics routines at the front of the pews, distracting the entire congregation. At home, Daniel and Clark once took a pound of butter (the family's entire supply), smothered the kitchen floor in it, then swung each other around in a sliding game.[7]

Their crowning achievement became a classic tale in Auburndale, Massachusetts. When their father was away in World War I and their mother was secretly sick, Daniel and Clark found a mangled, dead skunk in the middle of the road. The poor animal had been mauled by a car. Somehow, they managed to string the body up and drag it. Its stench was as repugnant as if it were still alive and spraying every enemy in sight. The evening settled in, growing darker. The two boys hauled their find up and down the streets of the village. Everyone who came near could smell it. The youngsters traipsed past nearly every house in town. After they had stunk up the entire community, they brought the carcass home. Apparently after considering their options—or perhaps after no thought at all—they deposited it in their next-door neighbor's yard and headed home. When the adults finally caught the boys, they forced them to bury the skunk and their clothes. As Clark's dad recalled, "they paid and paid again and yet again for their sin."

The conversion of Clark Vandersall Poling from belligerent youth to devoted minister began in the early 1920s, with the Quakers, and a panicked night on a dark mountain. For his middle and high school years, Clark attended Oakwood, a Quaker-run boarding school not too far to the north from where his family then lived. There, he found a mentor in the school's headmaster, a man named William Reagan, who taught Clark the importance of both spirituality and knowledge. Very quickly, Clark found himself immersed in lessons of science and art, scripture and history. He gobbled it up. His mind turned to things of philosophy, and he yearned to find himself.

After his first year, the boy had adopted and made part of his inner being the Quakers' teachings on peace and the commonality of all humanity. But Clark's transition was a process, not an instantaneous transformation. During the winter vacation after his first semester, when the family had all gathered to celebrate the Christmas season, Clark and Daniel found themselves in the living room. Clark shared his thoughts, apparently for far too long, on the importance of peace and brotherhood.

Daniel was fed up. "That's soft stuff," he said.

Clark immediately charged and dove into Daniel's stomach. They grappled, loudly enough that other people in the house could hear the noise.

Daniel got the upper hand, somehow knocked Clark onto his back, then sat on his chest. He couldn't hold it. Just as Clark was about to thrust his brother off, their father burst into the room, his face half shaven. He ripped the two away from one another. Though he listened in anger to an explanation from the two boys as to why they were wrestling, he couldn't help but notice the humor in Clark's fighting to defend his faith in pacifism.

Despite the starts and stops, Clark grew into his own man. With the pacifistic Quakers at Oakwood as a starting point, Clark developed his own philosophies on war, the commonality of humanity, and the importance of having love toward everyone, even his enemies. He was not extreme. Though he abhorred war and felt very little could come from it, he recognized that at times it was necessary. He became a leader at the school and an exemplar of what it meant to thrive there. As a student, he excelled in his English classes and did moderately well in others. But in terms of balance, in succeeding across multiple areas of life, he was a model. Years later, a student who never even met him wrote that "Clark Poling was an Oakwood tradition, and to be your best and finest was to be like him."[8] He became a star athlete with an unconquerable spirit, even though his build was far slighter than the physiques of his competititors on the football field.

The special relationship he developed with the headmaster deepened. Reagan had suffered a tragic loss: the death of his little boy.[9] By then, Clark had been elected the student-body president.

One day, during a period of grieving that was yet to end, Reagan returned to his office at the school. Judging from his letters, the time appeared to be in the evening, when no one would be around. His heart wasn't in it. He simply wanted to get acquainted with his workplace again. He held no desire to see or talk with anyone. Under normal circumstances, he had all the appearances of a confident man, with neatly cut hair and a sharp part, eyes that could be both caring and stern, and high cheekbones that left the impression he was always just a twitch away from cracking a smile.[10] On that night, however, it's easy to imagine the weight of the world weighing him down.

As he gathered his things and started back for his house, he found Clark outside his office door.

Reagan's initial reaction was that he didn't want to talk to the boy, not about school, not about the students, not about anything.

Clark gently grabbed Reagan's arm and said only, "I have waited to walk home with you, Mr. Reagan." Nothing else.

They exited the school and strode together. Clark never said a word. From the record we have, the principal didn't either. When they reached Reagan's house, Clark held open the door for his mentor and said, "Good night, Mr. Reagan."

With that, the headmaster entered his home, lifted by another's presence. "I could have faced anything after that walk with him," he later wrote. The boy who had always insisted on having the last word throughout his childhood had finally learned when to speak and when to let his presence speak for him.

In his own family, Clark transitioned from being a "trial"[11] for his parents to becoming truly conversant with his well-read father. Sitting on the deck of their home, in the family room, on hikes, during long walks through town—father and son shared and spoke about their deepest convictions. One thing became clear: the rigidity of Clark's youth had given way to nuance. He saw room for both spiritualism and the practical sciences. He cherished his own faith but was wary of absolutist positions. He was certain in the paths he followed but always left room for course correction.[12]

After Clark transitioned from Oakwood to Hope College in Holland, Michigan, he found the next step in the journey of his life. In the spring of 1931, when he was twenty-one years old, his father took a trip to Detroit to deliver a number of sermons. Clark drove across the state to see his dad. They spent the day together, enjoyed a hearty steak, took in a movie, and saw a doctor for an injury Clark had suffered to his wrist on the football field. Throughout the day, Clark was unusually silent. His dad didn't push him.

That night, in a small hotel room in the city, Clark transformed into a veritable fount of conversation. Though his dad was tired and wanted nothing more than to sleep, he let his son roam from topic to topic. Eventually, a quiet settled over the room. They lay in two twin beds, a tiny table between them. As the silence stretched on, something told the minister that it was stuffed with meaning. Though he had been sleepy, that intuition kept him from drifting off.

Finally, Clark reached across the two beds, touched his dad, and said, "Daddy, I'm going to preach; I've got to do it!"

A shock passed through Clark's dad. For years, given Clark's track record, the family had assumed he would become a lawyer. He seemed born for it, and his parents were fine with that path. But the moment Clark revealed his new plans, his dad felt the warmth of fulfillment, as if his own life choices were being validated by his son. They spoke late into the night, sharing their thoughts and feelings. Only when the stars had made their long journey across the sky, the glow of dawn approaching, did they drift off to sleep together.

How Clark reached his decision to become a minister may be lost to history. He received no pressure from anyone, including his parents or grandparents. Even if they had pressured him, it wouldn't have mattered. Always, his dad wrote, "he was God's man and his own, and neither from his father nor any other did he take his convictions and conclusions."[13] But on a dangerous night a short time later, he seemed to have confirmed his choice.

Around the time Clark was in his high school years, his parents had bought an old home near Deering, New Hampshire, they called the "Long House." A gargantuan house built around the time of the American Revolution, it probably had more rooms needing repair than were livable, but it became a sanctuary of sorts for the Poling family. With granite-studded hills, open fields, and even ancient cemeteries with lichen- and moss-covered gravestones where Clark would wander and explore and think, the property was special to everyone in the family.

One summer afternoon, while Clark was on college break at Long House, he found his father and said, "Dad, I'm going up to Wolf Hill tonight after dinner, and I'll not be back." He seemed to pause, then added, "Well, for some time."

Wolf Hill was a well-known rise in the area. It carried its own dangers. Though not high compared to the mountain ranges in the western United States, it still claimed plenty of granite cliffs and crags, boulders and ravenous wildlife.

"Dad," Clark said, "don't worry about me and keep Mother from worrying. My return is indefinite."

His father looked on, somewhat bewildered.

Clark grinned. "I may stay twenty-four hours or longer, but there are some things I want to settle, Dad, and I hope I won't be interrupted. I wouldn't have said anything, but all of you would have been anxious about me. Of course, you'll understand—and help me?"

His father later said he didn't understand, at least not fully. But he also knew he should help his son, that this was part of his spiritual growth. He was seeking something, and this journey to the mountaintop was part of that search.

That evening, after dinner, Clark packed up his blanket and canteen. His stepmom tried to get him to take some sandwiches, but he refused. Off he went into the settling darkness. It was a clear night. Out there in the woods, with no cities to pollute them, the stars decorated the black tapestry of the sky in milky patterns and endless combinations of constellations. Mr. and Mrs. Poling settled into it and eventually drifted off to sleep. Their worries about Clark were in their infancy, zygotes sparking to life, mostly in his stepmom.

By the next day, those concerns began to mature. The weather was perfect: "one of New England's finest" days, Clark's dad recalled. Still, after the sun dropped below the trees and the evening shadows grew long, Clark's stepmom had waited long enough. She whispered to her husband the fears that were now boiling in him as well. These were thick forests—the kind that struck such wonder in the Puritans when they had first arrived that they invented all manner of fantastical stories about what lurked in their murky depths. It would have been easy for Clark to break his leg. Or to have fallen off a cliff.

As evening settled, they watched the woods around their home for any sign of their son's return. The hours passed. Still Clark failed to show up. Mrs. Poling continued to nudge her husband. She reminded him of ledges, plummets, a precipice on Wolf Hill that could kill anyone if they weren't careful near its summit. The risk was especially poignant for a young man who had failed to bring any food—with just water and a blanket, he was no doubt feeling fatigue. Mr. Poling acknowledged his wife's worries, but he didn't act. Clark would be coming along soon enough, he figured.

But the young man never emerged from the woods. Twilight morphed into blackness, which thickened well past midnight. Still Clark had not come back. One a.m. passed—nothing. Two a.m.— still no sign. By three o'clock in the morning, Clark had been gone nearly thirty-six hours. Neither mother nor father could sleep.

Finally, when the moon poked out from behind the horizon, Clark's father could no longer wait. He dressed, prepared himself, brought along the family's dog, and set out into the darkness. Named "Fluffy," the American shepherd was a welcome companion that night. They traveled south, following a road that would lead them to the mountain. As they walked, they heard foxes tracking them in the forest, perhaps a hundred yards away, occasionally unleashing birdlike shrieks.

Father and Fluffy picked up their pace. By the time they reached the Wolf Hill ascent, they were in a jog. Peering into the darkness, Clark's dad realized just how dangerous the terrain truly was. The moon provided some hint of footing, but that was the only light. It showed little to a human and was just a sliver of help to the dog. With every step, Clark's dad berated himself. Why had he waited so long? Clark had said he would be gone for a day, for a while, but surely he hadn't meant *two* nights. He should have listened to his wife. What if Clark had broken his leg? He had only one canteen, which he would have finished off soon into his sojourn. He had no food. The air was chilly enough to be dangerous.

Pondering his own foolishness, Clark's dad turned to prayer. He asked God to help him find his son, somewhere in the darkness on this frigid mountaintop.

Harder and harder, he pushed himself up the mountain. As much as the tricky footing would let him, he ran up the mountain. When he neared the last bit of the climb, he paused to catch his breath. In the daytime, from the summit, he could see across the treetops to Mount Monadnock and other rises in the distance. Now all he could see were shadows, capped by billions of twinkling stars. He sucked in a long breath and yelled, "Clark!"

Nothing.

Fluffy stood by him, silent, still. If she smelled or sensed anything, she didn't reveal it.

He forced himself up the final climb, a steep rise of granite boulders, a few evergreens, and shrubbery. "Clark!" he screamed again, his voice carrying away from him into the black. With each step, he hollered his son's name.

Time seemed to slow. We don't know how many moments passed as Clark's dad made that final ascent, but to him, the period felt like "infinite anguish."

"Clark!" he called again.

He was alone. Wherever his son had gone, where he had ended up, it was not here.

Then he heard the rustling. From out of a crevice in the boulders, a shadow stirred, as if one of the rocks had come to life and now was rising for the first time. It looked as if it were uncertain. Then it spoke. "Dad!"

Clark stepped from where he'd been sleeping and walked to his father. Fluffy hopped and bounced and yapped all about, mirroring precisely how Clark's dad was feeling. Feelings of relief and love flooded over the man.

Clark didn't say much more, but gathered his things. Together, they navigated the night back down the mountain. When they reached the road, Clark finally spoke. He was glad his dad had come, but he was also thankful he hadn't come sooner. "I had some things to settle, and I thought I might hear The Voice." His words were methodical, searching, as if he were talking to himself. "I did not hear it—not The Voice. But, Dad, I am glad I went; yes, I'm glad. Some things are clearer now and other things will be, I know."

He stepped closer to his father so that their shoulders touched. "Gee, Daddy, I'm glad you came up." Then, in a voice just a bit more repentant, he added, "Is Mother worried?"

Clark never looked back. On that mountain, his father would later write, Clark "had met himself." With singular purpose, he finished his undergraduate studies at Rutgers University after transferring there from Hope College. He thrived academically and received a graduate degree from Yale Divinity School, then moved on to being a student assistant pastor at a church in New London, Connecticut. During these years, he learned how to serve those with every kind of need: spiritual, emotional, and financial. He ministered to those ready to depart this life. He shepherded troubled youth and children. To the elderly, he lent a listening ear. He mastered the subtle art of drop-in visits to those who may not have expected or wanted him there. Perhaps more than anything else, he developed his voice. It was one of subtle strength that, paradoxically, conveyed power in a gentle way. At least according to one account, he was not the gifted orator that his father had become, but his ability to minister, to connect to others and help them bond with each other, was unrivaled.

Far and wide, churches in need of pastors began to notice. Soon, after considering requests in the Midwest, Clark accepted an invitation to be the head pastor of the First Reformed Church (Dutch) in Schenectady, New York. There, driven by a grand vision for the church and humble aspirations for his own worldly gains, he took the struggling congregation from a membership of just a few dozen and helped it grow into one of the most impactful religious centers in the area.[14]

Along the way, Clark also fell in love. His success with his church was not his alone. It was as if providence had prepared the perfect companion to walk by his side on this path—someone who belonged on the trail just as much as he did.

His family had met Elizabeth ("Betty") Jung first, then conspired for months to try to connect her with Clark. Everyone in the family, especially Clark's younger sister, was confident that she was the woman Clark would marry. The only problem with their grand plan was Clark himself. And, of course, there was no guarantee Betty would want Clark. The first few times they tried to introduce her to him, he seemed indifferent or unimpressed. To them, his behavior was puzzling—Betty was, in their minds, perfect. She was spiritual, charming, beautiful, intelligent, tender, tough, and gracious. Why wouldn't Clark want to marry her?

But Clark was at Yale, then preparing for his position in Schenectady. The family was now in Philadelphia. He rarely saw this young woman Betty, and when he did, they didn't have time to form any kind of deeper connection. Then, one day, he showed up in Philly unannounced. His parents assumed he was homesick,[15] but on Sunday morning, as he and his dad were driving to church, Clark said, "Dad."

His dad waited for him to finish the comment. It hung in the air for moments.

Clark nervously cleared his throat, then continued, "Dad, do you suppose I could reach Betty Jung? I might stay over and take her to a show."

His dad played it cool. He commented that Betty's family had a telephone and Clark could call her, but his guess was that she would be "engaged"—she was very busy and *very* popular.

Clark V. Poling

Clark made the call. He wasn't the first guy to be caught up by her spell. Masses of other young men had fallen for her unique magic. Her perfectly smooth skin, infectious smile, trim figure, conversational ease, intellectual and spiritual depth, and eyes that exhibited both warmth and caring[16]—all of it, coupled with her profound sense of confidence, made for a charming elixir few could resist. She was actually already booked every night for the foreseeable future, but she kept that hidden from Clark. Instead, she told him she was free the following Thursday. As soon as the call ended, she canceled all of her Thursday night plans.

On that night, March 31, 1938, Clark and Betty shared their first date. Whatever happened that evening, whatever depths of their hearts they explored in a conversation that stretched on well past midnight, may be secrets only they hold. All we know is this: by the time the night was over, they were engaged. Clark burst into his home, swept his little sister off her feet, then regaled his family into the wee hours of the morning about how in love he was, how perfect Betty Jung was, and how quickly and deeply they connected. The engagement lasted less than three months. Though he was just starting his time as pastor of his own church, Clark drove back and forth between Schenectady and Philadelphia, motivated by the thrill he felt every time he was in Betty's presence. On June 21, 1938, they were wed.

In Betty, Clark had found his other half. Like him, she was inherently spiritual. His ministry quickly became *their* ministry. They lived in a tiny apartment in Schenectady, but they did everything together. They hosted singles nights. They taught the youth. They organized multiday camping trips for hordes of youngsters. As Betty once explained, "Clark's idea was to make your religion hard," so he and Betty would lead groups into the Adirondacks where, after climbing for an entire day with heavy packs, they would cook for the entire group, then lead them in spiritual endeavors where they could ponder "the wonders of God's world."[17]

Betty loved Clark's strengths, but also his quirks. He was loving but absentminded. He was generous but not always as sensitive to Betty's needs as he should have been, often inviting people for dinner without giving her any warning. On their wedding day, he even forgot to shave and needed to be sent back to do it. He was caring but forgetful, regularly needing Betty to remind him of people's names. But above all else, despite his foibles, Clark was selfless. And that altruism filled Betty to the brim. During their five years together in Schenectady, she never experienced homesickness. Her family chided her for it. But, she wrote, "How could I be? Clark filled every moment of my married life and I was completely content."[18] He seemed to have mastered the key to a happy marriage: "His desires," she wrote, "his wants, his comforts were last." She returned that self-sacrifice. They were living that most mysterious of all paradoxes, one that few married couples successfully unlock: by giving up entirely their own desires, by focusing solely on the needs of their partner, they were both receiving more than they could have ever hoped for had they put their own wants first.

In time, they brought a little boy into the world. They named him Clark as well and soon gave him the nickname "Corky." Their family seemed to bless the lives of everyone they touched. As one acquaintance commented, "Clark came to Schenectady and in five years transformed a church that was virtually dead into one that was fast becoming the most influential in the community."

Then the war started.

If Clark was hesitant to join the fight in World War II, we have no record of it. Like so many men of his generation, he saw the opportunity to serve and defend his country as an honor. In a conversation with his father, he expressed concern that he would struggle if he stayed behind as a civilian while other men went to fight. Clark still embraced much of the pacifism he had learned from his Oakwood days. To him, war was a fruitless exercise.[19] He was not eager to see battle. But he also felt that some wars were necessary, and if they were, he needed to do his part. What he saw spewing out of Europe toward the Jews was pure hatred and evil. It troubled him so much that he knew he needed to act. As one member of his congregation explained, Clark "saw the same seeds of evil among" people in the United States. He would not let them land in fertile soil. So, on multiple occasions, he invited a local rabbi to address the First Reformed Church, to squelch any sentiments of anti-Semitism before they could grow.[20] What he saw from Japan after the attack at Pearl Harbor was a threat to the very existence of the United States. It all left Clark with one unyielding conclusion: this was a necessary war.

The question wasn't whether he would join the military. What troubled him was whether he wanted to be a chaplain or a traditional soldier.

When he told his dad that he would not go as a chaplain, his father replied, "Why? Are you afraid?"

"What do you mean by that?" Clark said.

His father knew what Clark was thinking. Just as he couldn't stay safe at home while others went to battle, he didn't like the idea of receiving what he perceived to be a "cushy" assignment as a chaplain while other men put their lives at risk.

"Clark," his dad said, "you'll try to go in—if you go—where you can count for the most. That's first with you, I know; and in the second place, the chaplaincy had in the last war the highest casualty rate of all the services."

Clark's eyes narrowed. He had received a stellar education. He didn't just take claims at face value. "Are you sure of that, Dad?"

"Yes, I am sure. As a chaplain, you'll have the finest chance in the world to be killed. The only difference is this: you can't kill anyone. Along with the medical corps, you'll be unarmed."

By Christmas of 1941, just after Pearl Harbor, Clark had made up his mind. He would enlist as an army chaplain. He had proven one thing: he was precisely the type of man the army, with its focus on tolerance amid diversity and individual spiritual strength of chaplains, wanted. He had demonstrated the former on numerous occasions. His father once wrote:

> Always and constructively Clark was a man of peace and a peacemaker. Never could he in all the "world's wide border" hate any human being—any man, woman or child. In uniform one day I heard him deny the assumption that the American soldier must hate Germans to be a good soldier. Hate the evil system with all your might, yes; but not those who with us are equally, however misguided, its victims. The "love your enemies" of Jesus was real and timely to him. He did not dodge it. He loved his enemies, saying, "If our cause wins, they will be free, too. In this world you cannot isolate any evil or any good. We do not fight

to win for ourselves and for our children any good that cannot be shared."[21]

As for the latter, Clark himself had published what he saw as the key to lasting personal peace in a world bent on destroying itself. In July 1939, with Hitler and Tojo wreaking havoc on both sides of the globe, and with many Americans fearing war was inevitable, Clark penned the following in a church magazine:

> The most effective way that men have of achieving happiness is by creating personal sanctuaries which cannot be stormed by the forces of adversity, in which things of the mind can be cultivated and in which love, a modicum of physical comfort, and a measure of spiritual tranquility can be enjoyed. We can build such a sanctuary by returning to the fundamental pleasures of home and family, of good books, and, most important, to the joy of worshipping God. If our happiness is dependent upon these the outside world can tumble about us and we can still have peace. Let us therefore cultivate only those areas of living which bring love, intellectual enrichment, and spiritual contentment. Only as we possess these are we wealthy. Only as we lack these are we poor. With these we are never lost.

Clark carried the personal conviction needed to give of himself to others.

★ ★ ★

How Betty felt about Clark's joining the fray may be known only to the two of them, and perhaps only to her. To the outside world, she portrayed supportiveness and pride. At his farewell dinner with the church congregation, she sat by his side at a table in the front of a room, an amused smile on her face while he regaled the crowd.[22] Inside, she was likely aching. Her letters reveal that, deep down, she suffered from the worry and longing anyone would in her situation. "From the moment Clark enlisted in the Army," she wrote, "he never allowed me to believe that I would go with him." His concern was that people cannot focus on the tasks before them if they are looking backward.

So when Clark embarked for his first assignment, to report to Camp Shelby, deep in the heart of Mississippi, they said their good-byes. Both were convinced they would see each other again only after the war's end. A date uncertain; a time unknowable. Betty steeled herself for the long, lonely road that lay before her. She threw herself mentally and emotionally into work that would keep her mind and heart occupied. The most pressing was her running a "Daily Vacation School" at the church. In effect, she built a wall that would keep the loneliness at bay.

Then came Clark's first letter. Apparently, he had been in the foreign land of the American South less than twenty-four hours when the loneliness targeted him. Whatever emotional walls Betty had built for herself, he wasn't able to replicate them. He was out of his element. Unlike Alexander and George, he had not been assigned to chaplain school, as far as we know, so his learning was done on the job. He needed something from home. He missed his wife, their sweet little boy. He let Betty know that she could come and live with him near Camp Shelby.

Betty was floored. The letter didn't answer a desperate hope, because she had allowed herself none. Instead, it threw her mind into a tizzy. She was so thrown, she considered writing her husband back to tell him that it was impossible, that she had already started down a path she would inevitably need to follow once he went to the front. But the chance to reunite was too much to pass up. She closed the vacation school a week early, using gas rationing as an excuse, claiming that it made getting the children there too difficult and costly.[23] She was so anxious to see Clark, she could hardly bear it. She set out immediately.

In Mississippi, just a few weeks into his new assignment as a chaplain, he saw them. Fresh from New York, looking radiant and brimming with excitement, were his wife and two-year-old son.

"Da-da!" the little boy called.

For Clark, the moment was perfect. Everything about it—his wife, the way she'd dressed Corky, the way the little boy called out his name. It also ended what had been a lonely month for the new chaplain, in a land—the American South—that was as foreign to him as any battle front to which the army might send him.[24]

For Clark and Betty Poling, the next day and a half were a time in paradise. They stayed in a fine hotel. Clark doted over both Betty and Corky. They took in the ocean views of the Gulf Coast, dined at breakfast while Corky played with a doll, and basked in being together. This was a time to be cherished, clouded only by the reality that both Clark and Betty knew was coming; it was only a respite from a separation that had already begun.

Over the next month and a half, they waited. Clark thought his orders were coming, only to find he'd been reassigned. So he and Betty enjoyed each other's company. On Sundays, he led services, they read comics in the papers together, and they drank Coca-Cola while listening to comedy shows on the radio. Clark did his best to serve the soldiers at Camp Shelby. He christened the commanding officer's baby, and people from every walk of life and faith group attended. He counseled with young men who needed advice.

Along the way, Clark and Betty realized she was expecting again. Already, she was showing signs. The only question would have been if Clark would be there when the baby was born.

CHAPTER 9

SOMETHING DEEPER BENEATH

By September 1942, John P. Washington was stationed at Fort George G. Meade, in Maryland, and he was bursting from his skin. His desire, his goal, was to serve on the front lines, to do what chaplains are called to do. Instead, he had been rotting, first in training in Indiana, now here. The United States was eight months into the war, ships like the *Chatham* were sinking by the droves, soldiers were dying, most of the other army chaplains were receiving their training on the campus at Harvard, then receiving their assignments, and he was still lingering on a base. It frustrated him. He wrote to superiors, hoping for a better assignment. Nothing came.

John P. Washington

Instead, he was left alone with his thoughts, wondering why he had even bothered signing up.[1]

Washington had the air of a frustratingly unsolvable mystery. When friends thought they had him figured out, he would surprise them. He would dazzle them all night around the pool table, mastering angle shots and backspin, then drop a thought of such deep spiritual significance that it left them wondering where it came from. He was the ringleader in joking and laughing, but always put an end to it if the jokes turned dirty or involved swearing. As a Catholic priest, he would end mass just so he could hurry to catch a movie. He wore glasses—sometimes. People left meetings with him feeling as if he had just preached them a sermon or steered them in a particular life direction, only to realize later that he hadn't really said anything specifically on point to how they were feeling. There was just an air about John Washington, a depth radiating from him that made people want to follow his example.

But the mystery of who he was started much sooner than his life as a chaplain. He was born July 18, 1908, the firstborn of Irish immigrant parents who lived on a middle-class street in a middle-class neighborhood in Newark, New Jersey. His was an avenue of outcasts, though he didn't know it. They were all in it together. In other areas of the city, the state, or the country, they might not have been welcome, so they all ended up here. Germans, Poles, Irish, Catholics, Black families—they all lived together on Twelfth Street, in modest but respectable homes on maple-lined roads. The parents worked, the kids played, and they got along in a way too many in American society at the time seemed incapable of doing. Years in that environment taught John both to stand up for himself and to forgive and forget others' differences.

The lessons came early. Once, when playing with a friend, they imagined they were hunting in an African safari. The friend, a little Black boy named Harvey, was holding John's BB rifle. The two of them approached a hedge in the neighborhood. They pretended it was the jungle. Beyond it, they would find beasts drinking at a water hole. As they worked their way through the hedge, something caught on the trigger of the rifle. Just as John turned his head, the gun fired.

John felt a searing pain in his right eye and collapsed to the grass. His eye throbbed. He struggled to see.

Nearby, he heard Harvey weeping. "John, John, I didn't mean to shoot!" Then the gun clanged to the grass. Harvey was running. He was climbing the fence to whatever yard they were in. He was afraid he would be blamed. Who knew what punishment he might receive if John told on him.

John lay in agony, screaming, his eyes blurry, until his father finally found him. He felt himself being scooped up. Then his father was running, sprinting back to the house, John clinging closely to his chest. He laid his son onto the sofa in the front room. A bit later, a doctor came. Everyone was asking questions. A crowd had gathered—they were angry, making the types of assumptions that mobs often do with incomplete information.

Eventually, a police officer showed up. "Now then," he said. "What's it all about?"

John was adamant about one thing. He did not want Harvey blamed for what happened. "It wasn't Harvey's fault, I tell you," he said with a weak voice. He explained what happened. "It wasn't Harvey's fault."

John would not let the narrative go, not until everyone in the neighborhood knew: it was not Harvey's fault. Eventually, the message got through. No one blamed the little boy. It was an accident, nothing more. But John's eye never fully healed. Sometimes it would blur up or fill with pus. Other times it just hurt for seemingly no reason. He struggled to see well, and the doctor prescribed him glasses. John didn't like standing out, and the glasses left him self-conscious. For many years after, he wore them only when necessary. Otherwise, he kept them a secret.

For the most part, John was known as a goofball. He got in fights in the neighborhood, continued to play games all over the street, told jokes, laughed at everything, played pool, smoked cigarettes on occasion, boxed, learned the piano, and played baseball. All the while, unbeknownst to many, he was seeking and asking questions. The nature of God intrigued him. When he partook of his First Holy Communion, the day resonated with him the rest of his life. As he navigated through elementary and middle school, he joked and snickered with his friends during mass and even as an altar boy—always keeping up the appearance that he was just like everyone else. But he was feeling things—spiritual promptings that perhaps no one else seemed to notice. He felt a powerful spirit in the music. He sensed the divine in the words of the Our Father and Hail Mary. The world seemed to be changing. No, that wasn't it—he was the one who had changed. Despite appearing so ordinary, he was drifting apart from everything, to a different, more spiritual way of looking at his existence.

And he felt the calling. God wanted him to be a priest. He knew it, even as he let only the smallest circle of people—his parents and one Sister at church—in on his secret. Even so, it was hard to take him seriously. Despite feeling himself compelled in a unique direction, John was still an adolescent. His serious side lay buried deep down, and it was a legitimate question if it would ever emerge to play a dominant role in his life.

That question was put to rest when John was in seventh grade. One evening, in the middle of winter, he stepped into his family's home, his sister Anna there with his mother. "Ma," John said, "I'm sick."

She placed her hand on his forehead. Heat radiated off him. "You must have a cold," she said.

He agreed. "And my throat is *so* sore," he said.

She rushed him into bed, forced him to gargle with Listerine, rubbed his neck and chest with a menthol cream, and had him drink war lemonade. None of it helped. By the next morning, John's face was red. The fever left him mostly delirious. He stirred occasionally, moaning. When he was conscious, he refused to eat anything.

This was just a couple of years after the flu pandemic of 1918 that had killed millions. The memories of that tragic time must have left scarring memories. John's mother called the doctor. Outside, snow started falling again. Plows scraped by on the street outside. The doctor visited and tried a few remedies. As the day dragged on, they seemed to have no effect, and John's mother began to weep. Her son was not getting any better.

By evening, the doctor came to visit again. He checked on John, then visited with the family in the living room. With a weighty look, he shook his head. "I can't seem to get the boy's fever down," he said. He thought John might have a swollen abscess in the back of his throat, near his tonsils. "If we can't drop that fever, his case will be serious by morning. Continue to use ice packs. And give him two of these pills every hour. Call me if there is any change."

John's parents exchanged worried glances.

Later that evening, John slipped into full unconsciousness. His father, tears in his eyes, put on his coat and stepped out of the house. It was time to notify the priest.

The family doctor returned first and used what little medical equipment he had, but he was out of answers. Shortly on his heels, John's father returned. The family priest, Father McKeever, was with him. It was time to turn to faith, when nothing else would work.

With John lying still and silent on the bed, everyone crammed into his room. On a small table, John's mother prepared various items for a ritual sacred to Catholics: anointing of the sick.[2] Parents and siblings stood by while the priest performed his work. When he was finished, nothing had changed but the feeling in the room. John still lay quiet, his face red.

At the door to the house, Father McKeever turned to John's parents. "Don't give up now," he said. "Remember this sacrament of anointing is also a sacrament of physical healing. . . . Be brave."

"God's will be done," John's father said. "John is such a good boy, such a good boy." He hugged his wife.

"He's none too good for God," she said, perhaps resigned that God may have wanted her son with Him.

Father McKeever left. The encircling gloom of the night closed in. John's mother wept. The morning seemed so very far away. Outside, the snow fell soft and pure, like stars falling from heaven. Anna went to bed, likely wondering if she would ever see her brother again. They were close. He had become a hero to her. He was a star student, a leader in the neighborhood and at school, one of the chief altar boys, kind, funny, and gentle. He was everything a little sister could hope for. We don't know how much she slept that night. It seemed her brother lay in that place between this world and the next. Memories likely tossed her mind about, bright flashes of snowball fights and carrying his books, images that brought both joy and pain for fear they may never happen again. How long would the sickness last? Would it take him? Would it take him?

When she woke in the morning, her mind crawling to awareness, she sought out her parents.

Both were smiling. "He's much better," John's mother said. "Thanks be to God! The fever is going down."

Anna felt the relief that comes only when someone steps to the edge of a great loss and then is pulled back. Later, she found a moment to talk to her brother.

"I guess I nearly put on my wings," John said. He laughed. "But God must have kept me here for something. I'll try to discover what it is."

From that moment on, Anna noticed a thoughtfulness to her brother. To so many he was still the same carefree person he'd always been, but the important differences were subtle. His prayers around the family were longer now, more thoughtful. He had always been kind, but it seemed magnified, filled with deeper meaning. It was as if he were transitioning into a shepherd right before his family's eyes. When his little brothers fought, he guided them to resolve their differences. He did it with a calmness, a presence that seemed to change the home.

Though he was still a boy and still played with his friends, he would come inside sooner than he used to. Suddenly he was more thoughtful than he'd been before, more aware of others' needs. He was the first in a large family: six other siblings followed. The burden on his mother was immense. Minutes after finishing lunch, she would have been forced to turn to supper preparations. Dirty laundry would have piled up as if it were invading the home—a never-ending onslaught. Shopping, finding food to feed the ravenous mouths of her growing children would have been a problem without a solution, an itch that could never be scratched.

More and more, John was there. Instead of staying with his friends, he left them outside. "I'll help you, Mom," he would say without being asked. Then he would set the table, help with his siblings, or pick up the house. On Saturdays, when his mother needed to go shopping, John would take some of his younger siblings with him. His little brother Edmund, the youngest in the home, was still too small to be left alone. Toddling and scooting along, completely clueless of the risks the world posed, he would place himself in constant danger if someone wasn't keeping an eye on him. John would offer to take him so his mother could shop without having to worry about him. He would guide him on hikes, or hold his hand to the baseball field.

Perhaps his most important help involved his sister Mary. Just two years younger than he, she had always been weak, suffering from a sickness that left her tired and pale. Too often, she was cold, afflicted by a freeze deep inside her she couldn't ever seem to escape. She would huddle over the heating vent in the winter months, trying to stay warm. Even in the summer, it seemed her body was determined to stay cool. When John and her brothers and the neighborhood boys and even her little sister Anna would play and frolic about, Mary would sit alone, sometimes in a dark room with the shades drawn. Hers was a stalking illness, one that made death seem an inevitability. It was as if the entire family knew, for almost all fifteen years of her life, in the deepest recesses of their minds, the dark fate meant for her—that she would leave this earth prematurely. As John lay plates on the table for dinner, or cleaned up the clutter in a room, he would entertain her with jokes and stories. He, as much as anyone, had the ability to bring some color to her otherwise pale face. Through that relationship, it seems, they formed a special bond.

So it was that much more heartbreaking when, at fifteen, she passed away. All the prayers, all the rituals, all the medicine—it had given them hope, but it hadn't cured her. She slipped away. At the funeral, John stood looking down upon her coffin, wondering why he had been spared but she called home. Nearby, his mom shook in her husband's arms. John's eyes filled with tears. Why had his parents' prayers for him been answered? He was now a senior in high school. One thing he knew: Mary's often silent suffering was over, and she would now be in a place to look down on him and pray for him.

He would not waste those prayers. At Seton Hall, he dove into his training with a renewed intensity and focus. Mary's death was a shock, but it jolted John into action. He earned top grades at Seton Hall. His eyes were set upon the priesthood, though only those closest to him knew it. To everyone else, he was the same pool-playing jokester he had always been. By 1931, he entered the seminary. In 1934, he was made a deacon, and finally, on June 15, 1935, he was ordained a priest. Always, the mystery of who he was surprised everyone, even in his family. On the eve of his ordination, of his eternal commitment to God, he bounded into his parents' home and told so many jokes that his dad wondered if he wasn't fully appreciating just how solemn and important the following day truly was.

John's response was simple: "This is an ordination, not a funeral."

★ ★ ★

The years passed. John became the priest of St. Genevieve's Church in Elizabeth, New Jersey. He was soon transferred to St. Venantius in nearby Orange. There, he developed a true sense of selfless service. Part of his assignment was to tend to the sick. Within the parish boundaries was a large hospital. John served as the priest to those who were sick and dying. Whether he liked it or not, he became acquainted with death. It was a responsibility that prepared him well for things to come. Watching people pass from this life must have, in some way, informed his testimony of the eternal nature of things. And his duties never seemed to end. On his days off, he would travel to spend time with his parents. His father was ill; his mother needed caring. But even on those days, he gave the operators running the switchboard at the hospital his parents' number. Inevitably, the calls would come. So he stayed near the phone. When it rang, he would pick up, listen for just a moment, then say, "I'll be right over." Then he would kiss his mother and dash out the door. When someone commented on the extraordinary demands being placed on John's shoulders, he said simply, "The customer is never wrong. I can't ask people to die at hours to suit *my* convenience."

All the while, he wondered if he was fulfilling the destiny for which God had kept him in this life. He was seeking, always searching for God's will, unsure if he was what the heavens had wanted him to be. He was certain God had a plan for him, that he had been spared while Mary had not. But why? For what purpose? Though he spent his time losing himself in the service of others, those questions swirled in his mind, always there, a lingering, whirling doubt.

His familiarity with death carried him through dark days. By 1938, he had been assigned to serve over St. Stephen's Church in Kearny, New Jersey, still close to his parents. There, he found a new joy in serving youth and the people of the church. In many respects, he felt at home and wondered if he had finally found where the Lord wanted him to be.

One evening, he received an unexpected phone call. The message was simple: *Come home. Your father is dying.*

John slammed the receiver down and raced home. There was a possibility he might not make it in time. His parents' home was roughly five miles from the church. Traversing narrow streets, across the Passaic River, John rushed. He never explained what thoughts passed through his head during that drive. Regret at possibly not being there for the man who had done so much for the family? He was in a race against the inevitable, and all his experience with death told him that it was not a respecter of persons. His sister Mary, the many people he had ministered to in the hospital, his parishioners—when their times had come, death had not waited. In many ways, his father embodied all that John hoped to be. He had given everything of himself to his family throughout his life, as an immigrant, a provider, a husband.

When he arrived, John bolted up the steps. In the parlor, he threw off his coat. "Dad!" he yelled. In just a few strides, he reached the bedroom. In that quiet space, prayers were already being offered for his dying father. John pushed through to the bed.

His father lay still, his face a sunken shell of its former self. Then, a smile cracked through its broken façade. He raised one of his hands. John clasped it. The skin felt cold, empty. Life was draining from it. With a smile, the dying man said, "Now John is here, everything will be all right."

With that, he slipped away.

As before, death gave John new purpose. He dedicated himself to taking care of his mother, in addition to the people of his parish. When he wasn't serving his adopted family, he was by her side. He dropped in unexpectedly. He stopped by on his free days. He brought her gifts and flowers and took her to movies and dining out, anything to brighten her day. Whenever he ran into others, he introduced her as "my girl." This was John's life. His cause was bound to his mother. The woman who had given so much of herself for others was now a large part of his focus.

So it's not surprising that when Japanese planes peeled away in formation and dove for Pearl Harbor, John was driving with his mother. It was midafternoon. He had just finished celebrating mass, and as soon as he stepped from the pulpit, he had picked her up for food and a movie. The news of the attack burst over the car radio. They listened as the broadcast detailed the United States' reluctant entry into war.

John wept.

His mother placed her hand on his arm.

Later that night, John kissed her gently. He apologized for needing to leave, but he was the priest on call that night. Before walking through the door, he turned back to her. "Of course you know I must try to enlist. Everyone will be needed."

How his mother felt about that, we don't know.

In the coming months, John signed up to be a navy chaplain. They rejected him because of his injured eye. He was devastated. For months, he wanted to serve. He spoke with his mentor, another priest at St. Stephen's who had served as an army chaplain during World War I. He encouraged John to apply to the army if the navy wouldn't have him. John bandied the idea a bit and was apparently about to drop it altogether for fear he would just get rejected again.

Then another priest had an idea: "When they test you, just cover your bad eye twice and read the chart with your good eye twice. They won't notice the difference."

It was intriguing. And he figured it would work. But it also troubled him. He was a priest, a man of God. The ruse was, at the end of the day, a lie. How long he toiled over the decision, we don't know. What we do know is that he went through with it, then spent a great deal of time praying for forgiveness afterward. Finally, he was accepted. He would report to Army Chaplain School at Fort Benjamin Harris, then hopefully receive his assignment from there.

After enduring training similar to what Alex and George later received at Harvard, John received his assignment. It was to Maryland. There, in September 1942, he waited, frustrated. He wrote letter after letter to his superiors. In one, he penned, "Once more I ask you to consider my application for overseas duty. If I am too fresh in requesting it, then slap me down." He fired the letter off, then tried to make the best of his situation. Inside, he was still searching, looking for the path God wanted him to tread.

CHAPTER 10

SHEPHERDS IN DEATH'S SHADOW

The role of the chaplain is not to be envied. Or perhaps it is. On the morning of December 7, 1941, at Pearl Harbor, Father Aloysius ("Al") Schmitt had just finished celebrating mass on board the *USS Oklahoma* when the first torpedo blasted into the side of his ship. Two more followed almost immediately. The vessel listed to the port side. Within minutes, the entire ship had tilted about forty-five degrees, sending men and books and metal and food and gear careening and crashing.

Another torpedo tore into the ship. Then another. And another. And another. Father Al found himself in a chamber with a crowd of other men. The *Oklahoma* continued to groan and tilt toward the ocean, like a moaning beast lying down for a nap. It must have felt like a dream to the men on board. What had been the walls were rotating to become the floor and ceiling. Water started to flood the room through a chamber door now tilted at an odd angle. It appears the door was closed, and the men didn't believe they could escape through it.

Another torpedo rocked the vessel, shaking everything and everyone. Ocean water and burning oil choked the air.

One thing was certain: the ship was capsizing. In a matter of minutes, the entire vessel would be upside down. They would all be trapped inside. If the explosions and fire and noxious smoke didn't kill them, they would surely drown. But there was one possibility for escape. On the wall was a porthole, no more than fourteen or fifteen inches in diameter. As the ship squealed onto its side, the porthole rose higher and higher. For a short time, it would stay out of the harbor water until the ship completely capsized. Then it too would submerge. If the men could get through before that, they might be able to escape the ship before it flipped completely.

Father Al was young, just thirty-two. His skin reflected a babylike smoothness, his thick eyebrows the promise of what he might look like one day as a grandfather. He waved the first man toward him. It's likely that by this point, the porthole was nearly above his head, while he stood on the opposite wall. He hoisted the man through. One by one, other men surged for the escape. Father Al hoisted each one up, shoving them, while the sailors who were already outside helped pull them through onto the exterior of the *Oklahoma*.

The sixth man to go through was too thick. His body jammed halfway, his legs dangling behind him. The five free men latched onto his arms and chest—anywhere they could get a handle. He wouldn't budge. Father Al heaved from underneath. Everyone rocked him, jerking him side to side to force him free. There was a sickening pop . . . one of the man's ribs had snapped. Groaning from the pain, he bellowed, "Don't stop! Keep pulling!"

Finally, he burst free.

At last, with water now swirling around his waist, it was Father Al's turn. He was the last. He tried to get through the porthole. Whether it was out of reach without someone to boost him or something else blocked his passage, the men on the outside couldn't pull him through. They tried. Finally, they latched onto his hands. Yanking, grasping, the sailors managed to lift him part way.

"Boys," he hollered, "I'm having a tough time getting through."

Then he heard the sound. Behind him, in the room, more men had managed to force open the door. He was aware of them—keenly—sailors looking for an escape. As the already-free men geared up for one last jerk to wrench him through to safety, he said, "Men, you are endangering your lives and keeping others from getting through."

He lowered himself back into the room.

The men forcing open the door waded toward him. The water had risen to their hips. They must have been thrilled. They had been grasping at a desperate hope: that the compartment would allow them an escape.

Father Al helped them as well, hoisting each through the porthole. With each young man, he whispered, "God save you."

When the last started his climb, he asked, "Who's going to save you?"

Father Al smiled. "The same person who is saving you."

When all the men were free, at least one of them looked back down into the chamber. The ship would complete its rotation at any moment. Then the porthole would be submerged. In just a glimpse, before diving into the oil-slicked water and swimming to safety, the sailor saw Father Al, water swirling about him, his arm outstretched, blessing his shipmates.[1]

Minutes later, the ship was completely belly-up. Father Al went down with it, after saving the lives of twelve other men.*

Word of Chaplain Schmitt's sacrifice likely made its way to the four chaplains. Newspapers covered it well. None would have been surprised. In their brief military careers, Alexander Goode, John Washington, George Fox, and Clark Poling had learned what countless other chaplains had long since known. A chaplain's life was a sacrifice for others. If they performed their jobs properly, no other soldiers

---

* There may well have been other men still in the room with him. At least one account suggests that Father Al intended to lift other men to the porthole but the ship made its final turn before he could. After the sinking of the *Oklahoma*, Father Aloysius Schmitt, like so many other men, was lost. The navy could not identify the remains of many sailors, so they buried them in a cemetery in Hawaii. In 2016, he was finally identified, and on October 5, 2016, he came home. He was buried there, in Iowa, three days later.

would be at more risk than they. When assigned, chaplains lived on the edge on the front lines and tended to face the same perils as other soldiers but with the added complication of duties that required them to face enemy fire without any means of protecting themselves. They dug graves while enemies fired at them. They performed last rites over dying men while others ducked from shell blasts. It was a singular pressure that no one, other than perhaps medics, faced. Father Al was not an anomaly, and each of the four chaplains knew it. His life—and his death—was no different from what each of them might face. Father Al had met that unique burden. He was the first US chaplain to die in World War II.

But he was hardly the first chaplain to die serving his country. The sacrifices were legend. In a strange twist of fate, the last United States officer to die in World War I was also a chaplain. William F. Davitt, just thirty-two years old, had served faithfully for nearly a year. On November 11, 1918, midmorning, he was in the mood to celebrate. And he had good reason. Earlier that day, the Allies and Germany had signed "The Armistice of 11 November 1918," also known as "The Armistice of Compiègne," for the city in France in which it was signed. The Armistice declared that all hostilities—on ground, air, and sea— in the Great War would end at the eleventh hour of the eleventh day of the eleventh month of 1918. Chaplain Davitt, a Catholic priest, wanted to ensure a United States flag was flying when the clock struck the magical hour. He had been assigned grave duty, but he traveled all night until he was near the front. Both sides were still fighting, firing shells and bullets at one another. Davitt arrived shortly before the time the fighting would cease. In his arms, he carried the large flag. According to one report, he presented the Stars and Stripes to his regiment's commanding officer, then stepped from his room. As he walked across an open space, a German shell landed on the roof of a nearby barn, blasting shrapnel and flames into the air. One of those pieces of shrapnel struck Davitt and killed him.[2]

The bottom line: like so many other servicemen, chaplains serving near the front could never escape death's stalking touch. It could strike them at any moment. As Clark's father had explained to him, chaplains carried the highest casualty rate of nearly any service branch in World War I, and World War II was no better. Except for the Army Air Corps, the Chaplain Corps "sustained the highest per capita casualty rate in the army."[3]

But it wasn't just the prospect of dying that made the chaplains' service a unique, but special, burden. Their role on the battlefield was also different. In combat, the other soldiers' goal was to kill the enemy. It was a singular and necessary focus. Their eyes looked forward, through the trees, across the trenches, into the enemy bunkers. Likely, most rarely noticed other men scurrying about them: chaplains. They were not looking to the enemy. In many respects, they required the fortitude of mind to ignore their foes altogether. Instead, their minds lay elsewhere: on the dying, on the injured, to ministering, to bringing comfort. They carried no weapons. Instead, they offered prayers and blessings, absolution and penance, wisdom and counsel, burial ceremonies and impromptu funerals. They were expected to do all of this knowing that the enemy often would not spare them.

Davitt, though he died in such an unfortunate way, exemplified this. Prior to his death, he had already received recommendations for distinguished awards. One noted: "Chaplain Davitt worked single-handed without ceasing for anything, collecting the dead of his Division (32d) and looking after the burial. He did this under violent fire, to which he apparently paid no attention. While doing this work he stopped to encourage with cheerful words and advice the enlisted men along the line who also were under fire. The results of his work were 125 American soldiers buried, many wounded cared for, and soldiers in the line encouraged." On another occasion, during one of the major offenses of World War I, three soldiers were wounded on the battlefield between the trenches. Davitt saw them. With heavy German machine-gun fire blasting up spits of dirt all about him, he leaped over the top of the trench and pulled one of the men to safety. Then he climbed back onto the field of fire to snag the next man. He returned for the third as well.

The chaplains' other focus was ministering. Sometimes this was done on the front lines to both living and dying men. And with the advances of trench, air, artillery, and chemical warfare in World War I, it took on a frightening dimension. Soldiers suffered from new psychological horrors.[4] Not only did they need to worry about bullets and cannon blasts, they faced bombs raining down on them from above and noxious, poisonous gas that could burn and choke the air from their lungs. Even if a soldier wasn't physically injured, the mental anguish could be just as devastating. The chaplains' role was to help the soldiers navigate all of this while ignoring the exact same threat to their own lives. Aboard the *USS Houston,* Chaplain George S. Rentz experienced this firsthand. When Japanese fighter pilots attacked his ship, he left the safety of cover and joined the men operating the antiaircraft guns. As a chaplain, he could not operate those weapons. Instead, he darted back and forth behind the men, fully exposed, screaming words of encouragement, even as the Japanese pilots rained bullets upon them.[5]

In denying their own instincts of self-preservation, chaplains demonstrated remarkable endurance. Many paid a terrible price. Soldiers often experience post-traumatic stress disorder (PTSD), which manifests itself in part by nightmares, anxiety, flashbacks, and unpredictable breakdowns. Chaplains were supposed to be one resource in preventing that. But the chaplains themselves were not immune. In the trenches of World War I, one British chaplain wrote in his diary: "All along the trench, am stepping over dead bodies. Some men shot clean through the heart or head . . . most with looks of agony or horror on their faces—if faces were not blown away—nearly all mangled in ghastly fashion. . . . Blood, flies, and smell—I shall never forget it. As one crawled along the trench, hands and legs of dead hanging over the edge would strike one's face."

Upon surviving such horrors, in the Great War as in the many that would follow, chaplains reported their own psychological struggles. Their role was, among others, to boost troop morale,[6] but their own psyches were at risk. Chaplain Hiro Higuchi, who served in World War II in Italy, wrote to his wife in July of 1944:

> War is hell—I have seen what hell is like—I don't know if the censors will allow these words to go through to you—but I feel that the home folks should realize what these boys and many other American boys are going through. . . . its [sic] just hell— undreamable goriness and fear. The first time in battle, we were shelled for five hours straight—I crawled in a little culvert barely able to squeeze my body through and just sweated the whole thing through. . . . The fear of these screaming whining shells is indescribable and almost unbearable. . . . We hardly sleep when in action—busy with the casualties which come in. I have seen officers and men crack up under the intense shelling—just go crazy—so that we have to strap them in and there was a time that I was afraid I would crack after seeing an old friends [sic] body come in. A friend I knew in LA. I just sat down and cried like a baby—and I don't blame men for cracking up.[7]

Three months later, he wrote her again, "I am changing a lot . . . not in any great way but my temper is certainly shorter and once in a while [I] loose [sic] it. I hope I don't get that way after the war—maybe I will be so happy, it will be one long smile for me for the rest of my life."[8]

Russell Stroup, a chaplain serving in the Pacific, experienced the same. Writing home in June 1944, he painted a debilitating picture: "Most of the burials have fallen to me and a Catholic chaplain in a nearby unit. It's heartbreaking business . . . it becomes almost more than one can bear. . . . It is not an easy thing to hold in your hand the smiling picture of a sweet-faced mother, knowing that soon the word will come to her which above all she dreads to hear."[9] Later, he continued, "I have the feeling that at my age a year out here is about all I could stand physically or spiritually."[10] And on the island of Okinawa, near Japan, after the United States first attacked, Jesuit Chaplain William Leonard drove his jeep to the cemetery for American soldiers killed during the incursion. It was morning. The cemetery was a mile or two from the beaches. When he took in the scene, his heart sank. Row upon row of crosses, between three and four thousand, stretched out before him. He noticed a poignant odor in the air, simultaneously disgusting and sweet. Nearby, a young soldier toiled. Chaplain Leonard asked him about the smell. "Bodies, Father," the soldier said. "Those are our guys' bodies. We can't dig graves fast enough." Leonard walked among the grave markers. The ages of the soldiers struck him. Some were older men. Most hadn't even reached their twentieth birthday. Leonard broke down. All he could think was: "For this, some poor woman labored for nine months, brought the child into the world, took care of every need, watched him grow up, proud, and this is the way it ends?"[11]

Finally, there was the mental toll of delivering the worst news to families. That responsibility often fell to chaplains. It wasn't just that they had seen men die, ministered to them amidst the anxiety of battle, buried them, or held them in their arms as they passed from this life. The chaplains then faced the duty of penning letters of condolence home. The families did not always respond with kindness. Certainly some did. One family wrote to a Catholic priest that his letter was "a great comfort and blessing to us. It indicates the great Faith and good which your mission has accomplished and will never be forgotten by us."[12] Others were more harsh, directing their anger at the situation to the bearers of heartbreaking news:

> Did he die quick, with a rifle bullet or was he blown all to hell with a mortar or torn up by shrapnel. Did he last long enough to see the flag go up on Seribachi? . . . We spent eighteen years raising this boy and it took eighteen months for the Marines to finish

the job, and we have an engraved certificate to show that he died for liberty. You will have to admit that it is a damn sorry swap.[13]

In moments of clarity, chaplains could discern that the bitterness some families expressed was not truly directed at them personally. Nevertheless, it was a burden that fell on their shoulders; not others'.

In October and November of 1942, although the four chaplains had been scattered across the United States, each received a new assignment: they were to report to Camp Myles Standish in Taunton, Massachusetts. They now understood their duties, if not the specific theater where they would serve. They had been trained, both by life and by the military. What the war would place at their feet remained to be seen. Death, despair, soldiers in need of advice, burials, shell shock, boredom, survivor's remorse—any or all of it was possible.[14]

PART II

WAR

★ ★ ★ ★ ★

CHAPTER 11

THE FINAL GOODBYES

For *Oberleutnant* Wächter, the wait was over. He was an instrument in the Führer's hands, and his master was finally moving him into position. In early December 1942, he pushed U-223. They had completed their training. Months of preparation were now behind them. Launching torpedoes, fixing firing tubes, servicing his ship, feeling ready for sea, only to endure more training, tactical exercises—it had all likely grown to such monotonous levels that he and all of his men wanted nothing more than to sail in open waters, to hunt.

If they were like many U-boat crews, they found meaning in their service. The success of those who had gone before them was epic, the stuff of German legend. When the new empire reigned for millennia, the triumphs of the U-boats in the Atlantic would be new folklore. Wächter and his men would be a part of that. Their children's grandchildren would speak of their triumphs. Just as he won in games of dice and risk aboard his ship, so he would prove victorious over the Americans.

Then the orders came. They were to make fast for Kiel, where they would join with other members of their wolfpack. Then they would turn their periscopes to the ocean. They sailed from Danzig, in Germany-occupied Poland, along the northern edge of their homeland, through the frigid waters of the Baltic Sea, south of Sweden and Denmark.

No doubt, they were humming with excitement. Their day had finally arrived. Like those who had gone before them to rain hellfire upon the Americans and British, they were coming. Part of Operation Drumbeat. They were coming. They were coming.

Christmas 1942 was a special one for Clark and Betty Poling. It wasn't supposed to happen. They were in a crammed, two-room apartment near Camp Myles Standish in Taunton, Massachusetts. And every second meant the world to them. The day wasn't about presents or meals or decorations. It was about time. Betty recalled: "Values do change and we were so grateful to be able to have that Day together."[1] Every moment, every second carried with it the possibility that it could be their last. They cherished them, especially after all the false starts and stops. Several times, both in Mississippi and now in Taunton, Clark had expected he was about to receive orders to ship out, only to be delayed once again. The emotional bait and switch must have been exhausting. Yet it meant they could still have their moments together. Corky bounced about the room, playing with his dad, memories he still holds to this day.[2] Clark and Betty held each other. They dreamed of days ahead.

Part of those dreams would be their second child. Betty had been expecting for some time, and the new baby was already kicking and squirming. Clark would place his hand on her stomach and feel the little one punch and thump. Disney had released *Bambi* earlier that year, and, not surprisingly, Clark nicknamed the little baby "Thumper."[3]

Around the same time, Alex Goode must have seen with horror the headlines coming out of Europe. He had long known that Hitler's and the Nazis' treatment of his fellow Jews was inhumane. He had worried about it constantly in his writings, sermons, and letters.[4] By signing on as a chaplain, he was already determined to serve his country and his fellow Jews. But what had been rumors, unspeakable fears almost incomprehensible to almost any rational person, were now being confirmed. For several months, the United States State Department had been trying to confirm reports that the Nazis were in fact following through on what their leadership called "The Final Solution of the Jewish Question." Whispers had leaked out of Europe through the Polish-Jewish underground: 700,000 Jews already murdered, gas chambers, concentration camps, millions more at risk. Fragmented suspicion had been reported in various United States newspapers, but it was almost as if no one wanted to believe that Germany would act on its rhetoric. By late November 1942, the State Department confirmed the truth. Press releases and newspapers amplified it. On December 10, the Polish government—now in exile—released a report to the world:

REPUBLIC OF POLAND
Ministry of Foreign Affairs

THE MASS EXTERMINATION of JEWS in GERMAN OCCUPIED POLAND

NOTE
addressed to the Governments of the
United Nations on December 10th, 1942,
and other documents

*Published on behalf of the Polish
Ministry of Foreign Affairs by*

HUTCHINSON & CO. (Publishers) LTD.
LONDON : NEW YORK : MELBOURNE

It was shocking in its detail. Ignored for too long, the Polish government was determined that the entire world understand the atrocities being committed in its homeland. The report was meant to shock the nations of the world. For Alex, reading the graphic details of what he had always feared must have brought his upcoming mission into vivid focus. The great, coursing river of all his past worries had just broken through a dam with terrifying force.

Seven days later, on December 17, 1942, the governments of the United States, Britain, and the U.S.S.R., along with ten of their allies, issued declarations simultaneously:

> The German authorities . . . are now carrying into effect Hitler's oft-repeated intention to exterminate the Jewish people in Europe. From all the occupied countries Jews are being transported, in conditions of appalling horror and brutality, to Eastern Europe. In Poland, which has been made the principal Nazi slaughter-house, the Ghettoes established by the German invaders are being systematically emptied of all Jews, except a few highly skilled workers required for war industries. None of those taken away are ever heard of again. The able-bodied are slowly worked to death in labour camps. The infirm are left to die of exposure and starvation, or are deliberately massacred in mass executions. The number of victims of these bloody cruelties is reckoned in many hundreds of thousands of entirely innocent men, women, and children.
>
> The [Allies] condemn in the strongest possible terms this bestial policy of cold-blooded extermination. They declare that such events can only strengthen the resolve of freedom-loving peoples to overthrow the barbarous Hitlerite tyranny. They reaffirm their solemn resolution to ensure that those responsible for these crimes shall not escape retribution, and to press on with the necessary practical measures to this end.[5]

Alex's reaction to the declaration must have been layered with emotion. For many soldiers, the desire to fight was triggered by the attack on Pearl Harbor. For Alex, in a very real sense, this was about his and his children's survival. Little Rosalie's entire future was at stake. There, at Camp Myles Standish, he steeled himself for whatever tasks fate would send his way.

In Boston, the cutter *Comanche* docked into port just a few days before Thanksgiving. There, Charles W. David Jr. and Dick Swanson looked forward to some much-needed rest. They and their crewmates had been working the waters around Greenland, guiding in convoys trying to survive the journey across the Atlantic. Now they would enjoy some leave while waiting for their next assignment. If history was any guide, they would soon receive news of another convoy heading to Greenland, and their role would be to protect it from lurking U-boats.

Whether Charles was able to travel south to New York City to see Kathleen and Neil is a question only they know. He may have, or circumstances may have demanded that he remain in Boston, close to his ship. Certainly not all of his crewmates were able to travel to see loved ones. Dick Swanson's family was back in Nebraska, too far to visit on a short harbor stop, so he and Charles may have spent that weekend playing the blues.

Still, in New York City, Kathleen kept her husband closer to her heart than perhaps some might have guessed. Whenever she could, she volunteered at the newly opened Harlem Defense Recreation Center, where she and Neil supported and helped any coast guardsmen and other servicemen who came through its doors.[6]

In the port of Kiel, looking out at the water, Karl-Jurg Wächter had been pent up long enough. Two hundred and forty-four days— that was how long he and his men had trained and waited. Even after sailing from Poland, he had been forced to wait a month in Kiel for loading and for an assignment. Now, on January 12, 1943, he and his men were leaving Kiel as part of a wolfpack that would join in the hunt of American ships.

Operation Drumbeat had been an unmitigated success in the Atlantic. The numbers were staggering. His fellow U-boat captains had sunk 7.8 million tons of Allied shipping in 1942.[7] The latest success had just occurred, and news of it had reached Wächter that very morning. A pack of U-boats had annihilated a large and important convoy coming from the Caribbean.[8]

He had every reason to be upbeat. For Wächter, there was no reason to think 1943 would be any different. It would begin with him and his crew and their new wolfpack. They called it *Haudegen*. In English, it meant "Warhorse." There would be twenty-six U-boats connected to it—a veritable killing machine, each of them as deadly as the other. And Wächter's ship was indeed lethal. On its con tower, he and his men had painted a white and green shield with a cup and three dice in the foreground. The dice showed the numbers two, two, and three. And why shouldn't he have chosen dice? Wächter was the captain, after all, and this was now his ship. His command.

He eased the submarine away from Tirpitz Pier.

Nearby, on the wharf, a military band played only half-heartedly. In the bleak middle of winter, gray day trailed gray day. It was like the war. Would the sun ever come out again? Would the wind ever stop howling? Despite the optimism that permeated the German navy, not everything was going so well. On land, the German armies had walked into a frozen wasteland in Russia. News reports indicated they were being hammered relentlessly. They weren't ready for the ice and waves of wind of Russia's snowy prairie. And the air raids had tilted against the country as well. Nightly, bombers from Great Britain rained death and destruction on German cities. For civilians and army personnel who couldn't escape beneath the waves, silent questions hid in the recesses of their minds. Where was Hitler leading them?

If Wächter shared those concerns, he didn't show it. The frigid drizzle blowing off the Kattegat strait would have chilled even the heartiest soul. For Wächter, it was nothing more than annoyance. He steered U-223 backward away from the pier. A small crowd had gathered to see the U-boat off, but this was just the latest of hundreds. Whatever enthusiasm may have permeated the air when the first boats had departed was long lost down the drain of war. As soon as U-223 floated away, the people dispersed.

Wächter went on.

Beneath him, his crew performed their tasks to perfection. They were ready. Over the months, the long, painful, repetitive days of training had given him a crew he could trust. At just twenty-six, he found this a scene to behold. He conned his ship past the rows of gray destroyers. The wind would have sliced like a razor, straight through his leather storm coat. The drizzle and icy spray would have licked at his face and fogged his binoculars. None of it could stop him.

At the mouth of the harbor, he commanded the ship to pause. Ahead of him, a small tugboat opened up the boom-defense nets, like pawns opening the gates to the castle for the knights to ride through. The engines idled, gulping at the water.

Only then, at least one historian reports, did Wächter feel a slight sense of anxiety, the tiniest gnaw of apprehension. He had seen something, and it had caused him pause. The dreary mists had opened upon a vision that, perhaps on any other day, Wächter might have found inspirational. But on this day, it brought only grim thoughts. It was of a giant edifice, 236 feet high, constructed out of red sandstone bricks. It soared into the sky, a monument to German pride. In the gloom of that miserable day, it would have looked more pale than red, as if all life had been sucked from it. People said it looked like a towering submarine con tower, or the stern of a Viking ship. The Germans had built it as a monument to the 4,744 German U-boat men who had died in the Great War. But in that precise moment, for Wächter, it didn't honor the dead; it prophesied of his potential demise. And for just a moment, he thought of his homeland. Thuringian Forest. Mountains covered in the silent veil of snow. Instead of bands and bombs, towering trees in a forest so still it seemed asleep, as if it might never awaken.

The tugboat blew its siren, stirring Wächter from his reverie. His thoughts turned back to his mission. On the shoulders of young Wächter and men like him lay the hopes of a nation facing defeat. He needed success. And success came in the form of blasting Allied vessels to the bottom of the Atlantic. He commanded U-223 through the defense nets.

The next little while was silent.

Then, late on the afternoon of January 12, he spied through his binoculars what he had hoped to see: materializing slowly where the colorless ocean and sky met was the first U-boat he was to join. Soon he saw another. Then another. The long, arcing leviathans could have passed for more ocean waves but for their unnatural smoothness. Each one identified itself by flashing signal lamps. Eventually five other boats joined him. The rest of the Warhorse wolfpack would rendezvous with them another time. For now, the U-boats formed a small flotilla, lined up alongside one another, and steered toward deeper waters.

The hunt had begun.[9]

At the same time, Clark and Betty drove from Massachusetts back to Schenectady. He helped her get back and settled in the house after having been gone for so many months. In her tummy, "Thumper" was as active as ever. The congregation needed and missed their minister, so Clark spent some of his time visiting those who were sick or elderly.[10] The time passed too fast. But they didn't worry; they would see each other again, likely even the next weekend. He would be able to take some leave in just seven days.

Once he had the family settled, he said his goodbyes. It was Thursday evening, January 14, 1943. Betty drove him to the train station. Clark likely gave Corky a hug and Betty a kiss. For the little baby, all he was able to do was touch her through his wife's clothes—perhaps talk with her, even if all she heard was the hope that his voice might reach her.

Betty wasn't worried. This didn't need to be an emotional goodbye. She would see Clark again soon.

On the morning of January 15, 1943, Isadore Fox was heartbroken. She and George were now separated. She could have dealt with that, but this day, this special day, was their anniversary. After all they had been through together, the nearly twenty years of sacrifice and service, she struggled to believe he could be leaving soon. After Harvard, they had shipped to North Carolina together. Then the assignment came to report to Camp Myles Standish. With that, she was no longer able to stay with him, so she returned home to Vermont. Last she had heard, George's name was on the bulletin board. He was next in line to be shipped overseas. There were no cell phones. Even long-distance calls over landlines could be tricky. No email or text, quick blurbs just to let her know where he was or whether she might even see him. She pined for news that might never come.

She forced herself from her bed. Her legs likely felt heavy, her limbs weighed down with the depression that comes from loneliness and emptiness. That George could be shipping out soon was a possibility she had denied. She had locked it away somewhere deep in a vault that even she didn't want to open. She had prayed away its inevitability the way someone might pray away the rising of the sun. But on this morning, her thoughts were tumbling, churning, shattering. She was a thousand broken shards. As she trudged to ready herself for the day, she had no choice but to accept that George, her George, whom she had sworn to help heal from the toxic gasses and broken back of World War I, would be leaving her soon.

In fact, he might already have been gone, for all she knew. Their anniversary, a date in history so special to them and them alone, she would spend by herself: sustained by the memories of their love.

She had taken a job at a nearby defense plant so she could support herself and her daughter while George and their oldest son, Wyatt, were away. To get ready for the day, she plodded through the motions.

A knock at the door.

It would have been surprising. She wasn't expecting anyone. She sauntered over and opened it. A man stood there, a huge bouquet of flowers in his hands. Nineteen roses. For nineteen years. She thanked him and eased back into the apartment. If the flowers were meant to cheer her, they didn't work. What they likely meant was that George had sent them because he couldn't get the leave to come see her. The realization poured through her like poison, choking her hope away. The sentiment behind the roses was nice, but that was all it was: an unhappy consolation prize in lieu of holding her dear, sweet husband one more time.

But Isadore Fox had endured much. The years of combatting poverty, pigsties, bedbugs, infestations, and worn clothes were a testament to her strength. Through her dense fog, she got ready and set out to work.

The day was long, the labor tedious. For eight hours, she stood at an assembly line, churning out the machinery of war. She didn't finish until nearly eleven p.m. By then, she had likely worked herself into a sort of comfortable numbness, feeling neither joy nor misery, just acceptance. The day was nearly spent; it had come and gone—evaporated, really—without a trace of George.

Isadore's legs ached. Slowly, she left the factory. It was dark out, nothing more than a streetlamp lighting the area.

Then she saw something odd. In the shadows, a short distance away, stood a hulking man, a stranger. Who was he? Why did he look so large? It was almost as if he were the size of two men standing next to each other. For the briefest of moments, the sight might have brought fear.

But a joyful realization burned it away. Her lips parted in a smile she had never thought she might allow herself. Her heart was pumping, thrashing. She called out, almost too excited, "You may come out now, George. I see you."

From behind a stranger, George sprung. He sprinted to her, bounding to close the distance between them. When he reached her, he scooped her into his arms. One hour—sixty minutes before their anniversary would have dissolved into memory. Somehow, he had made it home.

A wave of happiness washed over Isadore. She forgot the ache in her feet, the gloom of the day. They sped back to the house, determined to make every second count. For three days and three nights, they alternated between cuddling in each other's arms at night and telling jokes and stories with their daughter and Isadore's sister during the day. They laughed.

On one day, Isadore's sister pulled George aside. Isadore was out of earshot. In a whisper, she asked, "Aren't you worried about going overseas?"

George didn't hesitate. "I have all the faith in the world. I am going over safely and coming back safely."

Drifting off beside him or in his arms each night, Isadore still saw a dark emptiness lurking in her dreams. It sent chills up her spine. As much as she treasured her time with her love, she could only hold the darkness at bay for so long. It was coming, stalking ever closer, a constant companion.

On Sunday morning, it was almost as if the country wasn't at war. George and Isadore attended church together. They sang in the choir. George conducted the services. That night, they drifted off to sleep together.

On Monday morning, George packed his things. He was to report back to Massachusetts immediately. He didn't know what his assignment would be yet, but they expected it to come any day. Outside, a heavy fog imitated the pall settling over Isadore. It masked everything, sucking the world of all its nuance and beauty and depth. Added to it was a chill that seemed like it might never end. Once he was ready,

George turned to her. "You do not need to take that long walk to the bus station on this cold morning. I would rather leave you here in the home that I'm coming back to."

Isadore considered the words for a moment. How could she let him leave? How could she not spend every possible last second with him? But she understood what he wanted. He would walk away with a vision of her standing at their house, and he would hold that in his mind's eye when the shells descended and the bullets burst.

So . . . she pressed her lips to his. It was the kind of kiss written about in the poems of old—*singular* would describe it—the kind that explodes into being a new universe, one that expands and revolves around that precise moment, the beginning and the end, light dividing the darkness from the face of the deep. The two of them likely struggled to sever that last touch, perhaps letting their lips linger for just a moment longer than was needful.

Then he walked away. It had to be done. He crossed the street. Each step took them both a little closer to an unknown future. Isadore watched him until he disappeared into a fog that had seemed to swallow the world whole.[11]

After refueling in Egersund, Norway, Wächter, U-223, and the other five U-boats set sail up the Norwegian coast. Alongside them, minesweepers trolled the water ahead, seeking out any explosives the Allies may have left to destroy them. The sky remained overcast. The air was frigid. Visibility was limited at best. For the men in the depths of the ship, the weather was a nonfactor. What they dealt with was the mugginess and heat and claustrophobia of a tiny metal coffin. For the men on the con tower, however, life was as close to death as any of them wanted to be. The wind pierced them. It numbed their fingers and left icicles in their beards. Still, they had no choice. They were needed on the watch.

U-boats were not true submarines. They couldn't stay underwater indefinitely. They were designed to navigate the surface, then submerge when it was time to attack or hide. They also traveled faster on the surface than when submerged, so to cover long distances, Wächter needed to keep his boat on the water. That meant ordering his men to keep watch. They were entering enemy waters, the North Sea. British ships and aircraft were searching for them. They were on the hunt. But they were also prey. Lookouts were crucial, no matter how bad the weather.

Traveling slowly to ensure there were no mines, the U-boats continued up the coast for nearly four hours. Then the minesweepers signaled that their job was complete. No one spoke. No radio. They flashed their lights, then headed back home. The U-boats were on their own. Even that wouldn't last. Each had been given a different assignment. One by one, they peeled away from each other, their gray shapes vanishing en route to their assigned wolfpacks. Wächter watched them. Within an hour, he and his men were alone. In his holds, he was well stocked, every spaced crammed with what he needed for at least two months of hunting Americans: vegetables, bread, smoked hams, eggs, coffee, batteries, ammunition, fuel, water, first aid kits.

Behind him was the Norwegian coastline—ahead, a never-ending tableau of choppy and hostile water. At approximately four p.m., Wächter ordered a test dive. The men on the con tower climbed into the bowels of the ship. The U-boat slipped beneath the surface. Ninety minutes later, it surfaced. They set their course: almost straight north, which would allow them to sail near the Arctic Circle, far above the dangers of the British Isles.

Wächter did not want his men getting comfortable. At nearly eleven p.m., he ordered a crash dive for training purposes. His men scrambled, alarms sounded, and they plunged into the depths—just as they would need to do once they finally happened upon their prey.

They seem to have performed to his satisfaction. Less than an hour later, they were on the move again at full transit speed.[12]

★ ★ ★

That same day, Alex Goode checked into a hotel in New York City. Theresa met him there a short while later. He was already choking with disappointment. When he saw her, it nearly suffocated him. One source of his frustration stemmed from his assignment. No one was supposed to know where they were going; there were simply too many possibilities that the enemy could find out. But soldiers were people, and scuttlebutt was rampant. Alex, it turned out, was being shipped to Greenland. Despite his near constant requests to be stationed at the front in Europe, where he could actually do some good both for the troops and hopefully for his own people, he was headed to an icy, wind-swept tundra of nothing. It wasn't any better than staying at one of the bases at home. Surely he understood Greenland's broader strategic importance: after Germany had taken Denmark, the island had become a territory without a home country. The United States had filled the void, using it for extensive facilities that aided in dispatching air support and ships across the North Atlantic, including radio stations, army depots, weather stations, ports, artillery posts, and search-and-rescue stations. Alex knew and understood all of that, but he struggled to wrap his mind around what good a chaplain would be in that setting. Men working a weather or radio station didn't need a chaplain nearly as much as soldiers liberating concentration camps did. And the place was bleak: almost all of it was buried in ice 5,000 feet thick, the temperatures in winter plummeted to -9° F, and the sun woke for only about four hours a day. "I don't want to go to Greenland," he told Theresa. "I'm not going to sit on a cake of ice. I want to go where there's action." His hopes of helping free enslaved Jews remained locked in a cage.

His other disappointment came from his daughter. He had begged Theresa to bring little Rosalie with her to New York, but when his wife appeared, their daughter was nowhere to be seen.

Why didn't you bring her?

Theresa, thoughtful and always sensible, had a very good reason: Rosalie had just been vaccinated and had a fever; she didn't think it made sense to bring her, so she let the little girl stay with Alex's sister.

Alex's disappointment was palpable, so much so that Theresa immediately regretted her decision. She didn't know if asking the girl to travel by train would have hurt or not, but the pain on Alex's face was almost too much to bear.

Alex overcame the setback quickly. He still got to spend time with Theresa, three days in New York City together. It was a dream. Soon, in their hotel room, in each other's arms, even Alex's frustration with his assignment to Greenland dissipated, at least for a time. It would probably never leave him, but his passion and love for Theresa would keep it at bay. No doubt, when the months in the icy outpost turned to boredom, he would pull his hair out that he wasn't doing something, anything, to help stop the slaughter of his kindred by the Nazis. But this was not the time for that. This was a time to create memories: three days with no other distractions; no worries, no wars, no assignments; just the two of them together in a world that was nothing more than a blurry dream.

Late at night, perhaps in Alex's own dreams, or maybe as he watched Theresa sleep peacefully beside him, the reason for his distress at not seeing Rosalie was more apparent. A few days earlier, he had felt a premonition. His mind had lifted from itself, freed from the constraints of time and the stifling environment of a military base. And Alex knew something, a detail about the future that shouldn't have been his, a prophetical footnote that came to him even before he knew where he would be serving: the ship carrying him was not going to make it to that destination. Like so many other ships trying to carry troops and cargo across the Atlantic, it was going to fall prey to the enemy. So perhaps there, in the quiet, was why he had so badly wanted to see Rosalie; to hold her one last time. It might explain also why, many decades later, Rosalie herself found some belief in people's abilities to glimpse the future, even if in the foggiest detail.[13]

Alex's prompting was not unique to him. On the day they had to separate, he and Theresa navigated the bustling streets of New York to the train station. They kissed their goodbyes. She climbed aboard the train. She was always so sensible: the one who had wanted to wait to get married, practical, never one to rush into anything. She seemed the type who would never follow her gut unless logic stood right there beside her.

But in that moment, as she looked at Alex through the train window, her gut spoke to her.

Tears had welled up in his eyes.

She felt them in hers as well. Her premonition was powerful, a feeling in her heart she couldn't deny: she was never going to see him again, and he would never hold her or Rosalie again either. The regret of not bringing her daughter swelled in a way that would never leave her. She likely knew it in that very moment. The train moaned from the station. The cold of the New York winter surrounded them both. And as the engine tugged her away, she wept.[14]

That weekend, John's taxi pulled up in front of his mother's house. He walked up the steps and inside, knowing this would be the last time he would see her for a while. It must have been a bittersweet moment. Like George, he didn't quite know his assignment yet, but he knew it would arrive any day. And he knew he would be headed overseas.

He was battling a severe case of the hives. Red, itchy welts had been plaguing him for days. If the symptoms were truly severe, his lips, eyelids, and even throat would have been swollen. The signs were bad enough that his mother noticed immediately and demanded that he stay at the house.

"I admit I feel sleazy," John said to her as they sat in the house, "but I've simply got to see everyone. I'm not going off on any boat without seeing my old pals. Not with my dog paddle."

He and his mom likely shared knowing smiles. John had never really learned how to swim. As a child, he had tried again and again and again, but he'd never progressed past treading water. The prospect of being on a boat over the depths of the ocean must have been terrifying. "Just to be on the safe side," he added, "I've got to see the nuns and everyone possible. I'm going to need all the prayers I can get."

Sometime that Saturday or Sunday, John made the rounds. He stopped to visit another priest, a mentor, in the hospital. They visited for a time. As he was leaving, John paused in the doorway and looked back at his friend. Their conversation had mostly been light, filled with jokes and stories, but in that moment, John's face had turned serious. "I feel funny about this whole business," he said. We don't know what he meant. But he followed it up with an ominous request: "You won't forget me, Din?"

Then he left.

His last morning on leave, John gathered his mother, siblings, any other family, and friends close to him. He held mass for them and said his goodbyes.

At long last he turned to his sobbing mother and folded himself around her. "Goodbye, Ma," he said. "No cryin'. You'll be hearing from me."

With that, he set out on his mission.

★ ★ ★

Charles W. David Jr. received word in early-to-mid January. His cutter would be escorting another convoy to Greenland. The ships would all meet in Newfoundland, then make the treacherous journey. Once again, the crew of the *Comanche* would be assigned to protect against hounding U-boats.

While they sat in Swanson's office, playing the *Comanche* Blues, Charles and his friend prepared. They knew their cutter wouldn't be the direct target of the Nazis—their aim was always the larger ships. But when the battles began, it was the men on the *Comanche* and other escorts who did the fighting. They pursued the U-boats. They fired the depth charges. They took the machine-gun fire.

Charles, of course, wasn't allowed to fight. As a man with brown skin, he prepared and served meals. This might have been comforting, but, for some, sitting in a position of extreme danger while not being able to do anything about it was as intolerable as being dropped into a pit of snakes without a weapon. The strikes were coming, but Charles seemingly was given no way to protect himself.

Nevertheless, he was prepared to do his duty and was ready for the next assignment, come what may.

Betty Poling was nestled in her home in Schenectady, her little boy, Corky, nearby, the baby, tiny "Thumper," squirming away inside her, when the phone rang. It was Tuesday, January 18, 1943. When she answered, Clark was on the line. He couldn't give her specifics, but something was happening. He just wanted her to know. She had been planning on seeing him the following weekend. Now it looked like it might not happen.

The next day, Wednesday, the phone rang again. False alarm, Clark said. Nothing was happening. He could still come that weekend.

On Thursday, Betty and Corky would have been feeling the excitement. The next day, their dad and husband would be home to see them. She likely was getting the house ready. Corky was probably ready to play horsey on his dad's knee, or have his dad drag him around the street on a bike or other toy the way he had done before.

Then a telegram came. Betty opened the yellow envelope. Inside, a slip of paper read only: "Can't phone again, with my dearest love. Clark."

She broke the news to her little boy, who was no doubt disappointed. She was now moving into her final trimester with Thumper, and as she and Corky settled into the realization that they would have no choice but to wait for letters from Clark, she wondered what life would be like without him. For her and Corky, their lives revolved around Clark, as his did around them. But Betty was determined not to complain—she would face the future "uncomplaining," she wrote, "for we were awaiting the day when Clark would come back and the four of us would take up our life, finishing to a happy end what had such a perfect beginning."[15]

What happened was simple: Colonel Frederick Gillespie had been sitting in his office in Brooklyn at the New York Port of Embarkation. Before him on his desk lay a list of chaplains. He had a problem. One of his many duties was to ensure the right people were on the right ships headed for Europe, and four chaplains were supposed to be on a transport ship known as the *Dorchester*, headed for Greenland. At the last minute, two of the four chaplains had been pulled from the roster, which meant Gillespie had to replace them, and fast. The *Dorchester* was ready to set sail. In Alex Goode, he already had one rabbi assigned to the ship, and a Protestant in George Fox. But he needed a Catholic and another Protestant.

He found them in Father John Washington and in Minister Clark V. Poling. He immediately sent notice to Camp Myles Standish. The four chaplains were to ready themselves to depart with the *Dorchester* immediately.[16]

Around the same time Betty received her telegram, Theresa Goode received a letter from Alex. This is what it read:

> *Darling:*
>
> *Just a hurried line as I rush my packing. I'll be on my way in an hour or two. I got back yesterday afternoon just before the warning. Hard as it was for us to say goodbye in N.Y. at least we could see each other before I left.*
>
> *Don't worry—I'll be coming back much sooner than you think.*

Take care of yourself and the baby—a kiss for each of you.
I'll keep thinking of you.

Remember I love you very much.
Alex

She tucked it away, along with some of his other letters, then prepared herself for the long winter.

★ ★ ★

Far to the north, Wächter drove his men forward, willing them through wave after icy wave. The wind blasted them. Visibility plummeted to almost nothing, leaving the men on the con tower to look out into a frozen and spitting wall of gray rain and sleet. The conditions were brutal. Still, Wächter's mission was clear: navigate around and through the dangerous waters between Britain and Iceland, then destroy as many American ships and men as possible. Though it may have been tempting to submerge and run more slowly underwater, doing so would only delay them and extend the time before they might run into British ships or airplanes. So Wächter drove his boat forward.

Finally, U-223 reached its most northerly point. They were close to a hundred miles from the Arctic Circle, north of Norway and the Faroe Islands and even in latitude with Reykjavik, Iceland. There, in that lonely world, with no land visible in any direction, where the pounding weather offered cover and safety, Wächter altered course.

There, U-223 began sailing directly for the Americans.

CHAPTER 12

ENTERING DANGEROUS WATERS

O n the other side of that ocean, on January 22, 1943, Alex, George, John, and Clark stepped off a train at Pier II on Staten Island in New York and readied to go to war. Thick, wet snowflakes blanketed the rails and glided almost leisurely to alight on the warehouses, the train, and even the water, as if they hadn't a care in the world. Convoys of army trucks made their way around the pier, hurling clots of muddy snow. Before them, dominating the scene, stood the ship that would take them to Greenland: the *SS Dorchester*. Despite the different paths that had led them to this point, the four chaplains were now united. They immediately set to work. Behind them, they knew, hundreds of soldiers were coming, many who had never set foot on a ship or, for that matter, even left their homes. They would be green, some would be scared, and many would struggle to get along with anyone who was different from the people they knew in whatever insular community they made their home.

The chaplains could help with all of that. Each of them seemed to feel at least some disappointment that they were headed to Greenland, but that was behind them now. It was time to provide whatever service they could wherever they had been called.

The four men got settled, then stationed themselves near the gang-plank.

Soon, hundreds of young, fresh soldiers were boarding. Not all were new or naïve. Three different groups of military boarded that day. The first was the *Dorchester*'s crew of between 120 and 130 merchant marines under the command of Captain Hans Jorgen Danielson; these were seasoned seamen who knew how to operate the ship. The second was a squadron of roughly twenty-four U.S. Navy Armed Guard seamen; under the command of Lieutenant William Arpaia, their task was to operate the guns that had been added to the vessel for protection. Finally, the third contingent represented the vast majority of the men on board: roughly 751 army troops or construction workers shipping out for service.[1]

Most of those were as green as the chaplains had expected. Some were older and had traveled before, even on this very ship, but the bulk were new recruits. They stumbled off the train and gawked at the size of the *Dorchester*. For someone who had never seen an ocean liner before, it was a sight to behold: looming riveted steel hulls, wooden upper decks, triple-expansion steam engines, and four oil-fired boilers belching steam into the entire system. On the sides, massive cargo doors opened like gaping mouths in the hull so it could swallow thousands of tons of cargo. The ship towered over the pier, a behemoth that invoked fantasies of days gone by. Like its sister ships, it had not been built for war; it had been a cruise ship, meant to take fancy, well-to-do people up and down the Atlantic seaboard while they sipped champagne, listened to melodies float off the grand piano, rolled the dice in the casino, or lay down in their luxurious cabins. The young soldiers looked up at it in amazement, fantasizing about the day when they would have enough money to take a trip of their own on such a ship.

As the young men hiked up the gangplank, Alex, George, John, and Clark stood by, smiling. Occasionally, one of them would holler "Welcome aboard!" if a young man looked like he needed it. To at least some of the men, the chaplains stood out. John, George, and Clark all wore uniforms with crosses on the lapels; Alex's brandished Hebrew tablets under a Star of David. This would not have covered the nuanced religious beliefs of all the men walking past them, but it would have told the vast majority that they had a shepherd on board. Or at least that it was time to set their religious differences aside. One soldier recalled thinking that the chaplains' camaraderie was odd. In his hometown, the Protestants had nothing to do with the Catholics or Jews, and the same was true for all the religions. He had never seen clergy of different backgrounds actually working together.

Not everyone was in awe of the ship. Some of the more seasoned veterans and sailors were downright terrified. The *Dorchester* may have, at one time, looked luxurious, but that was back when it was being used for its intended purpose of sightseeing in beautiful coastal waters or down near the Caribbean. Now it was worn and rusted in places; it looked tired, as if it would prefer just to retire and give up the dream. The months of fighting the frigid, terrible storms and ice patches of the North Atlantic had taken their toll. The gutting of the ship to make it suitable for soldiers and cargo made it look like nothing more than a skeleton of its former self. Painting it gray only added to the impression that the ship was one step away from the scrapyard.[2] And it had a reputation: as some sailors recalled while walking up the gangplank, the *Dorchester* wasn't exactly known as the heartiest of ships. Sometimes it would break down in the middle of the ocean, a floating piece of target practice for any bored U-boat captain. Or it would lose some of its escorts in the thick fogs that blanketed the waters around Greenland. In fact, the *Dorchester* ended up late to its destination so many times that there were many false reports of its being sunk, which would leave everyone in shock when it would materialize out of the fog at the base in Narsarsuaq, Greenland, almost as if it were a mythical ghost ship back from the brink. Some had taken to calling it the "suicide ship." And while the chaplains tried to lift the sailors' spirits, a crotchety man on the dock, who was also an undertaker, muttered, "This damn thing is never gonna make it!"

None of this helped the green soldiers who were already feeling queasy. For some, the mere act of walking on the bobbing pier and the prospect of crashing over ocean waves left them nauseous. One, in line on the pier and waiting for his turn on the gangplank, vomited in a barrel full of water. The retching was embarrassing enough for a soldier trying to impress his fellows, but his situation was even worse because he had false teeth. When he lost his breakfast, his dentures flew out of his mouth and into the barrel. In that moment, he realized he was about to cross the ocean, potentially to a war zone, with no teeth. Some of the other men tipped the barrel over, and he snagged half of his mouth off the ground.[3]

To all of these, the chaplains offered whatever comfort they could. They were some of the few men who knew where they were going. That was intentional. Destinations of ships were a carefully guarded secret—or at least that was the intention. The United States was highly concerned about spies and the potential that any leak could result in the U-boats gaining crucial intelligence about their mission. Given the *Dorchester*'s propensity for breaking down, and considering it was already a pretty slow ship, providing its location or route to the U-boats would result in a suicide mission. So the vast majority of the young soldiers walked up the gangplank, past the chaplains, and to their rooms with no clue regarding their final destination.

There was one other thing most of them didn't know: the *Dorchester*'s sister ship, identical in every way including its original purpose and manufacturer, was the *SS Chatham*, blown out of the water near Belle Island just five months earlier. There was one man who knew this, a gunner by the name of Roy Summers. By some twist of fate, he had been on the *Chatham* that day in August and had survived to tell the tale. Now he was marching on board its twin. At a minimum, he would have recognized how similar this ship was to the one he watched sink.

As the chaplains watched these soldiers step into a new and frightening world, they likely realized that they would be more needed than they had at first assumed. These boys would need to hear many things. They would require guidance. They would want perspective. As the last of them trudged aboard, the four men started plans to provide just that.[4]

Once everyone had time to get settled, Clark Poling found a quiet place. He had much to do for the troops, but at least part of his mind was on home and Betty and Corky and little unborn Thumper. In his cabin, perhaps, or in a quiet corner on the pier, he pulled out a pen and paper and scratched out a quick note to Betty:

> *Dearest:*
>
> *I can't write a "noble, brave" letter. I would be a little self-conscious writing that sort of a letter to you. All that I can say is that always I will love you and hold our happy memories in the most sacred part of my thoughts until that time when we shall be together again.*

He folded the paper, sealed it up in an envelope, and sent it on its way. Then he boarded the ship.[5]

On the morning of January 23, 1943, the *Dorchester* hummed and churned to life. A tug finally pulled it away from the pier and guided it to its place in a long convoy of fifty other ships. On board, she now carried 751 troops, as well as her own crew and gunners, for a total of 904 men. In addition, her bowels were stuffed with sixty bags of mail and more than one thousand tons of cargo.[6]

Most of the men bunked in the bowels of the ship. The officers, including the chaplains, were assigned to private staterooms on the main deck. John Washington settled into his room, then walked along knocking on doors and introducing himself to folks. He chatted with men on the upper level and got to know those closest to his room. Eventually, he found a stairwell leading to a lower deck. At the bottom of it, he ran into Alex, George, and Clark. After their time together at

Camp Myles Standish, they knew each other well enough. They talked about plans for helping the men and at some point put their arms around each other as if they were standing in a football huddle. Ideas about things they could do to lift the soldiers' spirits ricocheted between them.

At one point, at least a couple of soldiers walked by, thinking the gathering odd. One of them, a Catholic from an Irish neighborhood, had never seen Catholic and Protestant clergymen talking to each other. And he had never seen either ever talk to a Jew or a Baptist. To see them all huddled together like best buddies planning a prank was as odd as seeing Mussolini and Roosevelt shake hands.

The chaplains' first priority was to hold services, but they weren't sure how to let the men know the time and location. As one crewman walked by, they introduced themselves and asked for his thoughts. He looked relatively seasoned, and John had spoken with him up on the main deck enough to know that he'd actually been on the ship before. He suggested they post the information on the bulletin board near the mess hall. "Everybody goes there to eat, and they'll see it," he said.

That made sense. They broke the huddle.

The chaplains also knew that many of these soldiers were going to be in agony soon. As they descended into the depths of the ship, all of their concerns for their men were confirmed: this was going to be a painful voyage. The *Dorchester* had been built to hold a third of its current contingent. To cram this many people in, the army had gutted lower holds C, D, and E and stacked each room with two sets of bunks four beds high; the rooms were so narrow, only a couple of feet separated one set of beds from the other. The men were already on top of each other . . . it wasn't clear where they were supposed to put themselves, much less all of their gear, which included everything from helmets to life preservers to duffels to parkas to bags stuffed with contraband they had smuggled aboard. The air was muggy, the halls narrow—a metal maze of never-ending tunnels and doors. The space reeked of fuel, food, and bodily fluids, and it carried all the accompanying sounds, including one group of soldiers who had smuggled a guitar on board and were strumming it violently, completely clueless that there might be other crew around who didn't want to hear it.[7] To top it off, the sea did not promise to be forgiving— the same storm that had brought the snow upon them would bring a subtle (and at times violent) rocking that would make even the men with the strongest stomachs ill.

And the threat of roving wolfpacks lingered over all else. The chaplains could see it in the eyes of the young soldiers especially, some of whom had never even left their hometowns before this trip. If any torpedo blasted into the side of this ship, these narrow corridors and cramped rooms would flood, leaving little chance for escape. One soldier, so fearful of that possibility, had decided to sleep on a coiled-up fire hose in the passage, which would give him a quicker exit route.

Add it all up, and the place had the potential energy of a naval mine.

If tempers weren't already flaring, they would be soon.

High up above, the captain worried about routes and safety and spies and navigating troubled waters and narrow passages through harbors. Down below, the chaplains focused on calming nerves. In addition to the religious services, they decided they could host some kind of talent show—something, anything, to keep the men's minds off torpedoes, nausea, and their cramped conditions. In the meantime, they sidled and threaded their way through the lower holds, introducing themselves, joking, thanking the men for their service, learning who might have some skills for the talent show, and encouraging the young men especially that the *Dorchester* had already survived five previous trips just like this one.

As the *Dorchester* moved farther away from Staten Island, most of the men sprinted to the deck. The polished wood shifted beneath their feet, and they watched the New York City skyline melt away as the behemoth carved a path out to sea. The tug offered its final toot goodbye. *Dorchester*'s engines hummed in the water. For the briefest of moments, at least, before they separated from the rest of their massive convoy and distanced themselves from United States coastal waters, they could feel at least moderately safe.

Wächter was being cautious. The occasional times when the weather had cleared to reveal the brightness of the waxing, nearly full moon, it made sailing more tolerable, but it also posed a risk to the boat—that was when the enemy could see them. The Royal Air Force and its planes and their bombs were always on the lookout, ready to rain fire upon any U-boat blackening the flickering moonlight on the ocean's surface. Twice in the past two days, his men had spotted enemy aircraft overhead. Both times, he had ordered U-223 to plunge into the depths. Twenty meters beneath the surface, U-223 had floated along safely . . . but slowly. The bloated pace must have infuriated the young captain. This was a respite for his men, to be sure. The waves didn't toss them down here, and the thick, muggy air was preferable to the freeze up at the surface.

But he had just received new orders over the radio from U-boat headquarters, and he likely did not like being delayed. Apparently, new intelligence had come in. In his captain's journal, Wächter wrote: "New Objective for . . . Wächter." He ordered the men to change course.

U-223 was to head to a point just south of Greenland.

CHAPTER 13

THE SPIES OF
THE FIFTH COLUMN

The *Dorchester* had barely lost sight of the New York City skyline before men started throwing up. The holds had transformed from a chorus of men stepping on each other's toes to a melody of bedridden moaning. The ship lurched forward, then backward; up, then down; left, then right.

Little broke the agony. The chaplains were still trying to plan some sort of variety show, but that was days away at best. And they weren't immune to the sloshing of the sea any more than anyone else.

Bleak day followed bleak day. The thrill and anxiety of departure had been subsumed by the mundane concerns of trying to pass the time without vomiting. Many men gambled, playing cards or craps. John Washington walked among them, often chiding the boys for their games of chance, but always doing it with a joke; his time on Twelfth Street, thriving on the streets with the neighborhood boys—it came in handy. In more quiet moments, he would listen to confession. Clark was the same; he would sit with the men and listen to them, dig into their spiritual lives, drill down, down, down until he had learned what was truly troubling them. Then help them talk it through.

At one point, an "abandon ship" drill was ordered. It would at least provide some mild distraction. Alarms blared. Men were forced to sprint up flights and flights of stairs. For the men in E hold, this meant huffing up three levels until they reached the upper deck. There, certain men were ordered to snag doughnut rafts. Their assignment, should a U-boat successfully hit them: inflate the rafts, sidearm them into the waves, then dive in after them.

The men went through the motions. Perhaps because of the seasickness, maybe the weather, the drill was barely supervised. The men didn't perform up to snuff, but whoever was supervising them let the laxity go unchecked. Months later, when official reports were being written and a confused country was trying to make sense of what happened, at least one commander of a nearby ship would make note of this. In the moment, the men were grateful for the distraction, though several of them lingered on the top deck for a time, staring down into the choppy ocean below. They knew their duty: inflate the rafts, jump in after, blaze the way for men to follow. But all they could think was that leaping off such a great height would be suicide.

During the blurry line between the fourth and fifth days, a change occurred. They had been traveling in a convoy, zigzagging their way in a northeasterly direction with a multitude of other ships. There was safety there. U-boats were less likely to attack large convoys because the chances of being detected and destroyed were too great. But on January 27, 1943, most of the other ships peeled away, vanishing into the vastness of the Atlantic. The men on the *Dorchester* saw that they were largely alone now. Only two other ships had remained with them. If U-boats were lurking beneath the windswept ocean surface, they would see their opening to attack.

And where they were headed remained a mystery for most of the crew. As the day dragged on, the ship steamed northward. The boredom of the past few days gave way to a robust anxiety, an anticipation that something could go wrong.

Then word spread among the crew: they were approaching a port.

★ ★ ★

Few places on earth are harder for a large ship to navigate than the entrance into St. John's Harbor, Newfoundland. There is but one passage from the Atlantic Ocean into the harbor, and its name reflects its danger: "The Narrows." It is a gap between cliffs that loom like 500-foot sentinels; in some places, it is only 220 yards wide. For a ship the size of the *Dorchester,* in a space that small, even a minor mistake could be deadly. Late in the night of January 27, 1943, nearly five days into the journey, Captain Hans Jorgen Danielson guided the ship and its men through the space, then picked up a tug to guide it into the harbor, where it dropped anchor. Their passage north to Newfoundland had gone unnoticed. As they waited here, in the safety of one of the oldest ports in North America, they could only hope they would remain as lucky for the rest of their journey.

The scene around them didn't present much hope. All around the port lay ships with holes blasted into their hulls. How they had managed to stay afloat long enough to make it back to harbor was anybody's guess.

Everyone was eager to get off the ship. This was a friendly port, the last until Greenland, but these were dangerous times. No one could be trusted. All over the world, but especially in Newfoundland, fear of German spies drove many decisions. It was widely believed that the Nazi regime had created a dramatic spy network all over the globe known as the Fifth Column. Its job was to infiltrate nations and populaces, gather intelligence, and lie in wait until the Reich decided to activate its agents. Its existence was one explanation for how quickly Germany had managed to rise to power in the late 1930s and early 1940s. It also helped the Allies, and especially civilians, make sense of a world in which Germany had managed to sink so many North American ships throughout 1942. Someone was leaking information to Germany, they believed. In many people's minds, Nazi agents were everywhere.

Some of the hysteria over the Fifth Column had abated in Britain and in much of Canada by the time the *Dorchester* docked in St. John's. But not in Newfoundland. Rumors and paranoia ran rampant.

This was especially true the evening of January 27, when the *Dorchester* crew wanted nothing more than to escape the cramped stomach of the ship and experience the cool, crisp air of the harbor town. Tensions were high. Just the month before, the Knights of Columbus on Harvey Road in St. John's had hosted a dance party. It was filled with nearly four hundred servicemen and their dance partners. As the party carried on into the night, the building mysteriously caught fire. The blaze was unforgiving: it tore through the wood structure. Many of the people inside were trapped. In all, ninety-nine died; eighty were servicemen. Another 109 others were critically wounded. Immediately, rumors began to spread that enemy agents, spies from Germany, had caused the blaze.[1]

And just five days before the *Dorchester*'s arrival, another suspicious fire broke out at the Old Colony Club in a St. John's suburb, killing four people.

To Newfoundlanders, anyone and everyone could have been the enemy. Stories ran rampant. Civilians reported strange lights flashing signals between land and sea. Others claimed to have seen large oil drums being loaded onto suspicious schooners under cover of darkness.[2] *Newsweek* ran a story in July 1942 claiming that critical intelligence information had leaked from St. John's to Germany, resulting in the downing of several ships in the North Atlantic. If the Nazis were invading North America, they were doing it silently, not with bullets and bombs but through agents sneaking onto land at night on rubber skiffs. They were in the bars and cafés, the dance halls and churches— strange men and women with unusual accents. Anyone of German descent was especially suspect.

It was into this frenzied paranoia that the *Dorchester* docked. Seventy years later, historians came to question just how active the Fifth Column truly was, not just in Newfoundland but worldwide. Far more likely: the hysteria around the Fifth Column was a product of Nazi propaganda and unfettered paranoia. Hard evidence that Nazi spies actually operated in St. John's or caused any of the fires has been notoriously absent.[3]

Still, captains needed to be careful about who knew where their ships were headed. Information required protecting at all costs, and letting young soldiers out at a port like St. John's was not the best way to keep a secret, even if most of them had no clue where they were going. Often, captains and army officers made their orders clear: soldiers should keep their mouths shut or stay on the ship. On this night, however, leadership determined that it made sense to let the men off.

Never in the bar or barber's
Talk of ships or crews or harbours
Idle words - things heard or seen
Help the lurking submarine

Careless talk costs lives and ships

Poster displayed in St. John's in 1942 warning against
careless talk in front of potential Nazi agents

"All troops," a voice blared over the loudspeaker, "all troops, get ready to disembark, fully clothed with packs." Orders trickled down through the ranks. The men were to march through town to a United States military base approximately one hour away. Rumors spread quickly—some men speculated this could be the totality of their mission: travel to Newfoundland, sit out the war, go home. The chaplains knew better. Whatever this was, it was just a pit stop.

But it was also a welcome reprieve. Early in the morning, long before the sun would rise in that part of the world, the men trickled through the mess hall on the ship. The chaplains were all together, a common sight. Eating pancakes and coffee, they joked with each other and talked with some of the more senior men about life in Greenland. Almost everyone else still had no clue about the ship's destination.

Not so in the town. The chaplains marched down the gangplank with the regular men. They weren't required to, but it's likely they, just like everyone else, wanted to be free of the ship for at least a little while. To feel the fresh air on their faces and in their lungs, to get to mingle with the men in a space other than the tight confines of the lower holds, to get to send communications home—the chaplains welcomed all of these opportunities. But as they marched through the town, a disconcerting fact became apparent: their destination wasn't a secret.

The troops were a spectacle every time they arrived, and small children ran to them to scream and holler for attention. Some of these urchins hollered that the *Dorchester* was headed for Greenland. Others seemed to know even the schedule of the ship, suggesting it was a day late. It's hard to know how much of this was just speculation. Many ships came through St. John's. Many sailed on to Greenland. It wouldn't have been hard for the children and others to assume, even incorrectly, that this particular vessel was headed there as well. For the chaplains and other officers marching with the troops who knew the correct destination, the children screaming their guesses at the top of their lungs had to have been disconcerting, because one thing was certain: if German spies were lurking about St. John's, they would relay a message that a large United States troop carrier was headed to Greenland in the coming days.

Wolfpacks would be on the hunt.

★ ★ ★

As the men settled into the camp, the *Comanche,* with Charles W. David Jr. on board, pulled into the port as well. There it waited for the order to get the convoy moving to Greenland. This was a journey Charles had now made several times. He had yet to see any direct combat. His missions had largely been uneventful, and for much of the previous year, he and his crewmates had spent their time patrolling the waters around Greenland or escorting convoys into harbor who had already survived the most treacherous parts of their journey.

Charles and his crewmates were seasoned to a degree; they had spent time in the water, more than most. But how they would all react if actually in battle remained a mystery. Who would step up? Who would hesitate? Who would go above and beyond the call of duty?

None really knew.

They didn't even really know about themselves, even in their most honest and introspective moments. Still, as he served meals to the commander of the *Comanche,* its grey and green hull bobbing outside St. John's, Charles could sleep comfortably with at least one thought: he always met his duty . . . on the ship . . . with his family . . . no matter the circumstances.

At the camp, men showered and enjoyed a warm meal. Once again, Clark Poling found a moment to write home. He penned two letters, one to Betty and one to his parents. With the threat of spies intercepting mail, Clark was careful not to mention in writing where he was headed. He referred to it only in the vaguest of terms that Betty would understand. To her, he wrote:

> *There is a part of my mind that is quite satisfied with the turn of events that sends me to the safe but lonely post we have talked about. However, you know there is another part of me that is disappointed. Perhaps all of us are drawn to the heroic and hazardous. I have done all and more than is legitimate to get into the thick of it. . . . Dearest, I love you, and*

wherever I go and for all time I am yours, and you are mine. Read to Corky for me and spank him, love him, keep him away from the river, and feed him the oil! You must let me know how things are with "Thumper" and send me a wire. . . . God bless you, my darling wife. . . . [4]

Clearly, at some point after they had received their orders but before he had mailed the letter, he had told her where his destination was, perhaps by phone. This was the last letter he would ever write to her. To his parents, he penned another missive. It read, in part:

Dearest Dad and Mother:

In order for you to check on whether my letters are getting through, I will number each one and you can keep a record. . . .

So far I have stood up pretty well against the sharp arrows of loneliness. I miss Betty and Corky terribly and I find myself turning unconsciously as though to tell Betty something. It is not so much the physical side of marriage that counts, as the constant comradeship with all the taken-for-granted little details of living together that makes for happiness.

Corky is often in my mind. I have dreamed about him several times. The worse pangs come when I realize that he won't know me when I get back, and that he will be quite a different small boy. . . .

Incidentally, Corky loves stories. The last night I was at home he fell out of bed. . . . He was very much disturbed and frightened by the sudden bump. But he wasn't too tired to want a story. "Me tory" is what he says when he wants a story. . . . Several times I dozed off but Cork would wiggle and say, "Read me. Me tory," and wake me up; finally we both went to sleep. And when eventually I woke up, there he was, a warm ball against my side clutching his "book" tightly in one hand. . . .

I love you both,
Clark

Clark sealed up both letters and dropped them off.

★ ★ ★

John Washington wandered the camp. As a Catholic priest with no family of his own, he may have thought of his mother, or perhaps loneliness nipped at him. But another priest was already there, someone John had met at Camp Myles Standish. He looked on John with understanding eyes and high cheekbones made even more pronounced when he smiled at his friend. His name was William Bowdern. After Massachusetts, he had been stationed in Newfoundland. This was his temporary home. He and John found a quiet place and talked. Wherever else their conversation led, it found its way to the dangers of the trip ahead.

Father Bowdern expressed what a blessing John would be to the men on the ship. Should anything happen, he could offer them absolution. But things of eternity were clearly near the surface for both men. Together, they visited the Blessed Sacrament, which to Catholics is like standing before God. Presumably, they prayed together. When that was done, John went to confession to Father Bowdern, offering his own personal failings.

But it was time to say goodbye. This was just a minor respite from the storm. John was anxious to get back to his men. They shook hands, then parted ways.

With little time left, John found time to send a wire to his mother to let her know he was safe.

Alex Goode also took a moment to wire Theresa and little Rosalie that he was safe. As for George Fox, if he sent a message to Isadore from St. John's, we have no record of it. The rest of the troops likely dreaded returning to the ship, but if any of them had nurtured hopes for a longer stay in Newfoundland, those were dashed relatively quickly. By the afternoon of January 29, the men marched back to the *Dorchester.* On board, John, Alex, George, and Clark would have learned they would be part of a small convoy of just three ships, known as SG-19. The two other ships were the steamers *Biscaya* and *Lutz,* both of which were filled with supplies for the army bases in Greenland. Those three ships would not survive long if left alone in the North Atlantic. To protect them were three US Coast Guard cutters: the *Tampa, Comanche,* and *Escanaba.* There would be no air support. The cutters were supposed to be faster and more nimble than the *Dorchester,* but that was questionable at best in this case. Still, they at least boasted some 5-inch and 3-inch guns and other anti-U-boat weaponry in case of attack. They weren't the most hearty set of bodyguards and likely wouldn't completely scare away an eager U-boat captain, but they were something.

On the afternoon of January 29, the convoy navigated through the Narrows and out of St. John's harbor. The shores of Newfoundland slipped away, and then there was nothing but the gray waves of the sea. From that moment forward, until they reached the safe harbor of Narsarsuaq, the vast Atlantic would be their ubiquitous two-faced companion. It would lull them to sleep, yet rock them to nausea; it provided passage to help their allies in the war, yet threatened to swallow them whole. Its depths were already littered with the skeletons of torpedoed ships and the ghosts of U-boat victims. The *Dorchester*'s sister ship—the *Chatham*—already rested on its bottom. Every day the men were at sea, they knew they could join it.

★ ★ ★

Wächter was finally in position. After several days of joining other U-boats in the area, U-223 now sailed just south of Greenland. Wächter waited for orders and for any indication of American convoys. His men were now two weeks at sea. They were likely anxious. For the past few days, they had encountered various ships or convoys, mostly just by sound—faint traces that popped up on sonar but that were out of reach or may have been other U-boats.

But the same day *Dorchester* pulled out of St. John's, Wächter's day had been uneventful. He had ordered his men to crash dive for training purposes. He had demanded they work on the torpedoes to ensure they were ready for an attack. Around noon, he ordered his boat up to the surface. It blew through the ocean's seal in an explosion of mist and foam, then settled. All was quiet. The day transitioned into an early night. By midnight, snow settled onto the con tower and blew past the men on lookout. The moon would not rise for another four hours; even if it did, a thick pad of clouds would have blocked its light. Wächter detected nothing—no lights in the distance, no sounds on the surface or on the sonar, just blackness in all directions. There, in the darkness, Wächter and his men listened, waiting for any signal or intelligence from headquarters to tell them where to strike next.[5] The question wasn't if a convoy would come his way—everyone knew the Americans were shipping men and supplies to the front and to Greenland—the question was when, and whether he and his men would be ready to strike.

CHAPTER 14

INTO THE DARK

The convoy left the safety of St. John's in a defensive formation. Whatever comfort the commanders had felt during the passage out of New York had vanished. The *Dorchester* was now entering the most dangerous part of the journey. The three transports sailed side by side, with the *Dorchester* in the center and the freighters on either side of her. The escort cutters then stationed themselves around them, with the *Tampa* in the lead, *Escanaba* on the starboard side, and

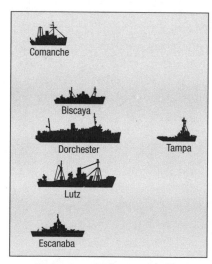

Formation of SG-19 as it sailed from St. John's to Greenland

Comanche to port. This meant the rear of the convoy was dangerously exposed.

To make matters worse, the cutters were relatively old. Only *Tampa* and *Comanche* carried radar. *Escanaba* did have sonar, but it covered only the 180 degrees in front of the ship. The *Dorchester*'s entire starboard quarter was its blind side. If a U-boat skulked up from that direction, no one in the convoy would have much warning. Ideally, there would have been a

144

fourth cutter to protect the rear, but the numbers were what they were. The larger convoys headed to continental Europe and North Africa received the most protection; smaller convoys to Greenland had to make do.

The convoy's captain, Joseph Greenspun, on board the *Tampa,* would issue all orders related to the convoy and had total control with regard to its formation and speed. The *Tampa* itself was under the command of Stephen H. Evans, who also followed orders from Greenspun. If he changed course, the others would follow his lead. He led the ships in a zigzagging line toward Greenland, which would make it harder for U-boats to lock on and strike. Radios posed too great a risk; the Germans could easily intercept them, then swarm like sharks to a bleeding fish. So Greenspun had ordered strict silence—the only way the ships could communicate with each other was through signal lamps, and even then, caution was warranted.

There was one problem Greenspun couldn't control. The *Lutz* was older, a coal-burning steamer. Its smokestack billowed a towering signal of black exhaust high above the horizon. On a clear day (and even on not-so-clear ones), it could be seen from miles away—a floating trail leading right to the convoy's exposed rear.

Most of this didn't trouble the enlisted men on the first day out of St. John's. The weather was relatively clear; the sea as calm as it was going to be. There were no signs of U-boats. The convoy carved a path to Greenland at a healthy clip, and all signs suggested they might arrive without incident.

But the question of the Puritan Mistake still lingered. The men on board the *Dorchester* had not gone through Army Chaplain School; unlike the four clergymen, they had not been selected because of their tolerance of others. Most were still in their youth, a breeding ground for prejudice. They had been picked from the cornucopia of American society—that diversity so derided by Hitler—because they were young and could fight a war. They came from all walks of life, small towns and big cities—places where tolerance was praised or bigotry was common. Crammed into those claustrophobic spaces were men who represented everything America had to offer. There were heroes, champions of the downtrodden, valiant soldiers, defenders of freedom, men who believed in equality, and men who would sacrifice themselves to save people who were different. But there were also racists, misogynists, anti-Semites, anti-Mormons, anti-Protestants, anti-Catholics, liars, cowards, anti-religionists, anti-secularists, anti-atheists, anti-agnostics, anti-Buddhists, anti-Muslims, and men who held many other prejudices. Most men belonged in many of those categories—the good and bad—all at once.

After six days of traveling together in tight spaces, these differences began to manifest themselves. That first day out of St. John's was a Friday. For the observant Jews on board, their sabbath (called Shabbat) would begin around sunset with a service to usher in the day, which would then last until the appearance of three stars in the sky Saturday night. The service was simple. It involved lighting candles and reciting a blessing.

Alex Goode, the lone rabbi, hunted for a space on the ship where he might lead some of the men to begin sabbath observance. With a small contingent, he finally found a space large enough: a room near the kitchen.

But as he was getting set up, a cook appeared. He wanted to use the room for a craps game he had organized, and he wasn't going to move now just because Alex and some of his Jewish men wanted to observe Shabbat.[1]

Alex was not one to back down. His was a life of standing for ideals, both intellectual and religious. And he would stand for them now as well, even if it meant standing alone.

But the cook refused to back down. We don't know much about him, except this: he valued a craps game more than Jewish religious exercise. So much so that he was willing to argue with a chaplain over the space. This isn't unusual—most people claim to value the rights of others to follow the dictates of their own consciences, unless doing so conflicts with something they value more. Then, making accommodations for others to live out their religion usually gets thrown out the window.

There were other men with Alex, most if not all of them Jewish, who wanted to have this experience. At least one of them was a non-observant Jewish man who simply needed the comfort that a belief in the divine provides. He was headed to war, he had suffered through some personal tragedies in recent years and months, and drawing a little bit closer to God felt like the right step for him. Others probably had even stronger desires for a spiritual uplift, a chance to ponder and think about a plane of existence beyond the here and now, to center themselves on principles and, perhaps for some, a heavenly realm after physical death.

It was for these that Alex refused to back down. They needed this. And there was no other room that would work.

The cook also would not back down.

As the two argued, Clark Poling happened upon the scene. He was immediately incensed at the cook's position. No one was asking him to participate in the service. All he would face was a minor inconvenience. The service to welcome in Shabbat generally happened at a certain time, and, given the number of men who wanted to participate, they needed a place large enough to fit them, on a ship where few such spaces existed. Craps could be played whenever and, quite frankly, wherever. Together, Alex and Clark pushed on the cook to change his mind. Judaism was not Clark's religion; it would have been easy for him to ignore the situation as someone else's battle. But that wasn't the point. This was the price of living in a religiously pluralistic society: a give-and-take, a gentle tug-of-war in which everyone experiences a taste of inconvenience while they accommodate others but, through giving, all receive what they value most.

The cook finally gave in. He would play his craps game somewhere else or even just postpone it a while.

With that, Alex ushered the men into the room. As part of the service, he handed out Bibles to each of them.

The chaplains encouraged the men to accept some burden—minor harms, if you will—as a price of mutual tolerance. But it wasn't enough to preach that principle. They needed to live it as well. John Washington staunchly opposed gambling. In his own parish, surrounded by the comfortable blanket of a people entirely similar to him, he would have demanded the abandonment of the practice. In his own life, he saw no allure in it whatsoever. But in the tangled depths of the *Dorchester,* where steel and saltwater narrowed the bounds of living as never before, the thrill of gambling was, to many of the young men, a siren song. Resistance was nearly impossible, and they didn't share John's religious qualms with it.

This meant he would need to find a way to get along with the men even if they were engaged in something he thought destructive. He found that way in humor. While navigating the smoke-filled halls of one of the lower decks, he happened upon a card game in one of the rooms. The pot had grown large enough to metamorphose the normally frivolous young men into serious players.

"Well," John said, literally looking down on them, "I see you're playing cards. Someday I'll tell you a story about cards."

Mocking him, in a playful tone, one of the players said, "Father, would you please bless my hand?"

The game was tense. Everyone in the circle partook in a dance of cunning and bluffing. At that point, those skills were far more important than the luck of the deck.

John looked at the man's hand. "I should waste my blessing on a lousy pair of deuces?"

Having blown up the game, he walked away, likely with a smile.

★ ★ ★

The next morning, on Saturday, January 30, 1943, everything started to change. The anxiety on the ships came not just from differences in ideology or race or background, but from a very real reminder that they were traversing a world intent on killing them. The winds started out of the North, as if the Arctic were releasing a long-pent-up sigh. The *Dorchester* glided over wide, lazy waves like a car rolling over country hills. But the gales soon turned into gusts, and the lumbering, gentle rollers morphed into towering, angry whitecaps. They hammered into the *Dorchester,* swallowing its bow with each blow, then lifting it up and dropping it into deep troughs. Again and again. To make matters worse, Captain Greenspun on the *Tampa* knew he could not stop proper maneuvers without exposing the convoy to the enemy; he continued to lead SG-19 in a tacking pattern should any U-boats be lurking about. As a result, the ships couldn't even attack the waves head-on but often approached them at indirect angles, which allowed even more water to flood the decks.

Visibility was near zero. From the deck of the *Dorchester,* the men on the guns peered through fog and phantoms of snow but often couldn't see any of the other ships. When they caught glimpses, the scene wasn't promising. The *Biscaya* and *Lutz,* significantly smaller than the *Dorchester,* looked as if they were struggling simply to stay afloat. The escort cutters seemed to have vanished altogether, as if the waves had finally gotten annoyed with them and consumed them whole. Staying alive was hard enough; maintaining position in the convoy while keeping an eye out for a wolfpack was nearly impossible.

The temperature plummeted. Soon, sea spray from the waves turned to ice—an ethereal, fine mist. It seemed harmless wafting through the air but soon covered everything in a clear, nearly magical translucent coating. Guns, riggings, lines, structures, decks, life rafts, the antisubmarine mousetrap guns—nothing was spared; all glimmered with a coating growing thicker by the second. The water spilling over the deck created a dangerous slick; when it froze, it only thickened the ice's stranglehold of the vessel. In some places, the ice sheet was over twelve inches thick.[2]

It added an immense weight—not just to the *Dorchester,* but to all the ships in the convoy.

★ ★ ★

On board the *Comanche,* Charles W. David Jr. must have felt his time had come. The *Comanche* had escorted the *Dorchester* on several trips to Greenland and back, but they had never encountered a storm like this.[3] In the vast maelstrom of the North Atlantic, Charles's ship might as well have been a cork for how easily the angry waves tossed it about. Given their size, the cutters couldn't take the bashing for long. The thick ice on their decks made the situation even more precarious.

It's unlikely anyone was eating on the *Comanche,* and it's equally improbable Charles and Swanson were playing the blues. The goals would have been simple: break up as much ice as possible to prevent capsizing, and hold on for dear life.

Lieutenant Commander Ralph Curry, to whom Charles reported directly, said the ice was so thick that the cutter would be useless even if it did detect an enemy submarine—all the weaponry was frozen.[4] All of the commanders, at roughly the same time, identified the same danger. If they didn't do something soon, some or all of the ships would sink under the additional weight. The commander of the *Comanche* estimated that his ship was carrying somewhere between 100 and 150 tons of ice.

The cutters slowed, dropping to six knots.[5] It was the only way they could navigate the waves and break the grip of the ice. But it also meant exposing the entire convoy to U-boats lingering beneath the surface.

Under the strain of the wind and added load, the *Dorchester* moaned and creaked. To the men below deck, she would have sounded as if she were about to split in two.

The card games were over. Sabbath observance was cut short. The

Men on the Comanche *trying to break up ice during the storm*

merchant marine crewmen were ordered into brigades. Clinging to railings or anything else they could grasp, they stumbled through the tight passageways to the narrow ladders and stairwells that led to the surface. On deck, whenever the storm relented enough to allow it, groups of them chipped and hacked away at the ice, sliding huge chunks back into the sea. They repaired damaged pumps. The more experienced navy men fixed guns and life rafts.

Through all of this, the chaplains navigated as best they could in the lower holds, trying to help army men who had not been assigned to go up and battle the storm. The ship's unpredictable pitching made walking nearly impossible. They latched on to rails, the ship knocked them into passage walls, and their stomachs churned. It's probable they were vomiting, like most everyone else, as much as they were assisting others. From the mess hall, they had snagged packages of crackers and fruit to help ease men's stomachs.[6] That and K-rations were about all anyone would be able to eat, assuming they could stomach anything at all. In the kitchen, pots and pans, along with anything else not bolted down, clattered and clanged out of cabinets and off surfaces—cooking was impossible.

Many of the men had taken to lying in their bunks. Suddenly, the *Dorchester* collided with a particularly vicious wave. The impact jarred the ship so badly, it knocked a number of bunks loose from their bolts, toppling them and their men onto those below them.

Three men suffered severe injuries; others more minor. The chaplains stumbled to the scene. Two of them—we don't know which—carried the men to some of the lower bunks in the lower holds. Once they had the men lying down, the two chaplains bandaged the wounds. They fed the men whatever food they had.

Hours passed. The storm pounded. The *Dorchester* climbed hundreds of mountainous waves and careened into just as many troughs, each one as deep as a valley. Through it all, the two chaplains sat with the injured men, offering what comfort they could. Up above, the other two continued to navigate the bunks, offering the crackers and fruit to whoever wanted them.

Captain Greenspun slowed the convoy to a crawl. He had no choice. Every ship needed time to deice. And the smaller cutters simply couldn't handle the heaving and thrashing at the same speed as the larger ships.

The pause allowed for survival from the storm; it also turned the entire convoy into target practice. The slower they traversed the swells, the easier it would be for a U-boat and its torpedoes to home in on them. For even the most carefree of the troops, the reality of the danger they faced was finally boring into their psyches.

Adding to the anxiety was the knowledge of what might happen should any of the men—on either the *Dorchester* or the cutters—survive an initial attack. By 1943, to survive a torpedo attack was miraculous enough. To survive one in the frigid waters of the North Atlantic in winter was perhaps one of the most formidable feats in the war, for two reasons. To begin with, the conditions were beyond brutal. The water temperature was hovering just above freezing, the snow didn't even melt when it landed on it, and the large chunks of ice bobbing in the waves were a testament to just how cold the open sea was in that part of the world that time of year. The air outside wasn't much better. It lingered between freezing and just above, with a wind chill so piercing it made even the best-dressed men feel naked.

Any man who fell in that water would have immediately felt the onset of hypothermia. The symptoms are dramatic. At first, the skin cools, and the surface blood vessels constrict to conserve heat for vital organs. Blood pressure and heart rate skyrocket; muscles involuntarily tense and shiver. For a time, this generates heat, but the victim begins to lose muscle control and agility. The shock to the system when hitting cold water is so intense, it generates a reflex in which people gasp for air. The reflexive sucking causes some to immediately inhale water and drown before they even have a chance to survive. For others, the reflex can lead to hyperventilating. The seeming lack of air and the tremors cause panic, which can lead to even more erratic breathing. At that point, for most people, all rational behavior vanishes. In other words, the body enters into survival mode, a state of being in which most people abandon values and standards and thoughts and instead look only for avenues to live. Many actions are completely irrational: people will resist help, turn on their friends, lose track of where they are, or attack others even when doing so provides no obvious chance of improving the odds of survival. Once the body's core temperature starts to plummet, it's almost as if the body rebels against its initial furious reaction. The brain slows, blood pressure drops, respiration rates plunge, and heart rate decelerates. The slingshot reaction can be so shocking, some will die from cardiac arrest or respiratory failure. For others, a dreamlike fogginess settles in. The shivering and panting yield to extreme lethargy, which eventually gives way to hallucinations trailed by unconsciousness.

For a human being of average height and weight, in waters the temperature of those surrounding the *Dorchester,* the amount of time it takes to lose consciousness is anywhere from fifteen to thirty minutes;

to die, thirty to ninety. The factors that determine life or death are surprisingly mundane. Many are not intuitive. Sailors would have a better
chance of living if they held still rather than swimming; if they had any
sort of personal flotation device that would allow them to tuck their
legs and arms close to their chest; if they huddled with others; if they
had some clothes on, even though that clothing may not be survival
wear; or if they had thoughts or memories or visuals that would help
them keep a positive attitude—in the words of University of Minnesota
researchers, "a will to survive really does matter."[7]

The attitude of the German navy was also critical to survival
chances. And that had changed dramatically just in the months prior
to the *Dorchester's* voyage. Originally, at the outset of the war, both
the Germans and the Allies followed a commonly understood set of
ancient rules on the open sea: if either side downed an enemy ship,
once the fighting ceased, enemy vessels could pick up survivors from
either side in the water without fear of attack. But several months
before the *Dorchester* set sail, those rules were abandoned because of
an event thousands of miles away off the coast of West Africa. After
U-156 sank the British transport *RMS Laconia,* it joined several other
ships in picking up survivors. It then broadcast on all open radio chan-
nels the following message: "If any ship will assist the shipwrecked
Laconia crew I will not attack her, providing I am not being attacked
by ship or air force. I picked up 193 men. 4°-53" South, 11°-26"
West.—German submarine." The U-boat sailed on the surface to rendezvous with a French ship, to which it would transfer the survivors.
En route, it draped a Red Cross flag across its gun deck. Despite the
pleas from U-156, which were transmitted in English and Morse Code,
an American B-24 Liberator bomber received orders to attack. It did
so, blasting U-156 with bombs and depth charges and killing many
Laconia survivors in the process. The incident was complicated, led to
accusation of war crimes against the Allies, and has been debated by
historians and legal scholars for decades.[8]

The men aboard the *Dorchester* didn't care about any of that. For them, it meant only one thing: their chances of survival in the water were even more diminished. In response to the *Laconia* incident, Admiral Karl Dönitz, leader of the German navy, issued the following order to all German U-boat commanders:

1. Efforts to save survivors of sunken ships, such as the fishing of swimming men out of the water and putting them on board lifeboats, the righting of overturned lifeboats, or the handing over of food and water, must stop. Rescue contradicts the most basic demands of the war: the destruction of hostile ships and their crews.

2. The orders concerning the bringing-in of skippers and chief engineers stay in effect.

3. Survivors are to be saved only if their statements are important for the boat.

4. Stay firm. Remember that the enemy has no regard for women and children when bombing German cities!

That order was a key piece of evidence against Dönitz when he was later tried for war crimes at Nuremberg. Prior to the Laconia Order, as it came to be known, U-boat captains had enjoyed at least some discretion to save Allied survivors. Not all of them exercised it, and Hitler himself opposed it. Not surprisingly, his view was that any and all Allied soldiers and sailors should be killed without mercy, and he grew infuriated when he learned that some of his captains were actually assisting in the rescue of enemy personnel. But some German naval officers still honored the old traditions of the sea. No longer—with the stroke of a pen and a radio signal, German naval headquarters had wiped that away. Hitler's view now controlled. For the men on American troop transports like the *Dorchester*, or for their protectors like Charles W. David Jr., no one was more alone than a man dumped into a frigid ocean with no ship and little help but floating blocks of ice.

All of the potential threats took a psychological toll. Some of the young recruits, especially, increasingly felt alone. This was their first foray into any of the complex difficulties of life's journey: their first exposure to the ocean, their first experience on a ship, their baptism by fire of meeting people different from themselves. And they had nowhere to turn. As one survivor, James McAtamney, explained, they couldn't turn to the officers, who were completely off-limits and whom they could salute but nothing else. The merchant marine crew who operated the ship didn't want to have anything to do with anyone— they were salty and seasoned and worried about keeping the *Dorchester* afloat; making time for coddling the troops they were transporting wasn't part of the job description. The navy gunners were the same.

"But the chaplains were different," McAtamney said.[9] They were approachable. They wanted to hear from the men.

The fury of the storm abated enough for the troops to start moving about the *Dorchester,* at least somewhat. The kitchen had turned into a pit of broken dishware. Bunks and supplies all over the lower holds needed repair. The harshness of the sea had not let up entirely, but it opened the possibility of cleaning and repair. For a day and a half, the army soldiers alternated between performing various duties and trying not to vomit. The kitchen had been so badly damaged, no one would be able to eat another properly cooked meal until the voyage was over.

To the chaplains' disappointment, the talent show they had planned had to be canceled altogether. Between sickness, destruction, and injured men, it simply couldn't be done.

Still, many of the army men sought out the chaplains. Clark, John, George, and Alex would listen to the youngsters, hear their worries and troubles, pray with them, offer counsel and perspective, and uplift with jokes and levity whenever they could. They held services in the mess hall, each focused on his own religious tradition, although there were some men who attended all four services.[10]

Lines formed to see them. To pass the time when the ship wasn't on the verge of total disaster, the men would lie and brag and gamble and tell fabulously tall tales about their exploits. Then they would wait in line for their time with their favorite trusted adviser, one on one, to discuss the truth, the feelings of their hearts they could share with no one else. And they had come to know that they could meet with any one of the clergymen. The chaplains didn't care what someone's religion was; they would serve if they could, and if men needed a service specific to one faith—such as a Catholic needing confession—then Clark, George, John, and Alex directed them to the right chaplain.[11]

The four had signed on to a life that could swallow men whole with anxiety. But for all its worries, there was an unmistakable allure to the chaplain's duty, one none of them could resist. Many American men in World War II naively wanted to be part of the action. They wanted to be heroes, and their perception of that term—*hero*—was formed by tales and fantasies, movies with the likes of Errol Flynn.

In the hold of a ship, so far from family, with enemies elemental and unseen, beaten and bruised, the storm raging, their stomachs in mushy knots, hunters on the prowl, the question of whether they would survive another day very much in doubt, the men had nothing to focus on but their worries.

If anything, in that environment, the chaplain mattered perhaps more than anyone.

On board the *Comanche,* the respite from the storm wouldn't have had nearly the effect it caused on the *Dorchester.* First, although the storm had eased somewhat, it wasn't over. For Charles and the rest of the cutter's crew, the battering was still intense, the waves still ferocious. Second, U-boats could still be out there. The convoy had survived nature's onslaught, but human enemies still abounded, and the somewhat calmed waters meant those foes would have an easier time firing their weapons.

Everyone needed to be extra focused.

So during the day on February 2, now nearly four days into the voyage, the gift the ocean bestowed upon the *Comanche* seemed, at the time, nothing more than an unwelcome distraction. Only later, in the most desperate of moments, would the crew appreciate it for the miracle it was.

As the cutter sliced the waves, one of the lookouts, while spying for any sign of a U-boat, noticed a massive cargo net floating in the water. Whatever it had been carrying had long since vanished into the depths. Now its thick ropes, tied together in squares, stretched out over the angry water with all the carelessness of a sunbather. Fighting against the waves slapping against the boat like giant hands, several of the crew, with Charles and Swanson looking on, grabbed huge pole hooks, jutted them out over the ocean, and fished the net toward them.

It was massive. Its load must have been equally gargantuan. The men tugged and yanked, slithering the beast over the rails until it lay in a huge clump on deck. It's not clear any of them had any idea what to do with it after that. Why they felt the need to haul it in from hostile waters or allow it to distract them while they should have been watching for U-boats was something no one ever explained.

CHAPTER 15

FULLY CLOTHED WITH LIFE JACKETS ON

At 1:10 in the afternoon on February 2, 1943, Wächter spotted a faint cloud of smoke on the horizon. He ordered the men to turn toward it. For the previous couple of days, while the storm had ravaged convoy SG-19, U-223 had received multiple orders to align with the *Haudegen* wolfpack in hopes of intercepting convoys headed for Europe or Greenland. But the same storm had caused Wächter problems as well. It had knocked the boat around like a weather buoy, crushing cooking-oil canisters in the diesel compartment and causing leaks in U-223's exhaust pipes.[1]

But now, Wächter had something. He had floated on the surface all day, diving every four hours to listen for any sign of American ships. For the next fifty minutes, he pursued the smoke. Snow tickled the con, but visibility was good. After days of angry waves, the boat now glided over smooth, medium swells.

No doubt, Wächter and his crew felt the thrill of pursuit. By roughly 2:05 p.m., they saw six mastheads jutting from the horizon. They also clearly identified three smoke clouds, which meant there were at least three steamers churning along as part of a convoy.

Wächter adjusted his course just slightly. Some historians have written that he had received orders to wait for other ships so he could attack as part of a true wolfpack. If that was true, it is clear the potential for a kill was too tempting. He maneuvered ahead. As he approached, he adjusted his bearings occasionally, but he had to shift slowly, deliberately. Anything sudden, and he might stand out to anyone on board the vessels.

Then a squall hit, a momentary blur of snow that offered him cover. He increased his speed, hoping to close as long as the weather would hide him. When the squall passed and he could see again, he now had a better sense of his victim: "I see 3 steamers and 2 escorts," he wrote. He couldn't be certain if that was the entire convoy, but he at least knew it was small.

Continuing to shadow the Americans, he radioed to U-boat headquarters what he had discovered. He was roughly fourteen to sixteen nautical miles away.* Then he reported, "Holding contact on smoke clouds, which are easily seen."

On board the *Dorchester*, though it was 3:30 in the afternoon, the northern winter darkness had already begun to consume everything. Lieutenant William Arpaia noticed signals flashing from the *Tampa* up ahead. He and the other men locked in. Through the snow, the bright flashing code was clear: "We are being followed. Submarines estimated in our vicinity. Inform all ships to close up tightly and stay closed for the night."

Captain Danielson immediately relayed the flashed message to the *Lutz* and *Escanaba*. The *Comanche* would have seen it too. All of the ships tightened into one another, circling around the *Dorchester*.

Arpaia had already been wary. His duty was to command the Naval Armed Guard, who, in turn, carried the weighty responsibility

---

* There are approximately 1.15 miles to a nautical mile.

of protecting American troops from the enemy. If the soldiers were the package, Arpaia and his men were the security, along with the coast guard cutters. He immediately buzzed his guards. They assumed their positions. Their guns were cocked and cranked—ready to rain fire on any Nazis who dared showed themselves. All of the navy men were to be on the ready for the possibility of immediate and prompt action. He directed his men further that if they saw a wake anywhere in the water, they were to open fire without waiting for orders. They should lay a barrage of bullets into the water immediately forward of the wake. If the worst should happen and a torpedo hit the ship, the men were to unload all of their fury into the water with the 20 mm guns in the direction from which the torpedo had come.

Ships like the *Dorchester* carried confidential information, documents that could not fall into the hands of the enemy. Arpaia discussed the situation with Captain Danielson. They agreed it was time to put security measures in place. Arpaia charged to Danielson's cabinet and found in it a metal, perforated box that contained the captain's top-secret documents. Arpaia shoved his secret papers into it as well, sealed it up, then placed it back into the cabinet. It was ready.

Captain Danielson ordered a complete blackout. Whatever lights had been twinkling in the night were extinguished. Below deck, all portholes were covered. The *Dorchester* was to become nothing but a shadow against the cloudy sky.

Then came the question of what to do with the troops—the hundreds of young souls crammed in below. Arpaia found their commander, Captain Preston S. Krecker. They consulted for a time and agreed it made no sense to cause a panic.

But the men needed to be ready. Krecker and Arpaia agreed they would be ordered to stay fully clothed with their life jackets on. They also decided they would increase the watch. In New York, before departure, the two commanders had concluded that none of the army men should ever be on deck, except to maintain a continuous series of seventeen lookouts around the entire vessel. Now they decided to double that number. At all times, thirty-four men would be stationed high and low, anywhere they could spot the telltale froth or periscope of a submarine. The men below deck would stay dressed and ready.

On the *Comanche*, Charles W. David Jr. would have been keenly aware of what was happening, since his primary duty was providing steward services to the ship's officers, including its commander, Ralph Curry. Many of the men on the ship were young, including those whose racism was so apparent. For some, this was their first voyage. Charles, on the other hand, was nearly twenty-six years old. He'd made the Greenland run multiple times. He was a veteran. While the cutter's executive officers tried their best to screen for U-boats, finding nothing, Charles watched and observed. Calm.

But he did have one problem: he was sick. Over the past couple of days, he could feel the effects of the virus, so small, but causing such a dramatic reaction from his body—the tickling in the throat, the chills from a fever, the mucus in the lungs. He brushed it aside and told no one.[2]

On the *Dorchester*, at some point, the commanders alerted the chaplains to the situation. They were some of the only men on the ship who knew what was happening. They were not to inform the men of the certainty of a submarine hunting them, but they could help with keeping anxiety down and with ensuring the men were ready should the worst happen.

All four descended back into the lower holds. By then, the troops knew something was going on; the announcement had blared over the loudspeakers. It was vague. The ship was entering into troubled waters, where U-boats were known to prowl; they were to put on their life jackets and clothes just to be safe. Tensions were rising.

Father John Washington headed to the mess hall. It was still a disaster from the storm. He put together a modest tray of food for the three men who had been injured during the storm. His mind was on how to offer some comfort to the soldiers. Walking from the kitchen, he ran into one of the more seasoned men, Michael Warish, who had actually been serving in Greenland for some time. He was smoking.

When they passed each other, they exchanged meaningful looks. John explained he was taking the food to the injured men below.

"Father," Warish said, "I guess you heard the news."

John was hesitant to reply. He didn't know who had been let in on the secret. Finally, he nodded, a painful look on his face. "Sergeant," he said, "I'm going to hold mass at six o'clock." John knew death. And he knew the power of prayer. What he wanted from Warish was clear: spread the word.

A couple more hours passed. As the chaplains maneuvered through the lower levels, they would have been disheartened. Many of the troops had blown off the announcement about clothes and life jackets. The C, D, and E holds were hot and muggy, a potent mixture of engine, body, and cooking heat combined with all the odors seven hundred young men can produce: socks, vomit, oil, exhaust, sweat, flatulence, food, waste, urine, feces, and cigarette smoke. The men were still reeling from the storm. Most were so sick that vomiting was always just an awkward movement away. Staying fully dressed, with shoes, with a life preserver on top, was just too much for some of them.

Their youth and inexperience were manifesting themselves. Some had become belligerent, thinking all of the precautions were overblown. Others just didn't have the willpower to stay wrapped in sweltering gear when all it did was add to the nausea already stalking them. Some may not have heard the order over the loudspeaker. Regardless of their reasons, a large contingent of the men on the *Dorchester* were not properly prepared if a torpedo pierced the hull.

Around 4:30 in the afternoon, Wächter's captain's journal reflects a hardening feeling: resolution. Visibility was good, despite snow showers. The waves had stretched themselves into lazy swells, as if the ocean were yawning. He knew for certain now there were only three steamers. The smoke clouds gave them away.

He instructed his radio man to send the short report.

At almost the same time, U-223 received another report from the German leadership. *Is it a larger England or a smaller Greenland convoy?*

Wächter didn't risk responding again. He was too close now. Any unnecessary radio blasts could give away his position. "I believe the question is settled by my last Short Signal."

★ ★ ★

As far as we know, John held mass, ministering to the men who sought spiritual comfort. Alex, George, and Clark continued their rounds, meeting with as many men as they could. By 6:30 in the evening, it had been three hours since the *Tampa's* warning about a submarine hunting them.

On deck, Arpaia surveyed his naval guards. He didn't want any letup. Despite the bitter cold, he kept half his crew at the guns at all times. The weapons remained cocked, with magazine tension cranked at 60 pounds of pressure. His orders remained in place: if the men saw something in the water, they were to unleash hellfire upon it. They needn't wait for permission. He also commanded a petty officer to roam the decks, checking in on all lookouts and inspecting the gun magazines every half hour to ensure they were operational in the cold. The rest of his crew stood by in their quarters, fully dressed and ready for immediate combat action.

After making his rounds, Arpaia visited the captain. The convoy churned ahead at 10 knots per hour, a snail's pace. If they could just survive until midnight, Captain Danielson believed they would be safe. By then, they would be close enough to shore that icebergs would

obstacle the entire course. U-boats generally can't maneuver in that setting . . . so, a little less than six hours.

Below deck, after services, the men and the kitchen were finally
mended enough for a real meal. Like ants in a line, the troops sidled
through to the food.

Then the loudspeaker crackled. A commanding voice boomed into
the room; it would have reverberated through similar speakers throughout the ship. It was Captain Danielson. This time, his message was
unmistakable:

> NOW HEAR THIS: THIS CONCERNS EVERY
> SOLDIER. . . . REPEATING, THIS MEANS EVERY
> SOLDIER. NOW HEAR THIS: EVERY SOLDIER IS
> ORDERED TO SLEEP WITH HIS CLOTHES AND LIFE
> JACKET. REPEATING, THIS IS AN ORDER! WE HAVE
> A SUBMARINE FOLLOWING US. . . . IF WE MAKE IT
> THROUGH THE NIGHT, IN THE MORNING WE WILL
> HAVE AIR PROTECTION FROM BLUIE WEST ONE,
> WHICH IS THE CODE NAME FOR THE AIR BASE
> IN GREENLAND, AND OF COURSE WE WILL HAVE
> PROTECTION UNTIL WE REACH PORT.[3]

Clearly something had lit a fire in the man. He no longer saw
any sense in maintaining pretenses or in keeping the men from panic.
They needed to know the truth, and they needed to act accordingly.
Before he finished, the captain reiterated exactly what he meant, to
ensure there was no chance of confusion: the men were to wear *all*
their clothes, including hats, gloves, parkas, and shoes. Boots would
weigh them down in the water, so they shouldn't wear those. If he cared
about the miserable heat below decks, he gave no indication—that was
nothing compared with what the men would feel if they were dumped
into the Atlantic with little gear or clothing. Before he squawked off, he
wished the men luck.

Reality hit like an iceberg. The chatter from before the announcement never returned. The men just stared. In the line, they shuffled

through with less enthusiasm. At the tables, they stopped eating. Those who had been angry earlier likely dished up begrudging respect for the very real danger outside the hull. But where would they turn? They already felt as if they had no one. It was almost as if the men were looking for something to happen, or for someone to break the silence.

The reprieve came from George Fox. The captain had wished everyone luck, but the chaplains were not the kind of men who relied solely on chance. They were spiritual enough to turn to the divine, believing there was real and tangible strength there. But they were practical enough to know they needed to help themselves.

What inspired him is hard to say, but George stood.

Hundreds of young eyes turned to him. For many, he was not their minister. But he had become someone they could trust—the older man who had broken his back in World War I wanted nothing but the best for them. They knew that. He had shown it again and again.

George announced that the chaplains had been planning a talent show, an amateur night to help pass the time. It had been called off because of the storm, but the worst was past, the sea had calmed, and it looked like people were feeling better. This was going to be their last night together; after all, by the next day, they would be safely at port. It was time to have the event. Everyone should get ready.

All four chaplains set to work. In a short time, they announced the show over the loudspeaker so anyone not in the mess hall when George spoke would know to come.

For two and a half hours, Wächter had crept closer and closer to the *Dorchester*. When the convoy adjusted its direction, changing bearing to make his hunt harder, he adjusted—two partners dancing at a winter ball. Back and forth they went.

In squalls, he made dramatic leaps, knowing there was less chance he'd be detected.

The wind was dying. The ocean had finished its outburst, and the waves were flattening. At the same time, darkness had cloaked the entire area. The smoke signals from the ships were useless now, in the dark, but Wächter didn't need them. He knew the direction of the convoy and its speed. Between that knowledge and sonar, he could track them now.

The convoy changed its bearing 10–20 degrees. Wächter continued to creep. He sent a short radio message to his superiors: "Intend to attack."

The wind had died completely. "The sea is mirror flat like a duck pond," he wrote. Then he called his men off the con tower. With a great sloshing, U-223 slid beneath the surface.

In the mess hall, the chaplains did their best to entertain anyone who walked in. Men came and went. Some were up on lookout, freezing in the dark. But when their shifts ended, they wandered into the hall to warm up and listen to the music. What was completely out of place: an old grand piano, still in the mess hall from the *Dorchester*'s prior life. It was dusty and out of tune, a relic, not a luxury. But Father John Washington could still play. He plopped in front of it and knocked out some of the popular songs of the day.

Clark, George, and Alex sang along. They each had some voice talent, given their backgrounds in church and other choirs. A few other soldiers joined the band as well—two singing and one on a guitar. The room was full. Men flitted in and out.

Still, lingering in the back of everyone's mind was the threat. It was impossible to escape. Even as they listened to the singing, they were wearing all of their gear and life jackets. Some men knew they had to go back out on lookout soon, so it was hard to relax and enjoy the tunes.

But the chaplains played on. The show stretched on for hours. Although the air was not nearly as festive as they might have liked, the sheer number of men in the mess hall told them it was working. They weren't naïve. They didn't expect the troops to let loose and truly party like they were on a beach in the Caribbean. What they wanted was to give the men a distraction—something, anything, to keep their minds off the threats they faced. There was almost nothing on the ship to do that. The men had no televisions, no downloaded movies or music, no cell phones with games on them, no laptops—with all the pressure of the ocean caving in on their minds, they needed some other way to find a release. The chaplains hoped they were providing it.

Whatever religious and other differences there were between these men seemed to have vanished for the moment, swallowed by their shared aspiration for survival.

Up above, Private First Class James McAtamney wondered how on earth he had gotten himself in this situation. He had been a construction worker before the war, just a young grunt digging holes or crawling up ladders or scaffolding. So heights didn't really bother him. But this was different. He found himself dangling on the side of the climb up to the crow's nest, with nothing to grab but a "narrow steel ice-covered handrail." In fact, everything above deck still seemed coated in ice: the canvas on the lifeboats, the ropes, the railings, the block and tackle.[4] All the clothes he wore—long underwear, gloves, parka, face mask, sweaters, and anything else he could find to stay warm—made keeping his grip nearly impossible. It didn't help that the tower swayed with the ship and the wind. All around him was blackness, a dark abyss of nothing that toyed with the senses and left the sensation of flying in a dream.

When he finally reached the nest itself, it was nothing more than a tiny compartment. If it was twenty feet above the deck it might as well have been a mile for McAtamney. That was what it felt like. If he tumbled off, he would fall forever. And toppling over the side was a real possibility: the rail that protected him was only about chest high and felt flimsy at best.

The wind howled, piercing even all those layers of clothes.

He had been one of those kids at the pier in New York who had fantasized about one day taking a cruise on a ship like this. Now all he wanted was to get off it alive.

He had received somewhat general and vague instructions: "Look for U-boats."

But he didn't know what he was doing. His mask clogged his vision. The wind licked at his eyes, which teared up. The boat rocked and flung him around. He had spent his entire life on land. Although he likely wouldn't admit it for years or even decades to come, he also felt exasperated by this assignment; he didn't understand why in holy heaven he was up there in the first place. He wouldn't have recognized a submarine if it exploded out of the water right next to him. At least a couple of times, he gave up altogether and huddled in the crow's nest, trying to stay warm from the stinging gusts. When he did try to look out at the sea, he found it produced an "uncanny luminescence" that played with the senses. Waves broke, puzzle pieces of ice interlocked in the water, snow landed on the surface but didn't melt, the *Dorchester* created its own frothy wake, and the cutters were out there somewhere. How was he to spot a U-boat periscope? Or a torpedo or submarine wake? Looking into the vast expanse, his mind and the water and the wind playing tricks on him, he knew he wouldn't "have been able to tell a torpedo coming toward us, or a sub for that matter, from a flying fish."

Between ten p.m. and midnight, Wächter had maneuvered so close he could see the paint on one of the escort cutters, most likely the *Escanaba*. He had stalked the convoy mostly underwater by sound but dared surface just enough to spy the enemy.

The escort was 1,000 meters away. Wächter noted "one mast, light gray paint."

He could tell the cutter was searching for U-223, but it had no sonar. That was every U-boat captain's fear: being detected by sonar. And it was shared by Wächter's crew. Kurt Roser, who served in U-223's control room, would later report in an interview that their biggest concern was being detected by the US's crude sonar systems. At this point, this close, if they were detected, they would be an easy target.[5]

But on this night, it became clear that the ship they were stalking didn't have the equipment to detect them, at least not where they were currently positioned. U-boats could hear the transmissions of the US sonar when it was in use. As they floated just beneath the surface, they heard nothing.

The snow was intermittent.

Wächter continued to search, but he saw nothing of the larger steamships he knew were there. In the gloom, standing in the blistering cold, gazing through his binoculars, he hoped to spy any hint of the larger transport ships.

He also worried about one nuisance: seagulls. Every time he raised his periscope, they pounced on it. "If I were an English lookout," he wrote in his log, "I would watch the gulls."

Around 11:30 p.m., the chaplains' show was over. They had given everything they had. They were almost in the clear. Midnight—they only needed to reach until midnight. As the troops shuffled out of the room, John, Clark, Alex, and George reminded them all to stay fully dressed and to wear their life jackets.

It seemed the party had worked, at least somewhat. Some men hummed the songs as they walked back to their bunks or up to lookout duty on deck.

Whatever stress relief the party offered, it didn't last. Captain Krecker, the direct commander over all the army troops, called all of his men together once again. He likely spread the word for them to gather where he could address them over the loudspeakers. Some were no doubt in the mess hall; others spread throughout C, D, and E holds.

He'd grown up in New Jersey. He was young—just thirty-seven. But the burden of preparing these men had fallen to him. Once they were ready, he said:

This will be the most dangerous part of our mission. We're coming through the storm and now we're in calm waters. And they can really spot us out there. I want you to go back to your quarters, lay down on your back with your life jacket. Be sure to wear your life jacket and even your parka. We're not here for a beauty contest. It's going to be a dangerous thing.

It was clear Captain Krecker had one goal in mind: help these young boys appreciate the gravity of the situation and be prepared. If he struck fear in them, in his mind, that was probably a good thing. It would motivate them. With that, he went back to his duties.

The responsibility for offering continued comfort fell to the chaplains. Clark, George, and Alex left the mess hall and followed the men back to their staterooms, where they did their best to help them stay positive.

John held back. He decided to hold one more Catholic mass for anyone who wanted to attend. Quite the gathering joined him. Many were Protestant. Some were likely of no faith at all.

While he proceeded through the service, Naval Armed Guards who had been on deck joined as well. At least one was Protestant. But he enjoyed the service "very much," he said. "I would have listened to any of them." The man's name was Roy Summers, the gunner who had survived the sinking of the *Chatham*. He knew what it was like to lose men to the blast of a torpedo. And he also knew this particular situation was far more dangerous. In August, the survivors of the *Chatham* had had time in the water to get picked up. It was summer. The freezing winter had yet to blanket everything in ice and snow. Tonight was different.

When John finished mass, he implored the men to pray. Even if they weren't Catholic, he told them, "All of you know the Lord's Prayer. Go and sing it, say it, whatever. It'll help you."

★ ★ ★

Wächter saw the *Dorchester*, though he wouldn't have known its name. The *Escanaba* had sailed away from him, and it appears he had slipped behind it so that he was now in between it and the *Dorchester*, right in the convoy's radar blind spot. He felt comfortable raising his periscope. Light snow flittered across his view. But he saw his targets. They were 6,000 meters away. Too far. "Shooting is senseless."

In time, he closed the gap enough to see the whole picture. He was certain now. There were three steamers. Two were smaller. One was fatter, clearly a "passenger freighter." Somehow in the night, through his binoculars, he could see its colors: light gray, nearly white. Both the forward and rear parts of the deck carried cargo.

Wächter was clearly of singular focus. He had seen a ship filled with men, and he intended to kill them. Questions that would be asked after the war, for decades, across so much of Germany: did rank-and-file German soldiers like Wächter understand what the Nazis were doing to the Jews and any other dissenters? Did they understand just how brutal the Nazi regime truly was, even to its own people? Did they know of the concentration camps? Did they know of the gas chambers? Had they read the report from the Polish government in exile? If so, did they dismiss it as enemy propaganda? Did men like Wächter understand what his cause was? Did he agree with Admiral Dönitz's order to let survivors die in the water? When it was all over, did he even know why he was supposed to sink a transport ship that, in his own estimation, was between 6,000 and 7,000 tons? Did he understand the difference between tanking a ship full of men versus one just full of supplies? Did he understand just how complicit he was in genocide?

For Wächter, whatever the answers were, they didn't matter in that moment. If he had moral qualms with what he was doing, he had buried them deep down underneath a sense of duty or pride or the thrill of the hunt. Or perhaps he was a true believer in all of Hitler's speeches and German nationalism; perhaps he, like Hitler, believed the only world worth living in was one in which everyone was the same, and anyone different deserved extermination. Either way, he dove beneath the surface and moved in for the kill.

CHAPTER 16

A MUFFLED EXPLOSION AND AMMONIA

An oppressive weight lifted off the entire ship when the clock struck midnight. It was as if a curse had suddenly been broken. In nearly every part of the *Dorchester,* men had the sense they had survived the gauntlet. Below deck, troops shed their life vests and heavy clothes. The cards came out. Some lay in their bunks, content to sleep until morning. With each passing minute, a sense of relief and normalcy settled over the crew.

Even the chaplains, likely exhausted from talking to and working with the men the entire voyage, had settled into their own bunks.

Lieutenant Arpaia couldn't rest. At least not yet. He toured the entire upper deck, personally checking every gun and every lookout. In his mind, nothing had changed. His armed guards were to open fire if they saw anything. The lookouts were to stay as vigilant as ever, at least until they started noticing large patches of icebergs. Maybe then, and only then, could they feel comfortable that the waters were too treacherous for U-boats to navigate.

At fifteen minutes after midnight, he walked back to his cabin to get some rest.

* * *

Around the same time, James McAtamney crawled down from the crow's nest and retreated into the warmth of the lower decks. Every part of him was either numb or aching. So grateful to finally be off the lookout, he wandered toward the mess hall, paused long enough to warm up with some coffee, then headed down to E hold. He stripped out of his extreme cold gear and put on more comfortable clothing. Then he started the long climb to the upper decks.

The last hours of February 2 and the first of February 3, 1943, were almost unbearably frustrating for Wächter and the men of U-223. They were so close to striking distance, but circumstances repeatedly impeded them. Just as they were ready to make their first attack run, the convoy shifted directions away from them. It made the distance too great.

They surfaced again, at least enough to look through the periscope, but a mist had settled over the entire area. Then a snow squall, thicker than usual, engulfed them. Between the two weather phenomena, the convoy passed out of sight.

Wächter, no doubt frustrated, perhaps a little angry that his prey was about to escape, ordered U-223 to dive. Just as the *Dorchester* was racing for the cover of the icebergs, Wächter needed to fire before he ran out of open space. The sub descended enough to use its sonar, pinging in multiple directions.

It found the ships again.

Wächter once again ordered his men to surface. Then they pursued as fast as they could. The ocean was calm. The waves had practically vanished. Still, in the darkness, with the occasional snow flurries and the persistent haze, keeping a visual on the convoy was difficult.

So they danced. They lost the convoy, dove, found it, surfaced, lost it, and dove again. Visibility had decreased to just one or two nautical miles.

The calmness of the ocean had made this a true chase. Wächter must have known the Americans were sensing the safety of the ice-bergs. They had picked up their pace by at least 2 knots. But they had also stopped zigzagging, which meant he could track them better and he was less likely to lose sight of them in a snow squall. Still, for the moment, even after he found them using sound again, he still couldn't see them.

Just then, two events seemed to happen simultaneously. First, there must have been a break in the clouds, because, second, while Wächter had surfaced again and was peering into the darkness from the con tower, he noticed the bright, wavy line of the Northern Lights—an eerie, silent, rippling glow from the heavens, most likely in shades of pale green and pink. Directly in front of them was the dark silhouette of the *Dorchester*. All around the ship, except for right there in the glow of the solar particles colliding with earth's atmosphere, the night was as black as pitch. Wächter's target could not have been framed better.

Suddenly, one of the cutter escorts appeared again. Then one of the other ships.

In that moment, Wächter realized he couldn't get any closer to the *Dorchester*. If he was going to fire, his chance had come. He estimated he was roughly 4,000 meters from the *Dorchester,* and he saw one of the other freighters as well, lined up perfectly so that he might be able to hit two ships at once.

From the con tower, he sent an order to his torpedo man: fire tubes I and III, single shots, "target speed = 12 knots, target angle green 70°, range = 4000 meters"; fire tubes IV and V using the same data.

Approximately 0055: Charles W. David Jr. couldn't play his music.

In the sonar room, the other member of his two-person band, Dick Swanson, was on duty. Swanson shared the sonar duties with another guardsman, but it was his time to be at the station, listening for the enemy.

Charles may have had his own responsibilities to worry about. But whatever he was doing at that precise moment was interrupted.

Up above, near the bow of the ship, another guardsman watched the water carefully. Just like with everyone else, it would have been difficult for him to make out a torpedo from a whitecap.

But when the young man finally saw what he'd been looking for, he knew it.

One of the long cylinders whisked right past the bow of the ship: a slender, pent-up tube of death. He watched it narrowly miss the *Comanche* and vanish into the blackness beyond. It must have been a surreal moment—to see something carrying so much potential chaos and destruction slide by in near silence, then disappear, almost as if it had never been there. It would've been like a half-remembered dream. But he was certain what he'd seen.

He called below, reporting to the rest of the crew.

Everyone who could raced to the deck. There, in the cold, they saw the foamy trail still lingering in the waves, a sign of how close all of them had come to death. They must have looked for other torpedoes, wondering if a second or third weren't on the bubbles of the first. For a few crucial seconds, nothing happened—perhaps just long enough for them to wonder if they and the rest of the convoy had escaped the best the Germans could launch at them. Down below, Dick Swanson was listening on the sonar; although he didn't know it, he was just seconds away from a complete understanding of where the other torpedoes were headed.

Whether it was then or later is difficult to say, but some of those young sailors began to lose their resolve. The reality of what they were actually doing out there was setting in—the possibility, even the probability, of blasts, shrapnel, flame, and the clutches of the icy water stealing their young lives. And as that reality set in, so did a crippling fear.

At least for some.

For Charles, a different sensation was settling upon him: resolve.

★ ★ ★

Roy Summers maintained a fixed state of indignation at the ocean, glaring at it with vindictive intent, searching every whitecap and snow flurry, looking for revenge for the sinking of the *Chatham*. Sitting at his post in the turret of his 4.5-inch gun on the starboard side of the ship, he didn't hold out high hopes of spotting a U-boat, given the night and weather. But he was ready. He had taken his life jacket and placed it on the gun mount in case he needed it. Now, if a U-boat did show itself, he would not hesitate to unleash the fearsome firepower at his fingertips. The Germans had nearly killed him once, and they had killed some of his comrades. Not again.

In a ridiculously unhelpful warning, perhaps just long enough for him to realize a life-changing event was about to occur, Roy might have heard, like so many other men did that night, a swishing sound. It was followed by a different noise, for the briefest of moments that seemed to last for an eternity—a muffled rumble from the side of the boat, as if the *Dorchester* itself were unleashing a monstrous cough into the water.

Then the dark space in front of Roy exploded with water and fire.

It seemed the air itself had reached out and grabbed him in a death grip. An unseen force lifted him off his feet and flung him backward, while a tower of mist and spray seemed to burn before him. He flew until his back slammed into something so hard it likely knocked the wind from his lungs. As soon as he hit, he crumpled to the deck, his back now resting against a wall of smooth steel: one of the ship's bulkheads.

Immediately, the ship lurched, listing about thirty degrees toward the blast. Around him was chaos. The engines immediately powered down; the *Dorchester* lurched to a passive float. Men were screaming. Some were already rushing to throw life rafts overboard. One of the other gunners on the 20mm gun nearby had been "blown out of the gun circle onto the gunwale and into the water."[1]

There against the bulkhead, his body likely aching and his vision spinning, one clear, sickening realization settled over Roy Summers: for the second time in this war, a German U-boat had torpedoed his ship. For the second time in five months, Roy needed to decide if he was going to live or die. In many respects, this was a question he had been answering his entire life. Roy was a survivor, a fighter. He had to be. In a mining town in Illinois, his father had become disabled when the roof of a coal mine collapsed, crushing and crippling him. In an instant of smoke and dust, the family's sole source of income and food and clothing and housing had vanished. Roy was one of six sons, and they suddenly needed to provide for their family. They moved to a farm. Roy worked it with his siblings to grow their own food. He toiled on other local farms as well, all while trying to get an education. If his family ate meat, it was because Roy went outside and hunted squirrels. The family couldn't afford more than a bullet per squirrel, so Roy had one shot each time he ventured off to find food. If he missed, they ate no meat that night. So he had known poverty. He had felt the pit in the stomach, the fatigue and irritability that come from starvation. He had experienced hardship.

With all of that history burning inside him, flames of survival fanned by an insatiable sense of vengeance, Roy stood. He likely leaned on the bulkhead, steadying himself against the tilt and tumble of the ship and the fog in his brain. He registered that it was time to evacuate, that he should probably start hunting for the lifeboats.

Instead he stumbled back to his gun.[2]

The moment of impact affected every person on the *Dorchester* differently.

Lieutenant William Arpaia had been resting in his room no more than forty minutes when the explosion rocked the *Dorchester* into chaos. He immediately processed some key facts he would later report to the vice chief of naval operations: the torpedo must have hit well underwater because the explosion was so quiet, it sounded muzzled; the blast was not minor, because the engines had ceased to function; all of the electricity on the ship cut off, and the giant beast powered down, as if it had decided to take a nap right there in the middle of the ocean; the ship was already listing, which meant a large hole had been ripped into its side and water was spilling in; everything on deck had broken into "pandemonium."[3] Arpaia stumbled from his cabin and ran on the tilted wood toward the bridge.

Below deck, most of the army troops were relaxing. They played cribbage or poker. They sipped coffee. They shot the bull. Some slept. Most had taken off their parkas and life jackets and warm weather gear. When the torpedo struck the side of the ship, it ripped a tear in the hull the same way a giant serrated knife might. The gash stretched from beneath the ocean surface to the open deck, where it left a massive pit. The ship's belly immediately guzzled water and ice, right near the engine room. As soon as the frigid flow hit the boilers, the change in temperature caused the metal to morph, and they exploded, unleashing lethal steam and killing anyone in the area. The generators—both the main and auxiliary—shorted or shut down. Water flooded the lower holds, drowning most of the men there instantly or sucking them out to sea before they could even attempt to put on flotation devices. In the areas that didn't flood instantly, steam pipes burst, searing anyone nearby; the lights blinked off, plunging the holds into darkness; and many of the bunks collapsed on themselves from the jarring. Some of the men sleeping on them were crushed and killed. Others were knocked unconscious. Some were alive but pinned underneath bodies and debris. Then a pungent odor slithered into every available space—in the dark, where no one could see it or touch it, men started to choke to death. It was a combination of gunpowder and ammonia from the ship's refrigerating system.[4]

On the upper deck, a few of the more seasoned men had earned staterooms away from the regular troops. Some were playing cards. Others slept. When the blast hit, they weren't in nearly as much trouble as the men below deck. They had time to hunt for the life jackets and other clothes, even if finding them was nearly impossible in the dark. Then they stepped out into frigid chaos.

As for Clark, John, George, and Alex, they were stirred into action like everyone else in the upper staterooms—a moment of shock, trailed immediately by realization, followed by gathering themselves together. When they stumbled from their rooms, trying to keep their balance against the lean of the ground underneath them, they would have had just a moment to take in the gravity of the scene before them: men streaming out of the lower holds, some clinging to handkerchiefs over their mouths to keep from inhaling the deadly ammonia; men with life preservers; men without life preservers; flashlights dancing about the ship like streaks of starbursts, illuminating and disorienting all at once; tiny red lights bobbing in the water and prancing about the deck— emergency lights attached to the life jackets; men screaming; groups of men trying to get into lifeboats or to lower them; soldiers flinging themselves into the water; the core-rocking blare of a fog whistle—six blasts followed by several more before the steam leaked its final sigh; panic in the form of men flailing and shrieking wildly; panic in the form of men being completely immobilized, just stares and white knuckles gripping icy rails; a strange calm from other men, as if they were certain the ship would never sink; a deck tilting more and more to the starboard side with every passing second; smoke; darkness in the sky—no flares or white rockets to notify the other ships that *Dorchester* needed help; one light flashing to try to get the attention of escort cutters. Most of the lifeboats on the starboard side of the ship had been destroyed by the torpedo blast, or, as the ship listed in that direction, swung away from the rail out over the water so that no one could reach them.[5]

In all of that chaos, both above and below deck, the time had come for every man on board who had survived the initial blow to decide how he would react. Human nature being what it is, especially when pushed to survival mode, the most likely outcome was that people would look out for themselves or descend into a sort of tribalism: protect your friends, the people you know, your clan. Everyone else could fend for themselves, or, if necessary, would become the enemy.

PART III

DECISIONS

★ ★ ★ ★ ★

CHAPTER 17

TWENTY-FIVE MINUTES IN FEBRUARY

William Arpaia burst into the pilothouse. Captain Danielson stood there, trying to keep the ship under control.

Arpaia asked if the captain had thrown out the confidential documents yet.

He had not. He ordered Arpaia to do so immediately.

Arpaia burst through the door and staggered to the captain's cabin. He threw open the cabinet with the perforated metal box, then bounded to the railing on the starboard side, likely needing to catch himself lest the tilt of the ship throw him into the ocean. The box soared through the air, landed in the dark, icy water, then slipped beneath the surface, where the saltwater would devour the secret papers and the box would sink to the ocean floor.

Once he had done the deed, Arpaia charged back to the pilothouse. Had the captain seen anything? Anything at all?

The captain said no. Some reports suggest the captain intentionally chose not to fire any rockets or flares to notify the cutters of the torpedo strike, for fear that doing so would only make the entire convoy even more vulnerable to lurking U-boats.[1]

It's hard to know precisely how the captain reacted at that point. From Arpaia's report, it appears as if the captain had determined he would go down with the ship, or perhaps he didn't fully realize just how certain it was the ship was going under. Regardless, he seemed to Arpaia determined to stay on the flying bridge.

Arpaia waited for just a moment longer. Then it became clear to him the ship would not recover. The *Dorchester* had no hope.

The line between Arpaia and the captain was not hierarchical; they were more parallel. Arpaia was navy; the captain a merchant marine. Arpaia commanded the Naval Armed Guard; Danielson the ship's crew. Arpaia's thoughts turned to his men.

He burst from the pilothouse, leaving Captain Danielson to make his own decisions. Then he sprinted up and down the deck. Given the list of the ship, most of the guns were no longer operable. And Arpaia had become convinced that, even if some could fire, doing so was "futile."

Screaming at his men as he stumbled along, he ordered all of them to abandon ship.

And having done his duty for the gunners under his command, he led a group to the port side of the *Dorchester.* It was slowly rising in the air as the ship rotated in the other direction. Of his twenty-three gunners, between eight and ten were with him. The others, he wrote, "fended for themselves."[2] There is no evidence they concerned themselves with the army troops below deck or any of the merchant marines.

Instead, they found a doughnut raft and tossed it over the railing into the ocean. With the ship on that side still rotating up and out of the water, they crawled over the rail and worked their way down until they were standing on the part of the hull that had risen out of the ocean.

That's when they noticed them.

A swarm of army troops had stolen the raft, swimming to it the moment it hit the water. And it appears that once they had control of it, they had paddled far enough away that Arpaia and his men had no hope of climbing aboard.

Arpaia scanned the water, searching for some other plausible lifeboat. Nothing.

Within seconds, two of his men volunteered to climb back up to the topside to snag another raft.

Arpaia watched them grip the ice-covered rails of the decks and stretch and pull until they slipped over the top and disappeared. Those must have been excruciating moments. It was unclear if the two men would be able to find a raft, or if they would ever return. Their names were McCoy and McMinn.

Arpaia saw them a moment later, raft in hand. They tossed it into the ocean, and Arpaia immediately jumped after it. No doubt, as soon as he hit the water, the icy blast would have sent his body into shock. Loss of muscle function would have followed. Shaking, he made it to the raft, then held it in position for the others until they could climb aboard. Together, the group clung to the raft, holding on against the waves.

★ ★ ★

Roy Summers gave up on his gun. Arpaia had issued the abandon ship order, most likely in sprinting past Summers on his way to tell other men. Roy didn't follow. Instead, he realized he hadn't put on his life jacket. When he turned to grab it from the gun mount, it was gone. Either the same explosion that had thrown him into the bulkhead had blown it off or, he figured, some other soldier had taken it.

He took comfort that he was at least wearing all of his warm-weather gear.[3] He climbed down from the gun turret and stabilized himself. The *Dorchester* was now listing at a 45-degree angle, making any hike across the deck an uphill battle, and any slipping on the icy surface might mean sliding into the ocean below. None of the lifeboats on his side of the ship were operational. Instead, he charged up to the top deck on the port side.

His options for escape had vanished.

He spied one lifeboat overflowing with men, but it was still attached to the ship. Roy pounced, hoping at least to set it free. He and another sailor tried to release it, but ice had frozen the moorings. No matter how hard they tried, they couldn't get it loose.

Nearby, another lifeboat was in the same predicament and wouldn't budge.

Roy scanned the area. The doughnut rafts were gone. Any other flotation devices had vanished. He was on his own, with no life jacket and no one to help him.

★ ★ ★

The plight on board the *Dorchester* and in the sea beyond had become one of doing whatever was necessary. Most men were focused solely on their own survival.

The signal to abandon ship likely reached the ears of the chaplains. It came from giant steam horns, but, like everything else, fizzled relatively quickly because the boilers had burst.[4] Protocol would have been to seek their assigned lifeboat, climb on board, and escape in an orderly fashion as quickly as possible. The four men ignored protocol.

Which one led the charge is lost to history, but they sprinted to a depository filled with life preservers under an antiaircraft gun.

Men faltered past them, stumbling from staterooms and the holds below. The stench of ammonia permeated everything.

The chaplains grabbed anyone they saw without a life jacket and helped him slip one on. As far as witnesses recount, the chaplains all wore their own jackets at this point.

So many soldiers stumbled to the railing and stared out into the night that they had formed an impenetrable wall. When others tried to get through, the frozen men clung to the rails with ferocity.

One soldier, trying to break the barrier, screamed that the ship was going down, that the men needed to jump. But no one moved. They just watched as the ship tilted closer and closer to the licking waves.

At some point, as he was helping people pull on their life vests, George Fox heard the cries; they may have reminded him of similar pleas for help he heard in the trenches of World War I: "I can't find my life jacket! I can't find my life jacket! I can't find my life jacket!" The panicky yelps continued on and on.

George identified the source. It was a young man, just a kid really, probably about the same age as Wyatt, who was off fighting in some other battle somewhere else in the war.

"I can't find my life jacket!"

This was a moment of truth for George. He stood at the opening to the vast labyrinth of life. He wasn't required to give up his jacket. It was no more a duty for him than it was for any of the other hundreds of men milling about the deck. And there was no expectation that a chaplain go down with the ship—captains faced that burden, but not clergy. A multitude of pathways opened up before George. He could have turned away, deciding to help less panicky soldiers. He might have grabbed the youth and told him he would help him find a jacket. Perhaps he could have just ignored him altogether and tried to find his own path off the ship—the trail that would most likely lead him back to Isadore and their children, to his church family, to that house in the fog where she stood waiting for him. Or he could have encouraged the soldier to brave the waters without a life jacket.

We will never know how George reached his decision. It's likely it came to him long before that particular moment, perhaps in World War I, when he lay in a heap with a broken back, knowing right then that he wanted to serve humanity a different way. We also don't know if, in that moment, he thought about Isadore. Or Wyatt. Or his twelve-year-old daughter, Mary.

Whatever thoughts rumbled through George in the moment of hearing the soldier cry for help, whenever he reached his decision, he got the young man's attention. "Here's one, soldier," he said.

Then he pulled off his own life jacket and helped the man into it.

★ ★ ★

Below deck, in a stateroom that once housed eight to ten bunks, First Sergeant Michael Warish knew he was probably going to die. It was likely a fleeting thought, a sensation that came to him through the dense fog his thoughts had become. He was lying in total darkness. Alone. The earlier screams had dissipated. He was sucking in ammonia by the lungful, gasping with all his might to free himself. When the torpedo had hit, a piece of wood had flown from somewhere, bashing into his head and knocking him to the floor. At the same time, all of the bunks in the room had collapsed on top of him and some of the other men, a twisted heap of metal, mattresses, and blankets.

The crash had broken his ankle. He was sure of it. And in the dark, all of the other men who had survived the initial impact had bolted for the door, trying to escape while grabbing whatever clothes or life jackets they could find on the way out. They had left Michael behind. Blood seeped from the back of his head.[5] He talked to himself to keep from panicking.

He had been in the army for eleven years, an enlistee long before the war had broken out—a seasoned veteran. And this was a trip he had made half a dozen times already, since he had been stationed in Greenland since 1941. This last voyage, he had been on furlough to attend his sister's funeral in Massachusetts. Now the only person he would leave behind was his mother.

He tried again to lift the bunks off his foot. In the dark, figuring out exactly how he was pinned was impossible. The aches in his back and head didn't help either. For a moment, he thought: this was where he would die. A second torpedo would surely come and finish what the first had started. And it had to be only a matter of minutes before water started creeping into the room. One way or another—from the ammonia, the smoke, by drowning, another fiery blast—Michael was going to die.

There is an incredible liberation that comes when all hope is lost. So it would have been almost disappointing when, somehow, Michael was able to free his foot from the wreckage. He couldn't walk. His shattered ankle couldn't handle the weight, and every step fired light-ning bolts up his legs and into his body. The tilting of the ship made maneuvering even more difficult.

He felt his way forward, crawling through the dark. If there were life jackets around him, he couldn't see them. He cursed himself. As a senior man on board, he had actually spent much of the trip encourag-ing the younger men to wear their gear. But after midnight had passed, he had convinced himself that they were safe. Now he was left with nothing, just a shirt and pants, no parka, no life preserver, nothing to keep him warm.

He fumbled into the hallway. In the days leading up to that mo-ment, Warish had walked these corridors enough to know where he needed to go. The exit leading up to the deck was, by his estimate, about thirty feet away. What he didn't know was how many obstacles would be in his way. With his hands, he felt hindrances spread all across the path before him. And if this hallway was like some of the others on this ship, what stood in his way could have included everything from fallen crates of soda bottles to the bodies of troops who had suffocated from the ammonia and smoke. If he had thought about it, he would have been grateful for the bunk beds and wood that pinned him to the floor. Ammonia is lighter than air, so, in normal circumstances, it rises. Pinned to the ground, unable to rise, now forced to crawl—these diffi-culties may have saved Warish's life. For the moment.

Into the dark, he inched forward. Given that the entire way might have been blocked, the thirty feet may as well have been a marathon.

★ ★ ★

The railing and lifeboats had become a magnet for chaos. The more men realized they had no option but to abandon ship into life-boats that were too crowded or no longer existed, the more their sur-vival instincts kicked in.

John, Clark, Alex, and George did their best to fight this. Unlike chaplains on the front lines, whose duty was to keep the men emotionally and spiritually strong in the face of a deadly enemy, their focus was to help these men stand brave against the unrelenting elements.

It would not be an easy task.

They had run out of life jackets. And the reality was this: dozens of men were going to have to enter the water without them. It didn't need to be that way; the ship had plenty for every person on board. There had been roughly 900 men and 1,400 life preservers—500 extra.[6] But so many troops had refused to wear them and couldn't find them once the water roared into the holds that now there was an extreme shortage. More important, even with the life jackets, the situation had devolved into anarchy.

Everywhere the chaplains looked, they would have seen mayhem. Even deciding where to start helping must have been excruciating.

Out in the waves, a stream of red lights bobbed in the water or trailed the ship because too many men had either been sucked out to sea or had leaped into the water before the *Dorchester* had stopped. The chaplains could do nothing for them. Their only hope—and it was slim at best—was that one of the cutters could pick them up before hypothermia slowed them to death.

On the deck on the port side, some men fought like animals for a space on any flotation device. They grappled and pushed, causing some to slip on the deck and slide over the edge into the darkness. Others, blinded from the smoke and ammonia and the chaos of the moment, fell into the maw the torpedo had created on the first-level deck. One kitchen worker emerged from the holds below wielding a meat cleaver. Facing a crowd that might prevent him from rescue, he swung it wildly, a crazed look in his eyes.

Men dodged out of his way. No doubt many screamed at him to calm himself.

He carved a path to one of the lifeboats, but who knows what he might have done in the close confines of a lifeboat once he got on it.

Finally, one of the officers shot him. He dropped dead to the icy deck. Otherwise, one survivor recalled, "he would've chopped everybody up."

At the lifeboat stations, every reaction possible to humanity seemed to be playing out before the chaplains' eyes. There had been plenty of boats, rafts, or floats on the ship: thirteen metal lifeboats, one motor boat, forty-five doughnut floats, and two square rafts—enough space for 1,286 men.[7] The 900 people on board the *Dorchester* should each have had a seat with legroom. But between the torpedo's blast, the listing ship, and sheer panic, the scene suggested not a single piece of lifesaving equipment had come along for the journey. At one station, a merchant marine helped some of the army men climb into a boat, then lowered them to the water with instructions that they should wait for him to climb to them. By the time he shimmied down the rope, they had abandoned him, leaving him dangling over the ocean like a worm on fishing line. At a number of other stations, the boats simply could not be lowered, either because their moorings were frozen or because the listing of the ship made it impossible. At another spot on the rails, a man decided to leap into a raft from the upper deck. When he hit, he smashed right through the bottom of it, plunging into the depths.[8]

In the air over the water and along the side of the ship, if people successfully boarded a lifeboat, they were still not safe. The ship was bobbing against the waves, and its tilt to the other side caused some of the boats to smash into the hull, knocking men loose and into the water. One raft had loaded properly, but while it was being lowered, someone on deck inexplicably cut one of its lines. The raft flipped. All of the men but one toppled out and into the water. The one still clinging to it had somehow gotten one leg trapped between its planks. He dangled upside down. He likely didn't realize it, but he wasn't alone. All along the port side of the *Dorchester*, men were swinging from ropes, hoping to climb down far enough to get themselves into some sort of lifesaving device. One cook from the kitchen had tried to climb through a porthole, perhaps because the way out of the lower holds was blocked, but had squeezed only halfway through before getting stuck. He dangled along the side of the ship as well, screaming.

Even in the water, the situation was precarious. Some men bobbed in the waves, frantically searching for lifeboats or rafts only to have them fall on top of their heads from above, killing them instantly. Others fought over space on the few boats that had actually made it. As more and more men climbed into boats, rafts, or floats, they capsized. At other places, while men tried to latch onto something, anything, that would keep them out of the stinging water, other troops beat them away with fists and oars. Even that didn't protect them, though—plummeting from above, death sometimes arrived in the form of sailors who chose to leap from the ship onto their mates in the boats below.

The chaplains were not part of the clamoring hordes. We don't know how they chose where to start helping, but each of them pounced to try to ease the chaos. They grabbed men and guided them to lines they could shimmy down into the water or into boats or rafts.

While they were doing this, John spied a soldier sprinting past him without a life preserver. The young boy was frantic—his body language and the look on his face suggested he was planning on leaping over-board without a life jacket. During all his time as a priest tending to people on death's door in the hospital, John was used to dealing with people about to leave this life. But now he could do something about it.

John grabbed the soldier by the arm and spun him about. "Wait, son," he said. He gave the boy time to collect himself. To his credit, the soldier seemed to return to the moment.

John asked where his life belt was.

"I couldn't find it."

Without another word, John unhooked his own life jacket. "Take mine."

The boy opened his mouth to argue, but John cut him off. "That is an order," he said in a surprisingly calm tone and slipped it over the soldier's head.

"God bless you, Father," the soldier said. Then he made his way to the rails, where John helped him grab hold of a rope that would lead down to a lifeboat.[9]

When he finished, John pivoted to find someone else to help.

Another army man, Acting First Sergeant Edward Dionne, then stopped him. They likely knew each other, since Dionne would have had a room near John's on the upper decks. Dionne, who had no life vest, noted that John no longer had one either. He asked if the chaplain knew where there might be any others.

John told him he knew where they might find some: on the top deck.

They sprinted up the stairs, likely clinging to the rails to keep their balance. But when they reached the place John thought the extra jackets might be, it was empty.

John gave a sorrowful look to Dionne. He was sorry—he had nothing else to give.

Dionne understood, then sprinted away, looking for some other avenue of escape.[10]

John watched him leave before turning back to help someone else.

★ ★ ★

Down on the main deck, Rabbi Alex Goode was helping soldiers either stay calm or find a way off the ship. Gloves warmed his hands, and he still wore his life jacket. Then he heard the cursing. Navy Lieutenant John Mahoney was struggling past him, swearing at himself for having forgotten his gloves in his cabin.

"Don't bother, Mahoney," Alex called, apparently not wanting Mahoney to waste the time to go back for them.

Mahoney stopped and turned back.

Alex yanked off his gloves. "I have another pair. You can have these."

Mahoney refused, but Alex wouldn't be denied. He insisted: he had another pair; Mahoney didn't need to worry.

It was a lie. Mahoney would come to realize that later . . . after the gloves had saved his life, after he had used them to hold onto the side of an awash lifeboat for over eight hours, after thirty-eight of the other men on that boat had died from exposure, after he was pulled to safety because of those gloves. Only then would he realize that Alex never had any intention of leaving the ship. Just why Alex chose to lie in that moment is known only to him. It was probably because he knew Mahoney would never take the gloves if he had told him the truth. Mahoney was not a Jew. Mahoney was not even army—the branch Alex was called to serve. Alex had no duty or obligation to help him. If anything, his duty was to his people, his synagogue, Theresa and Rosalie; he carried every right to leap from that ship himself and save his own life. But long before, after he had earned his PhD from Johns Hopkins and while he and Theresa were serving Temple Beth Israel in York, Pennsylvania, Alex had written a book. It was called *Cavalcade of Democracy.* It was one of the labors of love he left behind when he volunteered to serve. It spoke of the siblinghood of humanity, of great leaders from all different religious traditions bringing people together and uniting them in freedom. It was a vision Alex carried for humanity and a demand he placed upon himself. In all reality, Alex had no option but to lie so that Lieutenant Mahoney—this man so different from him—could live.

In that moment, Mahoney believed the falsehood. He took the gloves. He made his escape. "I owe my life to those gloves," Mahoney would later say.[11]

Roy Summers had reached that strange cliff where his only hope was to rely on God. The same God who had saved him on the *Chatham* and on his gun earlier would have to save him now as well, because he was out of options. He had given up any dream of finding a lifeboat or raft. And he had no life jacket. In reality, official reports after the sinking determined that many "rafts were still aboard when the *Dorchester* went down."[12] Had he hunted for one, he might have found it.

In the moment, with only minutes until the entire ship gurgled into the ocean, he was convinced he would need to enter the water without a single flotation device. He navigated through the pandemonium on the upper two levels and made it to the main deck. All around, the scene of men scrambling to survive would have been bewildering. He tried to orient himself. A plunge from the rail was his only option. He approached, ready to make the leap, confident God would save him. Just as he tensed his muscles, he remembered something: on the top deck, under an antiaircraft gun, there was a space with life jackets stored in it.

He backed away from the rail.

The ship had likely listed well past 50 degrees, giving everything a fun-house feel. Roy ignored the drunken sensation and muscled his way back up the stairs. He reached the jacket closet, flung it open, and felt inside. In the dark, seeing anything was nearly impossible. He fingered his way around, hoping to feel something other than empty space.

Nothing.

The jackets had all been taken. He couldn't have known it, but the chaplains had already given them all away. That must have been a plunging moment. He felt frantic to enter that water with something that could keep him alive, but he couldn't. He had no choice but to return to his original plan: brave the water and pray someone would rescue him.

He pulled his hand from the compartment to sprint back to the main deck; as he withdrew his arm, he brushed something. It was slight, but certain. He fumbled around more. The feeling of canvas and cork. Somehow, whoever cleared out the closet had missed this last life jacket. Roy yanked it from the darkness and pulled it on.

On the main deck, the situation had reached the point of no

return. The ship had listed so sharply and the angle was so steep that "some men . . . cascaded into the icy water."[13] Roy somehow managed to stay on his feet and decided to head to the rear of the ship. Clinging to whatever he could find in the dark, struggling against the ice on the deck, he reached what he figured would be the perfect place to abandon ship.

That was when he heard the screams—horrible, gargled wailing from men who sounded as if they were being eaten alive.

The night was so dark, Roy couldn't see precisely what was happening, but the shrieking locked him midstep. He peered into the black, trying to make sense of what he was hearing. With the ferocity of a bomb blast, the realization hit him: the engines had died but the ship's screw propeller was still churning.

Roy felt the tilt of the ship. It wasn't just listing to starboard—the bow was getting sucked into the ocean as well. The entire rear of the *Dorchester,* including the propeller, was rising out of the water, and some poor men had jumped off into it, only to be shredded to pieces. Their launch point was precisely where Roy had been headed.

In the cave of the holds, the water had yet to choke the life from Michael Warish. Time was a meaningless artifice at this point. When people are in moments of intense stress, time seems to slow. There is a term for this: tachypsychia. So, despite the chaos of the moment, Michael would have seemed to have an eternity, at least in his own mind. How many minutes had passed, he had no way of knowing, but given the shift in gravity all around, he knew it was only a matter of minutes before the water found him. His ankle broken, practically blind for lack of light, he had made tremendous progress. This thirty feet would be the longest distance he would ever traverse in his life. Piles of objects he couldn't identify in the dark blocked his passage, but he pulled and crawled and yanked.

Finally, he made it to the stairs leading to the main deck. His ankle throbbed. From where he was, he could likely hear the men struggling up on deck. He latched onto whatever he could find and started to climb. Step by anguished step, he pulled himself up. Cool air would have licked at him from above, reminding him that he wore nothing but a thin shirt.

He emerged onto the freezer of the deck to find the air snapping at him almost immediately. Lying there, he didn't have very many options: back down into the warmth of the hold was certain death, either from water or ammonia or smoke; on deck, with no one to help him and no life jacket or warm clothes, his chances weren't much better. The entire night on this part of the ship had grown eerily quiet. In the distance, men were still shouting. But right here on this spot, it was as if everyone had been wiped away.

The pulsing pain in his ankle snagged his mind away from his situation. He pulled his foot close and undid his shoe, then pulled it off to help slacken the ache from his swelling ankle. He took in his situation again. Blood was still gushing from his head. There had to be someone who could help him. But the longer he looked around, scanning for options, the more he realized how alone he truly was. The only light was red, emanating from the sea—a fiery, hellish glow, like embers from the deep refusing to let the ocean snuff them out.

Over the edge of the deck, in the water, bobbing, floating, radiating from the red lights on their life jackets, hundreds of frozen men drifted lifeless in the water.

On the starboard side, John, Clark, George, and Alex were still helping men over the edge, which by then was just a few meters away from the waves. A good distance from the rails, a young soldier screamed hysterically. Whatever sense he ever had of rational action had fled.

Clark climbed up the sloping deck to him and stripped off his life jacket.[14]

The young man, though seemingly out of his mind, recognized the significance of the act. That only led to more frenzy. "I don't want your belt!" he screamed. Whatever was going through his head, it appeared he didn't want another man to die for him.

Clark was seasoned. He had spent years training and teaching youth—he and Betty together, climbing mountains, forcing them to stretch their faith by extending themselves physically. To him, a father, battle tested from training, he had no qualms putting the boy in his place. He flashed his rank on his uniform. "Get into it, soldier," he barked, "and get into it fast!"

It may have been the flashing of the rank or the sternness in Clark's voice—either way, the boy obeyed. He slipped on the jacket.

Clark likely clipped it for him. He didn't wait for any more debate. With an open hand, he shoved the boy down the deck. The soldier slid across the icy surface until he hit the rails, Clark on his heels. When they both stopped, Clark lifted him and threw him into the ocean.

When Clark pivoted, he noticed another man watching him. With what seemed like a sense of exasperation, he stomped to him. "Soldier, what are you doing here? Get over that rail."

Before the boy could respond, Clark had latched onto him and spun the soldier around.

This particular man was more willing to go over the edge. He climbed over on his own, looking down at the churning water below.

Clark stayed with him. "Swim out," he said.

The man dove into the water. He struggled to a nearby boat and somehow climbed in.

Clark stood at the rail watching, and he unleashed a laugh so strange the soldier would recall it decades later. It's not clear what Clark was laughing at. It may have just been a nervous tick, something he did when feeling energized, but he may have been thinking of other things: the tragic irony that here he was saving these other boys but would never see Corky again, or Thumper, or Betty.[15]

Perhaps right then, maybe a few minutes earlier or later, he screamed words of encouragement to the soldiers still in the water.

Nearby, his good friend George Fox called out, "So long, boys. Good luck!"

History will not know precisely when John Washington resigned himself to death. But the moment came before the port side of the ship was abandoned and all that was left were men clinging to the railing on the starboard side, staring into a black abyss, stiff with fear, afraid to make the leap.

John walked among them. If he himself felt fear—of death, of an end to this existence, of never seeing his mother again—he showed no sign of it. He paused at each soldier, before their leap into the dark, and administered the Catholic sacrament of absolution. When he reached Charles Macli, who in another life had been a professional boxer, John encouraged the young man to join his fellow shipmates in the water. He had come to know Macli well. The boy had spent plenty of time talking with all four of the chaplains, and he had appreciated how open all of them had been to chatting with him. But now, John wasn't here to talk. Macli needed to abandon ship. It was the only way.

Macli howled, "Father, get off the ship yourself! It's going down!"

John had made up his mind. He seemed to carry with him the calm in the storm that comes from knowing one's destiny. "No," he said. "But you must get off."

Macli seemed to hesitate, but the longer he looked into John's eyes, the more he realized that John was a rock. He was not going to give in.

The young boxer scrambled over the rails and plunged into the abyss.

John pivoted to help the next soldier who needed him.

Roy Summers backed away from the screams of dying men and the grinding propeller. He pivoted back to the deck. He needed to find another way off the ship. Hugging the railing, he fought his way along the starboard side.

In the water, a field of red lights stretched out into the waves. Capsized doughnut floats and rafts bobbed in the water. Others were filled with men piled on top of one another or fighting for positions. What was absent: the cutters. No one was there to save them.

Roy couldn't worry about that now. His focus was just getting off the ship before it went down and sucked him with it. As he worked his way back to amidships, he noticed the chaplains trying to persuade two soldiers to climb down a rope into a lifeboat.

Roy didn't know the chaplains well enough to know their names, but one of them was shaking one of the soldiers, trying to get him out of a panic.

The boy was screaming, refusing to get off the ship, fighting the chaplains at every turn, as if shimmying down to the lifeboat was more dangerous than staying on the sinking *Dorchester*. It wasn't a completely irrational thought, given how chaotic the situation was in the lifeboats, with the men fighting each other for spaces. Still, staying on the *Dorchester* meant certain death.

The chaplain slapped the boy, yelling at him to calm down long enough to listen or think clearly.

The boy didn't respond.

The chaplain slapped him again. "Get on the lifeline and drop off the ship," the chaplain said. "You can save yourself."

It was hopeless. The soldier was too far gone.

Nearby, another chaplain was helping other more lucid men climb onto the rope that led to the lifeboat below.

Suddenly, the crazed young soldier flung out his arms, trying to free himself from the chaplain. He gripped the clergyman around the neck in a chokehold. The two grappled.

Roy pounced. He bounded in between the two of them and broke the young man's grip.

For just a moment, it seems, the boy stood there, trying to process this new arrival.

"Come with me," Roy said. "We can go down the rope together."

The man didn't even consider it. He turned and bolted away, lurching along the tilted deck. Where he ended up, Roy would never know.

At the same time, the chaplain who had been attacked had already turned his attention to helping some other men. Roy didn't need the help. He climbed over the rail, latched onto the rope, swung out over the water, and, hand over hand, lowered himself into the frosty depths.

Terrible, rolling minutes passed. There were some men George, John, Alex, and Clark simply couldn't get to move. They gripped the rails like children clinging to their mother. The chaplains did their best to help them, but they also turned their focus to the people in the water. They hollered words of encouragement. *Courage! Have courage!*

At some point, at least two of the chaplains, perhaps all of them, remembered the men who had been injured during the storm a day and a half earlier. There was no way they could have escaped the hold on their own. But with the ship listing to starboard, it was still possible they could be alive, as long as they were in the holds on the port side.

The details are gone, but it appears Alex led the charge. It also appears there were more than just the chaplains going for the rescue— other men had chosen to follow them in staying on the ship and trying to help others. Standing before the gaping black entrance to the depths, the stench of ammonia and smoke billowing out, they may have paused for just a second, wondering if it made sense to go in after the men, whose chances of still being alive hovered only slightly above zero. Whether they hesitated or not, they eventually faded into the darkness. Amidst the poisonous air, burst pipes, flooding tunnels, dead bodies piled on debris, and absolute oblivion, they hoped for a miracle, most likely knowing that even if they found someone alive, they might never emerge to save him.

★ ★ ★

For Michael Warish, there were only lonely, gut-wrenching sensations: the muteness from the bodies in the water, the unending ache of his broken ankle, the cold slap of the air, and then its razor grip on his fingers and toes. He knew he needed to abandon ship, but jumping into a sea of the dead seemed like a fool's errand—there was no chance of him surviving in the water long enough to be picked up, and any boat looking for him wouldn't be able to distinguish him from so many of the other men.

No, he needed to find others.

Gritting against the pain radiating up his leg, he pulled himself up on the portside rail—which was now high in the air—and began a lengthy journey around the bow of the ship. Every step brought with it the possibility of his losing his grip and sliding across the deck into a bulkhead. The rails would have been slippery; the deck would have been a hockey rink. With no shoe on one foot, he had no way of gripping anything.

He worked his way from the upper port side to the bow, which was plummeting fast. All around it, just a few feet down, water bubbled as if boiling. It wouldn't be long before the bow slipped beneath the surface. After that, the entire ship would follow.

Michael forced himself to push forward. Passing from the center of the bow to the starboard side made gravity shift.[16] It now pulled him into the rails, and he didn't need to cling to them as tightly. But he also needed to walk uphill the length of the ship, still hoping he would find someone who could help him get into a lifeboat. At a minimum, he hoped to find another group of men he could slip into the water with, since the cutters, if they ever came, were more likely to target a group of red lights rather than spy a solitary man between the waves.

★ ★ ★

Deep in the holds, the chaplains and other rescuers found at least one of the men still alive. He was too badly injured to move on his own. As with Michael Warish, he had likely survived the poisonous ammonia because he'd been knocked to the floor and the cleaner air lingering there. Most likely, alone in the dark, he had given himself up for dead, or had tried to claw and drag himself to an exit.

Somehow, the rescue team carried the man back through all the destruction in the guts of the ship and up to the main deck. They burst through the door and eased him down against a bulkhead. His shoulder was ravaged, useless.

If he had a moment, Alex would have taken in the scene to assess the situation: John, George, and Clark no longer wore their life jackets; John's glasses were gone; Alex had given his gloves away; the ship, now angling steeply to bow and starboard, had only minutes left; along the rail, still, were men too afraid to jump; about five yards away, an injured Michael Warish hung from the railing, watching; and this man they had just pulled from the hold was too injured to swim and, like Michael, wore no life vest.

No doubt, Alex was huffing for air; his hands would have stung. He was a goal-driven man, and there were many goals he had yet to accomplish: the book he had written but not published; one last time tucking in little Rosalie, whom he never got to see in New York City; writing that perfect sermon about the unity of all humanity and the freedoms we should all enjoy; helping others live in peace, without persecuting those who are different; serving the Jews in Europe and even in the United States; returning home to Theresa after that tearful goodbye near the train in Manhattan and holding her in his arms.

So much would be left undone.

But Alex chose to leave those goals to others—or to never be achieved at all in this life. He unbuckled his life jacket, peeled it off, and stretched it to the injured man.

Only one of the man's arms moved; the other was completely incapacitated—one of the injuries he had suffered during the storm.

Alex slipped the man's good arm through the armhole in the jacket and wrapped the rest of the preserver around his shoulders. There was no way he would be able to get his other arm through the second hole. It couldn't even move. And if the jacket hung off just one arm, it would do the soldier little good once he hit the water.

Alex leaned back and untied his boots. With freezing fingers, he worked the laces through the eyelets until he had freed them completely. He pulled the jacket tight around the man and knotted it in place with the shoelaces. It appears the man may have been too injured to make a run for the railing or to try to leap from the ship, so he stayed leaning against the bulkhead. Apparently the hope was that the jacket would pull him to the surface once the ship went down. And if he could fend off hypothermia long enough, he would at least have a chance of surviving.

"Thank you, Chaplain," the man said.[17]

Alex stood. That was it. There was nothing else they could do. The men at the rails who refused to jump weren't going to move. The chaplains had done all they could for them. And who was to say they were wrong? Given the frigidity of the water, maybe it was better to stay on the ship as long as possible. Maybe their fear would, at the end of the day, save them. What was troubling: they didn't seem to be making a conscious choice; they had simply stalled, as if they were bystanders to some horrible accident instead of participants in the middle of it. Most likely, in their catatonic state, they would get pulled to the depths by the ship as it went down, but it was hard to say.

The other three chaplains had shifted to stand before a bulkhead; a group of other men had gathered around them. Some wore life jackets; some didn't. Unlike the ones at the rail, these weren't immobilized by the gravity of the moment. For them, turning to the chaplains, helping them as they lifted others, had been a conscious choice. Like disciples of old, they had followed their spiritual leaders' example, and now they looked to them for strength before the ship made its final plunge.

Alex left the man with the shoelaces. The final moments had come. Grasping at a steeling resolution, he clomped in slack boots to join John, Clark, and George. Their next decision would prove crucial.

CHAPTER 18

HELP IN THE DARK

W hen all was said and done, the *Dorchester* would sink in roughly twenty-five minutes. A now-declassified memorandum found that, of the fourteen lifeboats on board, only two "carried survivors to safety." The numbers for the rest are jarring: five were not lowered at all; four made it to the water but capsized or were swamped from overcrowding; and three saw some progress but were still dangling on the ship when it went down because of damage from the torpedo.[1] This meant the vast majority of the men who made it off the ship had only a short time before the cold grip of hypothermia stopped their hearts. In the water, as opposed to on a boat, "body heat can be lost 25 times faster."[2] Even then, the men who did manage to climb aboard some floating object would be plummeting toward death at a terrifying rate. If they were going to live, they needed to be snatched from the ocean's icy grip. For most of them, their hope came from only one source: the coast guard cutters whose job was to escort them to safety.

On board the *Tampa*, at 12:55 a.m., when the torpedo struck the *Dorchester,* the realization that something had gone wrong rolled over convoy Captain Joseph Greenspun. His cutter was blasting through the waves at the head of the convoy, so close to the safety of Greenland and her surrounding icebergs that everyone could feel it.

But the *Dorchester* had violated the blackout order.

At first, it seemed searchlights were peering off its port side. For two minutes, Greenspun observed, trying to figure out what Danielson and his men on the *Dorchester* were doing. They were a razor's width away from safety—this wasn't the time to risk signaling the enemy.

When the *Dorchester* suddenly veered off course and flashlights and red dots exploded all over her decks, Greenspun realized the gravity of the situation. The *Tampa's* commander sounded for everyone to jump to their battle stations. Four minutes later, the *Biscaya,* one of the cargo freighters, fired two green rockets high into the air and made an emergency turn toward the *Dorchester.*

Greenspun immediately thought of what was likely still lurking in the depths: a wolfpack. The Nazi methodology was not to hunt alone; if one ship had fired, even if it fled, more were in the area.

While Greenspun considered how the convoy could best navigate the situation, the *Tampa's* commander ordered his men to sweep the area with radar and screen for other U-boats.

At five minutes, Greenspun knew for certain the *Dorchester* had been torpedoed.

★ ★ ★

At roughly the same time, men on board the *Escanaba* noted lights on the *Dorchester.* Commander Carl Peterson ordered his ship to change course and investigate. His thinking was that a man had gone overboard and the transport ship was attempting to pick him up. He signaled the *Tampa* his plan. The *Escanaba* immediately turned to port and started carving a path to the *Dorchester.*

Eight more minutes passed.

The *Escanaba* wasn't close enough yet to rescue any men from the water, but what Peterson and his crew finally saw when they got a visual lit fires under them: the *Dorchester* was listing badly, sinking into the ocean, and a steady stream of small red dots, visible from a distance, were plummeting off her decks and floating in the water.

Peterson ordered all men to battle stations.

His instinct was to charge toward those red dots. Time was melting away.

But orders from Greenspun on the *Tampa* floored him. The *Escanaba* was to ready for battle and return to its original position. As time ticked away, minute after minute, Peterson ordered his crew to push the *Escanaba* to full speed and swing out around the *Dorchester,* then head "back to station."[3] On the way, it's likely he and his men were watching those red dots, never dimming, floating in the waves. In his log, he wrote only, "Executed maneuvers per convoy instructions."[4]

★ ★ ★

On the other side of the *Dorchester,* on the *Comanche,* at the moment the torpedo hit, many of the men were above deck, still buzzing about the torpedo that had nearly blasted them out of the water. Charles was likely among them.

But his friend Dick Swanson was still at his station operating the cutter's sonar. Through the distractions of other noises clogging his listening, he thought he heard an explosion. He immediately reported it to his commander, Lieutenant Commander Ralph Curry, who in turn reported it to Captain Greenspun aboard the *Tampa.*

By that point, Greenspun already knew about the torpedo.

At nine minutes after the explosion, Curry sounded all men to battle stations. He expected to receive orders to pick up the survivors and prepared accordingly. Curry knew the men in the water would not survive long.

As a mess attendant, Charles had no obligation to prepare for battle. That was not his assignment—not for lack of willingness, but because the racism of the day forbade it. Still, his mind seems to have been churning. After months at sea, he had watched the protocols, he had seen rescues, he knew what the *Comanche* crew would need to do when the order to rescue the *Dorchester* men came. And he was in a welcome state of mind, ready to help however he could, whether he was wanted or expected.

But the order to save survivors didn't come.

★ ★ ★

On board the *Tampa*, Greenspun remained concerned about a wolfpack on the prowl. Instead of ordering the rescue of survivors from the *Dorchester*, he commanded the *Comanche* and *Escanaba* to screen the area for the U-boat that had fired the torpedo and to hunt for other subs as well.

Greenspun's decision has met considerable criticism over the years. He was, to be sure, following protocol. When any member of a convoy was hit, the general rule was to protect against further attacks by seeking out enemy subs. Saving men in the water would follow only after ensuring the area had been cleared. The protocol came from sad experience. In the year prior to the attack on the *Dorchester*, the Allies had learned, as ship after ship plummeted to the seabed, that the Nazi attack was relentless. Protecting other ships in a convoy after the initial strike was a crucial, lifesaving practice.

For the *Dorchester*, with 20/20 hindsight, it proved fatal. A series of assumptions turned out to be wrong: that U-223 was not alone; that it would likely attack again; that the men on the *Dorchester* would take advantage of their many lifeboats; that the *Dorchester* itself might not sink too fast. At least one expert has claimed it was impossible to comprehend Greenspun's order, since almost the entirety of the men in SG-19 were on the *Dorchester*; if the goal was to save men's lives, then protecting smaller, sparsely populated ships while men were most certainly going to die if left in the frozen water made absolutely no sense. And Greenspun did have some flexibility with his decision making; while normal protocol was to pick up survivors second, that was by no means a requirement. The United States Atlantic Fleet had issued a directive just two and half months earlier instructing convoys and their commanders to apply "common sense, good judgment, the seaman's eye, a sense of proportion, and sound imagination."[5]

But it's always easier to question decisions after the fact, with decades of research providing key facts that could affect crucial judgments. Greenspun enjoyed none of that. As far as he knew, from the recent history of the war, every ship in that convoy was on the verge of being sent to the ocean floor. And if that happened, no one on the *Dorchester* would survive anyway. He held to his orders.

Crucial time passed. Seventeen minutes after the torpedo hit, Greenspun ordered the *Comanche* to fire sixteen star shells into the sky. They burst over the ocean on the port side of the convoy, revealing the gray, ice-pocked, snowy surface of the Atlantic. There was no point in trying to stay hidden—the Nazis had already found the convoy; now the Americans needed light to spy their predators.

From what we know of Charles, he was likely on the deck with the rest of the crew, scanning the firelit ocean surface for any sign of the enemy. Neither he nor anyone else spied any submarines.

At thirty-three minutes, the *Tampa* launched twenty-one star shells over the ocean ahead of the convoy, trying to determine if the path forward was clear for the *Lutz* and *Biscaya*, which were still in the most danger.

Finally, at thirty-eight minutes, the *Escanaba* blasted twenty-one more illuminating shells over the starboard side of the convoy. By then, the *Dorchester* would have been completely underwater. Some men would have been floating for at least that long, others for somewhere near thirteen minutes.

As men from the *Dorchester* floundered in the waves, all three coast guard cutters failed to detect a single submarine.

Wächter was convinced he had landed three hits on the convoy. Whether he was padding his statistics to impress his superiors and men or genuinely believed his torpedoes had landed on multiple ships is unclear. But after the initial hit, he and his crew didn't linger long. They hovered in the sonar-dead zone between one of the escorts and the *Dorchester* for a few minutes. Wächter was certain two of the torpedoes had hit the large troop carrier right at the engine. He noted multiple high smoke pillars. But with one of the escorts still behind him, searching, hunting, Wächter ordered his men to turn the sub toward the escort so that it provided the smallest silhouette possible.

Finally, he ordered his men to sail straight south, away from the convoy. After a time, he paused. This was the most vulnerable moment for him and his men because, after firing the torpedoes, they had for the first time revealed their presence.

Wächter watched the star shells burst over the ocean, but he was far enough away that they wouldn't reveal U-223. Twice he tried to approach the convoy again, and twice he was rebuffed by what he thought were escorts stalking the area. The third time, he realized that what he had thought were escorts were actually icebergs. By then, he estimated he was fifteen to twenty minutes behind the convoy. He wrote in his log: "When I can next get in his vicinity the enemy will have reached the coast. With my uncertain navigation and in the bad visibility I do not want to go close off the coast." So he ordered a dive and disappeared into the darkness, gleefully reporting his success back to headquarters.

By forty minutes, the *Escanaba* stopped illuminating the sea. They waited. Bobbing in the waves, they listened; no sign of the enemy presented itself. Most likely, given their orders to return back to their original station, they could no longer see the *Dorchester* or the sea of red lights beside it. They had no hint as to the fates of their fellow servicemen. They had seen enough earlier to know the men were out there, freezing to death in the water.

The crew of the *Escanaba* also knew something else: until the orders were given, no help was coming.

CHAPTER 19

ALONE

After helping the chaplain escape from the chokehold of the crazed soldier, Roy Summers struggled down a frozen rope until he was dangling over the waves. He hit the water with a plan. Nearby, he'd seen a lifeboat—a floating mass of tangled arms and legs and screaming men. The cold would've hit him like a hammer, but he pushed through it. When he reached the boat, he somehow managed to climb in with the dozens of other men fighting for position.

The lifeboats were well equipped. Each possessed three fourteen-foot oars made of finely finished ash; one fifteen-foot oar; a bailer; a galvanized steel bucket; a flashlight with spare bulbs and extra batteries; hatchets; a lantern; a first aid kit; drinking cups; six blankets; bilge pumps; biscuits; forty pounds of pemmican; the same amount of chocolate tablets; an equal weight of milk tablets; lamp wicks; rowlocks; a compass; pilot charts of the North Atlantic; a tiller; a canvas cover, and a ridge pole. The boats were designed to save as many as forty-five men comfortably for a lengthy period of time.[1]

None of that mattered to Roy. All he wanted was to get free from the chilly grip of the water. Hordes more than the boat could hold were scratching and clawing for positions. As soon as Roy managed to pull himself aboard, the entire craft capsized. He plunged back into the water. Once again, its grip seized him.

The life jacket he had found pulled him back to the surface. He emerged in an arena of screaming and splashing men. Somehow, they managed to coordinate their efforts enough to flip the twenty-six-foot-long boat upright once more. But unless some of that group had succumbed to the cold already, the mathematics hadn't changed. As Roy climbed in again, fighting against the involuntary spasming in his muscles and the unsteady cadence of the waves, the boat flipped once more, a metal bludgeon that would have knocked unconscious any man not fast enough to move.

For a second time, the scrum of troops managed to overturn their only chance of living. Once again, Roy latched onto the side with numb fingers. He pulled himself out of the water.

"Stay offa here," a man shouted. Somehow, he had managed to pull himself up the fastest and had latched onto one of the oars, a fourteen- or fifteen-foot sword. Swinging it wildly, he attacked anyone else trying to climb up. He clubbed some of the others who were half-way in, knocking them back into the water.

He whirled the oar at Roy, who managed to duck away but once again found himself bobbing in liquid death. All around, all he could see was chaos, masked by crashing waves. Roy was a navy gunner; he had respect for the sea, for the sailors who navigated it, for the coast guard. They had saved him once before, after the *Chatham* sank. But this time, when he scanned the horizon from the crest of a wave, he saw a vast expanse of nothing.

Lieutenant William Arpaia floated on his doughnut raft somewhere off the port side of the ship. Time had become obsolete, a mysterious concept that existed in another life, a different world. Alone in the dark, he bobbed on the waves, past feeling, existing only in his mind.

When all was said and done, only four of his gunners made it onto the raft with him. Now he lay with them on a raft with a rope floor and walls not high enough to keep out the water. With every wave, the frothing, icy mixture of the sea washed up and over them.

Help had never come.

After the *Dorchester* bubbled into the ocean and vanished from sight, a strange silence settled over everything.

If the cutters were out there, Arpaia couldn't see them. One of his sailors, Seaman First Class Ralph Leslie Taylor, was seeing something else. Arpaia wrote in his report that Taylor "lost his mind." He provided no other details. Most likely, the young man began to hallucinate from hypothermia. This was happening to many of the men still alive in the water. One, clinging to the side of a wooden raft, had seen the non-existent rising sun. "It's melting the butter on the pancakes," he said. "I'm going over to get some of them." Then he swam into the dark water and vanished. Another seemed to have departed the ocean for his home. In his last moments, he must have seen his mother. He was shaking, but before he disappeared beneath the surface, he announced that he was going to ask his mom to bring him "another blanket."[2]

Ralph Taylor experienced something similar. His mind quit, and his body followed. It happened all over the *Dorchester*'s gravesite. At first, men pleaded, prayed, and moaned, calling for help. Then, one by one, they froze to death.

Arpaia did everything he could to keep Ralph alive, but his comrade went too quickly. Arpaia had brought with him, from somewhere on the ship, a package of morphine syrettes. He had stuffed them into a pocket in his shirt. With fingers too stiff to bend, he fumbled them loose from his clothes. He gave an injection to a man named McCoy, who in turn gave Arpaia and McMinn injections as well.

By the time they thought to use the morphine, Taylor had already passed. The science is not clear as to whether the morphine actually helped the men, but it gave them something to cling to, an idea to hold, as they settled into the net of the raft and their bodies stiffened.

Michael Warish finally decided he had no choice but to swim to his death. At the part of the ship where he had stopped, the rail was still too high above the ocean surface. With his hurt ankle, jumping in felt impossible. He hobbled back to where the vessel was bubbling into the water. Finally, he reached a spot where the waves were just a couple of feet from the deck. Fighting through the ache in his leg, he swung himself over the railing and stepped into the Atlantic.

At least for the first five seconds, it appears fate may have been on his side. Just as he plunged into the water and felt the utter shock of its cold embrace, a wave of saltwater and ship's oil carried him away from the *Dorchester*.

As he rode it into the field of sparkling red lights, his mind had slipped to another place: resignation, or perhaps acceptance. Without a life jacket or boat, he would pass from this life, a nameless, frozen corpse alone in the dark. Michael had never been a religious man; he likely had no definitive sense of the nature of God or the afterlife. But in those lonely minutes, as his body's systems transitioned from hyper-activity to sluggish drowsiness, he figured death wouldn't be so bad. Maybe, after all the dreariness and heartache of this life was over, there was something on the other side, a place worth being.

Roy Summers's entire existence had been reduced to one of two possible outcomes: freeze to death in the water or be murdered by a bludgeoning shipmate. It seemed there were no other alternatives.

In the moment that realization dawned on him, he noticed a possible lifeline in the water, a third path he hadn't dared dream possible. In front of him, riding the waves, were the shattered remains of one of the rafts. Several men sat on wooden bench seats on either end of it. The entire floor appeared to have been shattered, perhaps by falling men or from being bashed into the hull of the *Dorchester*.

But it was floating.

All around its frame, men clung to the wood. Roy estimated there might have been thirty or more. He swam to it. By then, his blood was no doubt congealing, making all of his movements stiff. The water would have felt like tar. He found a space alongside the other men and hugged the skiff. At least he could pull himself slightly out of the water. Perhaps he could hold on long enough for the cutters to save him. He knew they were coming; they had to be.

Next to him was another navy gunner. Roy knew him; he went by the name of Red. He was just a kid, and what his real name was, Roy didn't know. His fingers were wrapped around a rope tied to the boat.

Looking him up and down, Roy could tell the boy didn't have much time left. "Can you hang on?"

"I think so."

The ocean seemed prepared to prove him wrong. They rode the waves: up, down, up, down, up, down.

Red was slipping. Indecipherable words emanated from his mouth. When the swells knocked them about, he swallowed gulps of seawater.

Roy wrapped his arm around the boy, grasping the raft even tighter with his other hand. "Hang on! They'll pick us up soon."

But Red died in Roy's embrace. It was so subtle, Roy didn't even know it at first . . . after all, the boy may have just been asleep.

Then Roy checked his pulse. It had stopped, the same way a breeze stops. One moment it's there; the next it just fades, and no one notices until later. Roy let go. Red's body drifted away with the waves, joining his red light with what looked to Roy like a wheat field with a lot of lightning bugs on top.[3]

Everything was glazed with frost. The waves churned on their broad course. The cutters Roy was so certain would come never materialized. The *Dorchester* had long since dived into oblivion while Roy had been fighting for survival. On the raft, he could perceive the passage of time by the falling away of men. Some swam away chasing hallucinations, mumbling to themselves about better images only they could see. Others simply disappeared; one second they were there, the next, they were gone.

Somehow, Roy hung on. Roughly ten men had found seats on the raft out of the water. Even they fell, one by one, leaving vacancies.

Against all odds and the predictions of scientists, Roy urged his muscles to work enough to pull his body onto the raft so he could sit on one end, where the floor hadn't entirely been smashed away. He huddled. The ten men had dropped to nine, then eight, then seven . . . a countdown to Roy's inevitable demise.

One young man slid off his seat, nearly plummeting into the water. Roy and some of the others grabbed him. *Sit up,* they said. *On the seat.* He tried, held himself for a moment, then slithered again toward the ocean. *Sit up. On the seat.* But the man's legs had abandoned him. No matter what his mind wanted (*hold me up; on the seat*), his legs refused. Eventually, he tumbled away.

There were moments when Roy felt he might perhaps try to save some of the men chasing after their visions. But it was a futile effort. He remembered the man on the ship's deck choking one of the chaplains. People did crazy things when they lost their minds, and they manifested an otherworldly strength. Roy had seen it before. He knew if he tried to stop one of them, they would just drag him down to death. Except he wouldn't enjoy the hallucination during the ride.

As the night continued in its rhythm, all of the roughly thirty men holding to the raft disappeared. Of the ten fortunate enough to find seats, only four now remained. It was only a matter of time before another of them slipped away. Then another. Roy knew his end would be soon—his legs and arms had grown numb. How long before they could no longer hold him? Before he slipped into the sea as the others had? Sitting in the silence, seemingly abandoned, alone, Roy, it seemed certain, would die on this night.

Michael Warish existed in a state somewhere between life and death. He would die, he had no doubt. The moment would come like drifting to sleep, and then he would be in heaven. Floating without a life jacket, he somehow managed to keep his head above the surface, but he was barely conscious. Everyone around him was dead. He saw no reason not to join them.

CHAPTER 20

THE WORST DISASTER

Not long after the *Dorchester* slipped beneath the waves, coded messages started arriving in the office of the commanding officer at the Boston port of embarkation. Marked with the word *SECRET* in multiple locations, decoded by naval experts, they represented broad strokes that, layer by layer, painted a bleak picture. The sinking of the *Dorchester* was quickly turning into the worst disaster of the war for a troop transport.

Of the 904 people on board, 678 were lost.* The vast majority froze to death, their corpses bobbing in the ocean. In twenty-five minutes, one torpedo from one U-boat had killed more than a quarter of the number of personnel lost during the entire attack on Pearl Harbor. After the initial rescue efforts, in the two days that followed

---

* This number is almost certainly inaccurate to some degree, and different authors and scholars have reported within a range of ten, plus or minus, over the years. There were stowaways on the ship—at least one teenager who managed to sneak on in New York, naively hoping to make it to the front lines (see Kurzman, *No Greater Glory*, 52). A now-declassified Informal Action Sheet from the War Department also explains that there were at least thirteen Danish citizens on board, and the War Department did not keep firm records on them. Also, a large number of civilian construction workers were being sent to Greenland to help construct infrastructure for mines and military bases. The army did not have perfect records of these individuals, either. Regardless, the figure is still in this range and still represents a staggering loss of life for a troop transport.

the sinking, army B-25 planes orbited over the *Dorchester*'s last known location, gliding in expanding circles over an area with a fifty-mile radius. They found no boats or men hanging on to life—just wreckage, overturned rafts, search crafts, and bodies.

Hundreds of bodies—their dead eyes frozen in an eternal stare. Limited daylight hours and lack of resources "precluded taking time to recover" them.[1] In the days that followed, the life jackets absorbed the saltwater and eventually ceased to float. One by one, yet as a group, the dead released their grip on the surface. If someone were below, gazing upward through the water, it would have been a stunning, somber sight. The ocean, with all its secrets and mysteries and tales and history, had likely never produced anything to rival it: hundreds of bodies descending like a horde of falling balloons once the life has left the party, a ghostly invasion from the shimmering water above to the darkness below.

Those men who died on rafts or clinging to floating debris would not sink on their own. Search ships who found them did not want to leave their bodies exposed, nor could they take them aboard. After brief ceremonies to honor them, the searchers fired on the crafts to ensure they would plunge, giving the men a brief burial at sea.

A little over a week later, 678 separate telegrams fanned out across the United States, sent to families, parents, wives, and children.

Betty Poling was home with Corky, her little baby thumping away in her womb. The telegram arrived from the adjutant general's office. It read that Clark was "missing in action in the North African area." She immediately called Clark's parents.

The language of the original communication gave families a sense of false hope. Given the short amount of time since its departure, there was no way the *Dorchester* could have been in North African waters. So perhaps it was a different ship that had been hit. Or perhaps there had been a clerical error. For days, the families would have held on to hope.

Clark's father told Betty not to worry; he was certain it was a mistake. He knew the realities of war, "knowing always" that it "is no respecter of families," yet he prayed that the telegram would in fact be an error. There is no record or memory of how or whether Betty shared the information with Corky. During this period of hope, she may have hid her fears from her little boy, not wanting him to worry unnecessarily. Or, perceptive as children are, she may not have been able to avoid the many questions he would have fired her way.

A few days later, the hope turned even more fleeting. A correction came: "North African" was updated to "North Atlantic."[2]

The emotional whiplash must have been devastating. Most likely, the modification was issued because families were asking questions. *Could it have been a mistake? Was it really a ship in the North African area? Hadn't their boys just left New York and St. John's? How could they have been in North Africa? Is it possible you made a mistake? Please, sir, a word, any word.*

Still, hope continued to persist. Betty and hundreds of other family members just like her would have imputed to the word *missing* all of its weighty implications, the most important of which was that if people are missing, they can be found. Perhaps they had been saved but simply hadn't been identified yet in a field hospital in Greenland. Or maybe the Germans had taken them captive—not ideal, but at least they might still be alive.

To make matters worse, and to add to the tragedy, letters from some of the men who died were still arriving for their loved ones after the "missing in action" telegrams had arrived. One woman, Joan Swanwick in Connecticut, simply couldn't believe her father had died.

For good reason.

She received the adjutant general's telegram informing her that her dad had gone missing in action on February 3, 1943. A short time later, she received a letter bearing a postmark of February 10, 1943. It was from her father. He was writing to her seven days after he had supposedly disappeared. Clearly he was still alive. For months, she wrote letters to the adjutant general's office. Eventually, a lengthy investigation revealed what happened. He had written the letter in St. John's, when the ship had docked there for that day and a half. Because of fear of spies, strict censorship "was enforced on all mail written aboard [the *Dorchester*] and while it was in Newfoundland."[3] Her father must have post-dated the letter because he knew it would take the censors that long to approve it and finally send it on to its destination. Like so many others, Ms. Swanwick must have been crushed.

Isadore Fox experienced the same. On February 13, 1943, she was at home with her niece. They had skittered into the bathroom with a "recording machine to make a crazy record to send to George." The acoustics were best in that tiny space.

She was feeling upbeat. Just a couple of days before, she had received a letter from George. It read, in part: "I am feeling fine in case you are wondering. I know you were anxious to hear from me. I haven't a trace of a cold any longer and am seldom bothered with anything else. . . . Many men come for counsel. This is the reason I am here and I am glad." To her, this meant he had arrived safely at his post, and she really had nothing to worry about. Greenland was not a battlefront—once the war was over, George would travel home without a scratch.

While she sat with her niece, feeling giddy, the doorbell rang.

Isadore set aside the recording and slipped out of the bathroom. She opened the front door of the house, a smile most likely still lingering on her face.

A boy was there. He handed her a telegram. The words screamed off the slip of paper: "We regret to inform you . . . MISSING IN ACTION."

The message rolled over Isadore. She wouldn't accept it. In her mind, it was as if George's letter and the telegram were engaged in deep, primal battle—only one could be true, not both. The battle created so much dissonance, she couldn't stand. She stumbled through the house, back to her bed, where she lay trying to process two worlds that couldn't possibly exist at the same time and yet seemed to be doing exactly that.

Somewhere deep inside, she felt she heard a voice, God speaking to her. *On land, on land, on land,* it whispered. Again and again. Sometimes it added more. *Safe and well.* The voice strode alongside her as a constant reassuring companion. *On land, on land, on land. Safe and well.* But it also drove her. Weeks and months passed, and she couldn't shake the message and the hope it gave. She wrote to the War Department, begging them to "make a further search for my husband to ascertain if he may not possibly be a German prisoner, or on some island in confinement where he cannot write or get a word to me."[4]

On a Saturday morning, while she tugged and tucked by herself to get Rosalie dressed, Theresa fought back tears. Days earlier, she had sensed that something bad had happened to Alex, but not a sliver of news had reached her.

The phone rang. It was her sister. "I just received a telegram—"

"For God's sake, open it!" Theresa said. But she knew what it said, even before her sister could read the words. The urge to cry, which had been so dominant just moments before, suddenly vanished, replaced by a steely denial. Theresa would not believe that her husband, her Alex, was likely gone. She nestled Rosalie into the car and drove downtown, where she bought the little girl leggings and a winter coat. Something was happening, something absolute. She knew, just as she had intuited in a hidden layer of her brain, that Rosalie was now hers to raise. Alone. But the thought progressed no further.

Days passed.

Theresa's mind—that practical, intelligent, sensible instrument—constructed a wall so tall and impregnable, no emotions could break through. Nor could any people. She refused to speak with anyone about the situation. When she traveled about town, on a bus or streetcar, she saw Alex in the faces of people she passed. Every glance over a shoulder or stare through a crowd reminded her of him. Deep down, tucked away in a place she didn't want to discuss with others, she had buried a hidden hope that he was coming home; he was just "lost and would be coming back."[5] So she went about her business: bathing and dressing Rosalie, running errands, keeping up the house . . . for when Alex came home.

In Harlem, Kathleen David received a telegram. In contrast to the messages sent to the chaplains' families, its news left little hope: her husband, Charles, was lost in action. He had died in a field hospital in Greenland, where he was buried.

No other details.

A man was on this earth, part of her life—then gone. She would never see him again. Nor would her son, little Neil, not even three years old.

Tears couldn't capture the wave of emotions she felt. In just three years she had become a wife, a mother, a widow, and now a woman with a child and no means to support herself.

That last concern was pressing—Charles had been her sole means of survival, and now she was cast out into a cold and dark world—but it couldn't compare to the emotional toll the news took on her. Her feelings weighed her down with a guilt she would carry the rest of her life. Perhaps they weren't fair, or even accurate, the pangs that crept into her heart and mind. But they were real nonetheless, as tangible as people looking her in the face.

Charles was dead, she felt, because of her. She had driven him away. In the very early days of their marriage, she had believed the relationship was thrust upon her, and she resented it. Not that the wedding was Charles's fault; he had only wanted to help her. But life—an unfair world and time—had forced her into it, into pregnancy and motherhood, long before she had wanted to embark on those journeys. So, after the wedding, she had been less warm, less loving than she believed she could have been. In her mind, in that weighty moment of Charles's death, she constructed a narrative: with her coldness, she had pushed Charles into the service, and were it not for her refusal to love him with all her heart, mind, and soul, he would still be in her son's life.

Try as she might, she couldn't shake that feeling. It lingered with her like a constant whisper, as did its inescapable conclusion: he left because of her, and so he died because of her.

While trying to process all of those emotions, somewhere deep in the recesses of her mind, she turned to the necessary task of living. How were she and little Neil going to survive?[6]

Around the same time, Mary Washington, the mother of Father John Washington, was sitting in her home when the phone rang. She answered. The voice on the other end broke the news to her. She shrieked so loudly that her neighbor next door, Marge, heard it. Within a few seconds, Marge burst into Mary's house, wanting to know what happened.

Mary still clung to the phone. "John's gone! Oh, dear heaven, John's gone!" She leaned back in her chair, wailing. Marge was by her side, but Mary could only barely have sensed her. She wailed. She tilted back so far that her chair nearly fell over.

Marge kept her from falling. With her free hand, she took the receiver and spoke into it.

Mary released her grip on the phone.

Marge finished talking, apparently having confirmed what Mary had just heard. She hung up. "Don't worry," she said, her voice piercing through Mary's cries. "They'll find him. You've got to think positively."

But on April 10, 1943, the military sent the same number of telegrams. All those men designated as "missing in action" were now considered "lost in action." The same news Kathleen David had already received was now typed into telegrams and set for delivery. They would have arrived at 678 different houses and apartments across the country.

For Isadore, George would never come back out of the fog. She was inconsolable; people tried to comfort her, ministers and family members. But their words were empty, bereft of meaning: *George died a hero,* they said. *She should be proud,* they said.

Through her tears, she surfaced enough to swat these empty sentiments away. Looking at the wall of her home, she said, "I do not want a hero; I want my husband. I always knew he was a hero, the way he worked in those small churches and never complained, even when the pay was so small he could not get proper food for his children."

She was falling, tumbling away from everyone and everything around her, including her children.

Because George was her whole life. They were one, two beings whose spirits were so closely intertwined they may as well have been the same. Without him, "she felt only a shadow."[7] She and George were of a piece, torn asunder into fragments—and in her mind, one fragment could not go forward without the other.

She didn't want to live. Not without him. How could she? How could half of an existence survive?

Voices tried to bring her back. Friends, family members: *Think of your children. They need you.*

But her plummet was too great, the distance too far. She was a shred of her former self, blown off the edge of a cliff and tumbling with the vacillating motion of a leaf in the wind. She could see her children in her mind and knew they needed her, but "with George gone," she wrote, "there seems to be a gap of a million miles between the children and me." It seemed to be a chasm too far for her to bridge.

When Theresa finally received the confirmation of Alex's death, she still didn't believe it. But the wall broke, obliterated into a million emotional shards through which her tears rushed. For days, she told herself that he had to be alive somewhere. His thoughts, his forward-thinking way of looking at the world, his ideals of peace and freedom for all—they were too important for him not to be alive. The world needed his message.

But the abomination of his death transformed from nightmare to reality, cloaking everything in her world in gray.

Nine days after she received the confirmation that Clark was lost, Betty gave birth to little Thumper. Her husband would never hold his little girl. He would never watch *Bambi* with her. There were no more mistakes, no more clerical errors or possibilities of miracles. Betty lay with her baby, surrounded by family. But she was alone. She named the baby Susan.

In a hotel room off Grosvenor Square in London, word of Clark's death reached his father, to whom he had been so close. It came over the radio. He sat alone with his thoughts. They traversed through time and locations, all the places he and Clark and the family had spent their days. And all he had were memories.

As for Mary, she remained inconsolable. Her son John was gone. Soon she would receive the news that two more of her sons, Leo and Francis, were killed in the war as well. She had sacrificed more than anyone should. Not wanting any more of what the world had to offer, she closed the door to her home and refused to leave.

During the war, the United States shipped troops all over the globe. Between seven and eight million men and women traveled overseas, to nearly every corner of the earth.[8] They did so in convoys, and some were attacked en route to their destinations. But the sinking of the *Dorchester* would go down in the annals of history as the worst single loss of US personnel of any American convoy during the entire conflict.[9]

In the days and weeks after the news became official, the families of the four chaplains were beside themselves with grief and denial. This was a bitter end to their men's stories. All had wanted to comfort troops on the front, to bring peace and a message of hope to men in situations where those feelings seemed bombarded out of existence. Instead, they had perished in a frozen wasteland, sucked into the ocean, drowned or chilled in the darkness. Alone. Killed by Nazis.

CHAPTER 21

A LIGHT IN THE DARK

L ess than a month after the disaster, H. V. Stebbins, a lieutenant in the United States Naval Reserve, was tasked with seeking and summarizing statements from survivors of the sinking. It was an unenviable task, equal parts mundane and depressing. But several consistent themes were emerging. Among them was this paragraph he recorded in the memorandum he sent to superiors:

> Survivors spoke of the calm attitude of the Army Chaplains who were passengers aboard, all of whom were missing. It was reported that the Army Catholic Chaplain gave his life jacket to one of the men, and that the Army Jewish Rabbi supplied one survivor with a pair of gloves.[1]

The statement represented the dispassionate, incomplete, and truncated nature of his report; he didn't embellish and apparently asked no further questions. Nor was he required to do so—that was not his job.

But his comment triggered more investigations; the families continued to ask questions, wanting to know more about how their husbands, sons, fathers, and brothers had died. Over time, in contrast to the dreary portrait painted from initial reports, a grander landscape emerged . . . a work of art that would cast Charles, Alex, George, Clark, and John into immortality and that would lift families out of darkness. Its final stroke was breathtaking.

★ ★ ★

On the main deck of the *Dorchester,* Alex had just given up his life jacket and, in unlaced boots, joined his companions by a nearby bulkhead. Around them, a small group of eight or nine men stood. Some wore life jackets; some did not. On the rails, the men too afraid to jump or join the chaplains still held their positions.

Alex, George, John, and Clark each had a decision to make at that point. They had done all they could for anyone who wanted help. Now was the time to save themselves. They likely knew they had no chance of surviving. Without life jackets, given the dire situation of the life-boats and rafts in the water, with the ship about to conclude its swift descent, the most likely outcome was they would be pulled down with it.

No one could have blamed them for going their separate ways. Alex, especially, would have been justified in feeling he owed nothing to the others. As a Jewish rabbi, he had watched his people in the United States fighting for equality and recognition that had still not come; in Europe, his people were being murdered. Too many Protestants, Catholics, and even other nonreligious Americans had remained silent to their suffering, and Alex could have blamed these men in his circle for that, even refused to forgive them. To a lesser degree, John would have been justified in feeling the same. Catholics had not seen much better treatment at the hands of the majority in the United States. At the same time, Clark and George could have followed the path trod by so many before them and just protected themselves, no one else. Even more tempting, perhaps, would have been the desire to retreat to their own religious traditions at this point. And why not? For just these last few minutes, each of them could have abandoned the others and transitioned out of this life however his religious tradition saw fit. It wouldn't have been unusual; if anything, they would have been follow-ing the broader culture of the United States at the time. As one witness recalled: "Remember, this was 1943. Protestants didn't talk to Catholics back then, let alone either of them talk to a Jew."[2]

★ ★ ★

It's hard to know if any of those temptations whispered in their minds. If they did, the chaplains promptly batted them away. Instead, it appears they noted the men surrounding them, watching, seemingly looking for inspiration or one final sermon. They looked to each other. At some point in the melee of the night, John's glasses had been removed from his face. He was likely struggling to see as well as he might have otherwise. Alex stood without gloves or bootlaces. None of the four wore life jackets; they were probably numb from the cold. Which of them reached out first remains a mystery, but in that moment, all four chaplains linked arms.

The *Dorchester* was in its final death throes. Water bubbled all around the bow and had crept so close to the deck, it would begin spilling over at any moment. The ship had listed so badly that it would only be a matter of minutes before standing was impossible. The bow would get sucked under, the propeller would rise into the air, and the entire vessel would dive straight into the ocean, as if it had never existed.

Arms locked, the chaplains bowed their heads and began to pray. Alex offered his in Hebrew. Clark and George prayed in English. John spoke in Latin. The gaggle around them joined.

It was a moment many probably wished would last forever, the kind of ephemeral glimpse that proved Hitler wrong and humanity right. People with vast differences could unite and thrive together; they could lift each other, forgive, ignore the temptation for prejudice, embrace common causes without sacrificing their core identities, and set aside their disagreements to focus on areas where they did agree. Unity didn't need to come at the expense of identity.

But it was not to last. It wasn't long before the water started to spill over onto the deck, a frothing, creeping menace. Men peeled away. Some jumped over the rails. Others may have stayed with the ship. Perhaps some followed the chaplains until the very end.

It appears from witness statements that George, John, Alex, and

Clark left their bulkhead and started climbing to the stern as it rose out of the sea. The ascent would have been arduous. With fingers inflexible from the cold, ice glazing every handhold, and the deck a dangerous slide, reaching the rails on the stern would not have been easy. Somehow, they made it. As the ship entered its final dive position, its back half jutting vertically out of the Atlantic, they managed to climb over the rails so that they were standing near the keel and the giant propellers.

Along the entire starboard side, men who had refused to jump into the ocean still clung tightly to whatever they could grab. Many wore life jackets, their red lights twinkling in the dark. To one man watching from a life raft, the ship looked like a giant Christmas tree drilling into the sea.[3]

Near the keel, the four chaplains found a way to regain their footing. They stood.

Beneath them, the water churned and growled, devouring the 368 feet of the *Dorchester* foot by foot, along with any troops still left onboard.

Once again, the chaplains locked arms.[4] They looked to the sky. What prayers did they offer in that moment? What thoughts traveled through their minds? Did they pay heed to the gurgling and screams beneath them, or had each in his own way transcended to a different place? Alex's thoughts may have been on Theresa and Rosalie—a prayer for them, that they could have strength to carry on without him. He may have lingered on his long lineage of rabbis and hoped he had lived up to the family tradition and name.

For George, the days of poverty he and Isadore had endured were over. But how would she do without him? She was a fighter, he knew. If anyone could survive the difficult days ahead, it was his wife. Their long list of memories was at an end—there would be no more entries. So perhaps he prayed for her, that he might get to see her one last time. Did he know, even suspect, how painful his death would be for her, how far it would fling her into the pit?

In his letters home, Clark expressed tremendous concern for his little family and for his congregation. In those final moments, he may have considered a sentiment his father would later express to baby Thumper: "He never saw you, but you were in his dreams, I know; and perhaps, my dear, as you were coming in and he was going out your spirits met as ships that pass in the night. Perhaps he heard—yes, Susan, I am sure he did—heard your first cry and was glad." So perhaps that was where his mind traveled in those final moments: to a mountaintop in New England, his wife and two children by his side, his parents there as well, including his mother who died so long ago, and a still, small voice he finally heard riding on the breeze.

For John, who had sent so many out of this world, both on the ship and also in the hospital in his parish, the moment was ironic, perhaps not so much sad. Considering his tremendous sense of humor, did he catch the irony? Did he wonder what this next step would be like now that he was to make the journey on which he had sent so many others? Throughout his life, he had always used humor to hide his true, spiritual self. On the keel of the *Dorchester,* it was exposed for all to see.

At the last, the ship gave one final lurch, as if determined to knock these men from their pedestal. When it did, the four chaplains slid off into the water.

CHAPTER 22

STEPPING FORWARD

Two things were responsible for saving the lives of so many of the *Dorchester* survivors. One was the inspiration provided by the actions and prayers of the chaplains. The other was the answer to those prayers: Charles Walter David Jr.

Out on the water, a lot of men were dead. A lot more were going to die. In one of the two lifeboats that launched successfully, David Labadie could not shake from his mind the vision of the chaplains sacrificing themselves for others. Just before he had escaped from the ship, he had tried to persuade one of the chaplains to come with him, to save himself. The man had refused, showing a steely resolve to sacrifice himself for others.

Labadie would not let that sacrifice go in vain.[1] On his boat, space was already sparse. They had passed capacity long ago. He didn't care. Hailing from Massachusetts, he had been a shipfitter and a worker in a wool factory before enlisting in the army; having grown up around the waters of the Northeast, he knew boating, and he held a begrudging respect for the power of the ocean. Given his background, he convinced the other men that he was the right one to handle the rudder.

They consented, but a brutal argument erupted. Many of those already on the lifeboat didn't want to go back for fear that too many men would capsize the boat. This wasn't a trivial concern, and it wasn't completely irrational, given how many boats and rafts had already flipped.

Labadie had seen the chaplains. He had watched the choices they made. His view was simple: he would rather risk the lives of everyone and go down with their fellow soldiers rather than choose who would live or die. They had to take the risk.[2]

But it would not be easy—the men floundering in the water didn't stay in one place. Almost immediately, the currents and the waves continued on their course, scattering the survivors. Many had jumped or been sucked out before the *Dorchester* had stopped, so the trail of men stretched over a mile. Labadie could reach only a few, but he directed the lifeboat to try. With others manning the oars, he steered to as many groupings of red lights as he could. In time, he tried to remove his hand from the rudder and realized it wouldn't move. His fingers had frozen to the handle. He forged ahead anyway.

Over the objections of some on the boat, he steered toward a gaggle of men flailing for their lives. When they hit the first group, some on the boat screamed, "Don't let them on or we'll sink!"

"Pull 'em in," Labadie roared. "Pull 'em in!" He ripped his skin from the rudder handle, then helped, latching on to three men floating in the waves and heaving them aboard.

The argument didn't end, but Labadie flipped the script. He knew his fellow sailors wanted nothing more than to survive, so he played to that. "The more men you have on here, the more they'll block the splashing of the waves, so the boat won't fill up with water so quick." It was nonsense. Whether they bought it or not, David didn't care. But since he was the only one with any experience with the ocean, no one dared argue.

He kept searching. He couldn't give up. The image of the chaplains propelled him forward. After a short time, he spied a man in the water. No life jacket. The chances of seeing him had to have hovered just above zero, given the waves and the gloom of the night. But there he was. "Pull him up!" Labadie shouted.

Some of the others used a retrieving pole on the lifeboat to hook the man and bring him aboard. He was barely conscious. Under his breath, he moaned, "No, no, no!"

Labadie and the others ignored him. The man was clearly delirious, hallucinating. For some reason, he was missing a shoe. The only question was whether they could keep him from dying before help arrived.

Michael Warish felt the men from the lifeboat pulling him aboard. He didn't want to be saved. He had resigned himself to passing from this life, in part because of what he had seen on the deck of the *Dorchester.* Before stepping into the water with his broken ankle, he had watched Alex Goode give up his life jacket and shoelaces and had seen the chaplains lead the others in prayer. He had never found much solace in the practice. But in that moment, the faith of the chaplains washing over him, he wept. He cast himself into the arms of God. He offered his own prayer, stretching his mind to the divine he had so long ignored, with just the vaguest sense—a hope, at least—that someone was listening.

Then he had turned to the ocean.

Given what he had witnessed, heaven felt like a welcome place—a realm where men like the chaplains would be, where he would find his sister. It didn't seem so bad. The longer he drifted in the water, the closer he was to it. It was as if the visions of what heaven could be had always been a part of him, and he only needed to close his eyes and let them fold around him like a warm blanket. Dying, it turned out, wasn't nearly as unpleasant as he had expected.

So when he heard the words—*Pull him up!*—as if they were coming from a distance, he rebelled. Even as arms and hands wrapped around his body and pulled him into an overcrowded lifeboat, he wasn't sure it was what he wanted. *No, no, no!* But as he looked through hazy eyes at faces he recognized, he also wasn't sure where he was. Perhaps, he thought, perhaps this was heaven after all.

★ ★ ★

The coast guard cutters finally did return. By 1:43 a.m., convoy Captain Greenspun on the *Tampa* determined it was safe to hunt for survivors. He ordered the *Escanaba* to start searching. There was some back and forth as to which cutter would escort the *Lutz* and *Biscaya* safely into Greenland, but by 2:26 a.m., the *Comanche* received orders to return to the site of the sinking as well. The *Tampa* would finish the run into Narsarsuaq with the other freighters.

By 3:02 a.m., the *Comanche* eased into a watery cemetery. Its directions were not to pick up survivors but to screen for enemy submarines while the *Escanaba* searched for any sign of life. This troubled Lieutenant Commander Ralph Curry. He and many of his men were already furious they had been forced to wait so long to pick up survivors. Now to be here but unauthorized to help was agonizing. From the looks of things, it didn't matter. When they arrived onsite, the details were disheartening: men, stiff like statues, bobbed in the water; the only sign of the *Dorchester* was the flotsam and oil slick it left behind; though they had held out some hope the ship might still be afloat, they could neither see nor detect it on sonar.

They proceeded slowly, through lifeless men in life jackets. Acres and acres of them. At first, Curry followed his orders. He focused on screening and not on saving lives—there would be no point. He stared into the darkness, trying to comprehend what he was seeing, and he noticed his men doing the same. All along the *Comanche*'s rails, the young sailors under his command were in something close to a trance. "Many . . . were green," he would later report, and you couldn't look at a scene like that without it sucking the emotions from you. They just stared, trying to process the lifeless eyes looking back at them.

Several times, the guardsmen on the rails used a hook pole to retrieve someone from the water, to see any crumb of life. Every time, when they pulled a body to them and turned it over, the greeting in response was nothing more than the open-mouthed, staring eyes of a statue.

If the time ever came for his men to move, Curry wasn't sure their minds would respond.

And then: something peculiar.

From the bridge, Curry detected a different shape through the mist. He peered, trying to process it. When he realized what he was witnessing—a lifeboat surprisingly living up to its name and brimming with life—the orders from Greenspun slammed into him like an iceberg. He was not to search for or pick up survivors. That was *Escanaba*'s job. His was to guard the area.

But that other cutter was nowhere close. By the time it made its way to this location, these men could well be dead or hard to find again. Who knew where the uncaring currents of the ocean would carry them?

The ramifications stunned Curry. Greenspun had good reasons for his orders. If Curry ordered the rescue and the *Escanaba* were blindsided by an enemy torpedo, not only would all the men on the *Escanaba* die, he would be court-martialed. And he understood why— he was a man who appreciated the structure of the military, and following orders was important. He would court-martial his own men if they disobeyed his orders.

But war required tough decisions. The situation demanded common sense and flexibility. Hours had passed since the attack. If another U-boat were lying in wait, it would have already fired its tubes. Enough men from the *Dorchester* had died. His career lay before him, bare, exposed, subject to severe discipline . . . whatever decision he made, someone could die: either the men on the lifeboat or the guardsmen on the *Escanaba*.

Crucial seconds passed.

Curry gave the order: save the men on the lifeboat. The *Comanche* would screen for the enemy as best it could, but it was time to start looking for more survivors.* Under normal circumstances, when the commander gave such an order, the ship would have sprung to life like a disturbed anthill. This time, the reaction was modest. Three officers, trained in rescuing people from water, stepped forward, as was their duty.

Curry would need more—volunteers from the enlisted men.

As he expected, his junior men stiffened, unable to move. It wasn't a physical paralysis, just a strange immobility—of the mind, a fading of their collective will. The bodies, the bodies, the bodies, frozen and stiff, dead eyes, sprawling before them, seemed to have gathered them all in a flaccid trance.

Crucial moments passed. For the men in the water, they were seconds that could literally mean life or death.

And unless something spurred the *Comanche*'s men to action soon, the survivors on the lifeboat would die.

Charles, still weak and sick from his cold, watched the hesitation among the enlisted men. He had no obligation to lift a finger. If anything, he had every right to refuse to move a muscle. The coast guard's insistence that Charles was not a good candidate to serve as anything other than a cook simply because of the color of his skin was, of course, repugnant nonsense, born of bigotry and ignorance. But it was also an example of the ongoing suppression Black men and women faced in the United States in the 1940s, even outside the Deep South.

Charles would have been justified in feeling that the United States was not his country, that it had done little for him, and, therefore, he should do little in return. If the Puritan Mistake is seeking liberty

---

* In their official logs, neither Curry nor Greenspun mentioned Curry's conflict. If Greenspun was upset, we have no record of it. Curry wrote that he was ordered to pick up survivors, and Greenspun logged that the order he gave was for both the *Escanaba* and the *Comanche* to search for survivors with at least one of them screening for subs at all times.

only for ourselves, another facet of it is seeking revenge once we are in power. But like Alex, John, George, and Clark, Charles W. David Jr. saw the situation with a different perspective. There was, it seems, a single hour that all the days of his life and his family's heritage had pointed toward. The journeys from Antigua, carving out a life in the Bronx, marrying Kathleen, needing to find a way to provide for her and Neil, his willingness to meet that challenge . . . when we look back on the labyrinth of decisions he and his parents had made that led to that moment, all the destinations where Charles's life journey might have arrived, we find, in fact, that the choices had always been leading him here, along this road, to find that this was his path—chosen for him, perhaps—all along.

He stood at a fulcrum, a moment in time and a place in space saturated with significance for both himself and a hundred other men and their posterity. He could go downstairs, tend to washing metal coffee mugs, prepare the next meal, mind his demeaning duties.

Or he could stay on deck and propel himself forward with a force his shipmates had lost.

In a moment of perfect clarity, Charles chose an act of pure charity. He would save people different from himself, many of whom likely thought less of him for all the wrong reasons. It was a decision of both fearlessness and forgiveness.

He volunteered to help. His friend Dick Swanson was quick to join him.

If Charles's eagerness didn't surprise anyone, it should have. At the time, he was the fifth-lowest-ranked man on the ship—dozens of others should have volunteered before he did. They didn't, but the eagerness of Charles and Swanson to join the fray spread. By the end, nine other enlisted men followed.

As the *Comanche* approached the lifeboat, Commander Curry projected his voice through a megaphone to the men below: "We're only going to stop for one or two minutes, and we've gotta board you during that time!" It's hard to know why Curry felt the need to be so rushed; he may have been driven by a worry that a boat standing still was an easy target for roaming Nazis. Or perhaps he was worried that screening would be impossible while they were floating in one position. Whatever his reasons, he continued, "So when we come alongside, you get up as fast as you can!"[3]

It was a fantasy. Charles and crew realized just how difficult their task would be. The waves had grown violent again; at six and eight feet, they angrily clapped against the hull of the *Comanche*.

The pole hook was no good, given the rough seas and the sheer number of sailors who needed saving. And the preferred method—the coast guard had been perfecting it—involved men in rubber wet suits setting out with ropes. Once they found someone to save, they would loop the rope around the person; then someone else would pull him in. But that wouldn't work here. The *Comanche* carried only three of the suits; between the gelid ocean, snapping wind, crashing waves, and numbers involved, too many would die before they pulled even half of them aboard.

They needed a miracle.

It is a mystery precisely who remembered the cargo net—that bulky, massive, clump the guardsmen had pulled from the water the day before for seemingly no reason at all, with no understanding of whence it came. There lay salvation.

They scrambled to it and hurled it over the side. It slapped against the hull and tickled the surface of the ocean. Their hope was that any survivors could climb up.

The wind grew fierce, the waves more deadly. The *Comanche* slowed, easing to the men in the boat.

It was nearly swamped. It held so many sailors that it sat just eight inches above the surface of the water: a mass of tangled humanity. And few were moving. Some tried to get to the net. They scrambled over each other, but their movements were as if some video controller had forced them to struggle in slow motion. For the rest, their muscles wouldn't obey. They were clearly too weak to save themselves.

When the first few men reached the cargo net, the rising and falling waves, in their perpetual motion, made latching on nearly impossible. At one moment, the lifeboat rested at the bottom of the net; the next, it rose eight feet and was nearly at the *Comanche's* rail. When the first soldier attempted to climb aboard, he was at the nadir of the cycle. He latched onto the netting and pulled himself free from his comrades. With muscles like glue, he started the long haul up.

Then the waves lifted the lifeboat. It smashed into him, bashing him into the side of the hull. He crumpled into the water. Lost.[4]

After all they had already been through, despite their efforts to improbably survive the sinking, then the long wait in the cold, these men seemed to have no chance of taking the final, salvational step.

Charles recognized immediately what needed to happen. The guardsmen would need to do more than merely help sailors on the final rungs of their climb, or most would never make it.

He swung over the side and climbed down the net. Swanson joined him, as did Ensign Robert Anderson, one of the officers to whom Charles had served meals a thousand times. Anderson crawled onto the lifeboat itself, searching for any men still alive. It was a gruesome task. The only way to know was to turn the men to him and look into their eyes; too often, the gaze back was empty. But just as many still maintained a flicker of life and were merely comatose. Anderson helped these men to Charles and Swanson, waiting on the net.[5]

Together, they eased men out of the lifeboat and up the side of the *Comanche* until their crewmates could take hold of them. They tried to time the waves just right, freeing men at the highest possible point.[6] Within minutes, the irony of the military's policy to limit Black soldiers became apparent. Charles W. David Jr. was a natural leader who instinctively knew precisely where to be and what to do as the ship set about its rescue efforts.[7] He gave orders, directed some of the men, and largely took charge of the situation. The younger crewmen followed.[8]

In time, the guardsmen entered a welcome routine. With Charles and Swanson on the cargo net, Ensign Anderson shepherded delirious and confused *Dorchester* survivors to safety.

The waves continued to pound, soaking Charles and the others in water that was essentially liquid ice. They didn't stop. With heave after heave, they brought the men to safety. The cold was no doubt having an effect, crippling their muscles, numbing their fingers. But they pushed forward, hauling to safety every living man sitting or clinging to the lifeboat.

Charles climbed back up the net. Drenched, frozen, no doubt gasping for air that nipped at his lungs, he felt the *Comanche* lurch beneath him.

Lieutenant Commander Curry must have received word that everyone who could be saved from the lifeboat had been. So he had given the order to move on to look for others.

But Charles peered into the dark. He struggled to make out what he was looking for, but then he confirmed his suspicions: Ensign Robert Anderson was still on the lifeboat, refusing to leave until he had verified that every last living man had been found. He blended in with the bodies still on the boat. They were leaving him behind. And once they sailed into the darkness, he would be lost to the night.

On the lifeboat, as he worked his way among the lifeless, frozen men, Ensign Anderson first heard, then saw his ship leave him.

So that was it. This was how he would die—forgotten by his own men when all he had wanted to do was save as many people as he could. That was typical of him. To anyone who knew him during his childhood in Brooklyn, his wanting to stay and help, his generosity of spirit, would have come as no surprise. He was a warm-hearted, fun-loving man who could make friends with anyone, and usually did.[9] His hair and his cheeks seemed to be in a competition with each other for which were puffier, and that led to a warm smile that brought people into his orbit.

We can only guess what went through his mind at that moment the *Comanche* growled to life and churned away. Most likely, his thoughts turned to his love, Muriel. Childhood sweethearts, they had married just days before he had shipped out on the *Comanche* and had never really had any chance to see one another since the wedding day. Prior to the *Comanche* taking on the assignment to escort the *Dorchester,* Anderson had penned Muriel a letter: "I have been dreaming about you for the past three months," he wrote. "Seems like heaven on earth just thinking of seeing you!" She was his "sweet," his "honey," his "wonderful one," his "dearest." They had grand plans. Because the *Comanche* most often ported in Boston, Muriel had left her job in New York, squared away all her loose ends there, then rented an apartment in Boston so she could see Anderson anytime the *Comanche* came to port. She was likely there now, waiting, hoping for his return after this latest voyage. "Very soon now," he had written her, "we will be together in each other's arms and all the months apart will be forgotten."[10]

There, on the boat, his dreams of seeing her again now seemed like nothing more than fantasy—thoughts that would accompany him out of this life.

Charles pushed through the other guardsmen, sprinting to the control room. It was not his place, as a steward's mate, to tell the commander of the vessel what to do, but Charles had built his relationship with Curry by doing his duty and doing it well. With heavy legs, he tore the length of the cutter, burst in on Curry, and told him what was happening.

It could've been a tense moment. A lesser commander may have considered it an impertinence. To his credit, Curry listened. When Charles finished explaining what was happening, Curry stopped the vessel and ordered the cutter to return to the lifeboat.

It would take nearly thirty minutes, long enough for Anderson to die, plenty of time for a U-boat to fire off more than one torpedo.

By the time they circled close enough to the boat, Anderson had been so ravaged by the cold, he could no longer climb up himself. Charles tied a rope around his waist and, with no protective sea gear on, clambered down the net, tied the rope around Anderson, and helped carry him back onto the boat. The next year, in a radio interview, Anderson recalled, "Well, I'd probably still be there if it weren't for [Charles,] who was on the other end of my line. He was a big strapping fellow and managed to pull me up in time. I'm certainly grateful to him."[11]

The lifeboat the *Comanche* found was number 13. David Labadie sat at the rudder. Michael Warish lay among the men. The boat was designed to hold forty-five. Because of Labadie and his desire to follow the chaplains' example, Charles and his crew managed to save far more than that.[12]

But the night was not over.

The survivors waited an otherworldly amount of time—some for three hours, others as long as eight and a half. They all should have died. For those who managed to survive the long night while the cutters searched for them, different things kept them alive. For many, there was a physical aspect—proper clothes, a pair of gloves, extra body fat, huddling with other men; one man even managed to stay dry through the entire ordeal. But for all of them, the mental dance was far more important. Every man plucked from the sea that night found his own source of motivation. For some it was the idea that morphine injections would shield them from the weather; for others it was an unending optimism from birth; for still others it was faith that God would protect them. But for many, the images and voices of the chaplains kept them going.

Private First Class William Bednar summed it up well: "I could hear men crying, pleading, praying. I could also hear the chaplains preaching courage. Their voices were the only thing that kept me going."[13] Henry Goguen likewise recalled the men in the lifeboats: praying, their eyes to heaven, clinging to the idea that somewhere in the expanse of the cosmos, some divine being noticed them . . . and would send help.

While men clung to life and the *Escanaba* searched for survivors on one end of the debris field, Charles and his fellows on the *Comanche* had fallen into a routine. Though they had long since left Lifeboat 13 behind, they were, miraculously, still finding survivors. Their pattern was simple: wearing the rubber suits, they would dive into the water if they thought they had found someone still alive. When they did, they would wrap a rope around him; then men on board would tug both the rescuer and the survivor to the cargo net, where two others would lift them up. The men on the net—usually Charles and Swanson—were often waist-deep in the water themselves.

The same nine men continued this routine again and again while the rest of the crew, still unwilling to get into the water, helped on and below deck.

They would never find a large group like Lifeboat 13 again, but they were finding stragglers, pockets of men, and that kept them going. The wind, the waves, and the water were taking their toll, sucking the life from the rescuers with every entry into the icy sea. Charles's cold was still lingering. He was likely coughing through it at this point, but he refused to quit.

At one point, the *Comanche* coasted up to a broken raft. Its floor was missing, shattered planks dangling over deadly saltwater. Just four men sat on seats around the edges. They were barely conscious, their legs no longer working. They were minutes away from toppling into the water. Charles and the others helped them onto the ship. Only later, in Greenland, would they learn: one of the men was Roy Summers.

Fatigue was setting in. In and out of water so cold it may as well have been the grave, Charles and Swanson were losing energy. Swimming, hauling, roping, climbing nets—the human body can only endure so much. They were no more immune to the effects of the weather than the *Dorchester* men. But still they searched.

Finally, Swanson succumbed. With water crashing against him, the wind howling, he found his legs and arms would no longer follow his brain's commands. They had just saved another survivor, and he and Charles needed to climb back up over the rails while the *Comanche* continued its course. But no matter how hard he focused or tried, he simply couldn't climb up the net again. His spirit was willing, but his flesh had lost all power. He dangled, the waves licking him like a salivating beast.

"Charles!" he yelled. "I can't go any further!"[14]

Charles had reached the top and was up on the deck. He looked back to see his friend hanging over the black. "C'mon, Swanny!" he hollered. "You can make it!"

But halfway up, Swanson had nothing left to give. His legs simply wouldn't move. It would be only a matter of minutes, maybe less, before he lacked the strength even to keep his grip. Then he would fall, another victim of the depths.[15]

Charles grabbed another man, a boatswain mate named Art Backer. They climbed back down the net. The cutter rocked in the swells. On either side of Swanson, they draped his arms over their shoulders. One handhold at a time, with one arm each, they slogged back up the handholds, carrying Swanny to safety. Once they had pulled him over the rails, they collapsed onto the deck. "He saved my life," Swanson later recalled.

★ ★ ★

As the night wore on, exhaustion and the early symptoms of hypothermia led to mistakes. One proved crucial. During one rescue attempt, the ship's executive officer, Lieutenant Langford Anderson, ended up stranded in the water. Reports differ. One suggests that a *Dorchester* survivor, in a panic for fear of drowning, was pulling him into the water. The other implies he slipped and lacked the strength to swim back to the cargo net.

Either way, Charles didn't hesitate.

He dove in after Anderson. The cold ravaged him the way it would any human. His muscles were already racked from fatigue. But the years of swimming in high school, set in motion that day when, as a boy, he was pushed off the pier by a friend, paid back in spades. He latched onto the fallen lieutenant. With one arm, he swam back to the *Comanche.* Saltwater in his mouth, sea spray in his eyes, waves lifting and pumping and clawing, the mercury on the thermometer creeping lower and lower, the very elements conspired against them. But Charles could not be stopped. He hoisted Anderson out of the water so others could pull him up. By some reports, he saved the other drowning *Dorchester* man as well.*

By the time Charles ascended the net for the last time, he had given everything he had. He collapsed onto the deck. All the symptoms of hypothermia were setting in. His fellow crewmen rushed him down to the medical bay. They helped him strip out of his soaking clothes, dressed him in fresh ones, and wrapped him in warm blankets. Coughing, shivering, he settled into a long rest. As the *Comanche* sailed into Greenland, the symptoms never seemed to abate. If anything, they grew worse. The cough morphed into hacking, and his breathing grew clipped. Even after an ambulance rushed him to medical care on base and doctors watched over him, he struggled to get the oxygen he needed. As several weeks passed, he continued to deteriorate.

When he lay sick, in and out of fever and dreams, it's fair to guess where his mind took him. In one night, he had poured his whole life into so many others. Its comprehensive burdens. Its bitter injuries and longing regrets. His love for Kathleen and little Neil, and their long

---

* There is some confusion about the report of Charles saving Langford Anderson. Official reports confirm that he did so, but some personal interviews revealed the story of Langford Anderson's rescue may not have occurred but was merely confused with Robert Anderson's rescue. Because there were two Andersons that night, it's not surprising some confusion might emerge. Still, most records indicate he saved both Andersons.

sojourn through life without a husband and father. His friendship with "Swanny." The question of whether his little boy, just three years old, would even remember him—a father reaching into a crib to scoop him up and hold him in his arms. The concern of whether anyone would remember him . . . in 1943, as a Black man. Figures, places, faces of his past and future—his bride, smiling, radiant, in a white dress, holding a bouquet of flowers, or alone, dressed in black, sitting on her bed in their tiny room, wondering how to navigate the future without him. All of these possibilities were a part of him, and perhaps he was grateful to have them, and to have imparted them to the other men he saved.

Because he was one of them.

Because he was they, and they were he.

Because in his efforts, he bore witness to his humanity.

On March 29, 1943, in a Greenland field hospital, Charles W. David Jr. passed away from pneumonia brought about from exposure to cold and a virus he kept secret.

The night of the rescue, the *Escanaba* picked up roughly 134 *Dorchester* survivors (including William Arpaia and the men who had used morphine syrettes to stay alive).[16] On the *Comanche*, Charles and the men who followed him saved 93.

CHAPTER 23

LEGACY

He came to her one last time. Perhaps he came to say goodbye . . . until we meet again. Or it was God letting her know he was okay—a subtle moment between her and the divine. Either way, she didn't realize its significance until later. At roughly the precise moment the chaplains slipped into the ocean, perhaps a little after—it no longer mattered, for time was a continuum at that point, one eternal circle—Theresa Goode's eyes snapped open. She was a world away, sleeping in Alex's parents' house in DC.

She gasped, feeling as if she'd plunged into ice water. For a fleeting moment, she was frozen, chilled to her core.

The light was wrong. The entire room seemed to be glowing, yet she knew it was the dead of night, as dark as dark can be. But no lights were on. As sleep departed and clarity came, the source of the radiance came into focus: Alex's picture, which she had placed on the dresser. She remembered the feelings she had experienced in New York—that she would never see him again—and she was filled with dread.

Weeks later, after his death was confirmed, she looked back on that moment not with dread, but with gratitude. Alex, her love, the other part of her, who made her whole, was not gone. What was time? What was death? He was far away; he was close. The world still needed him. In her quiet moments, when she wasn't dressing Rosalie or tucking her in or helping her out of the bath—all by herself for many years—she collected Alex's letters, manuscripts, sermons, notes, and belongings. Even after she remarried, she raised Rosalie to know the story of her father, and Rosalie passed it in turn down to her children. Eventually, Theresa donated her collection to various archives and foundations, ensuring that the world would remember her beloved Alex. Because, in her view, he still lived, and when the day came that she departed this life, she would see him again—in another existence, on a different plane, but he would still be her Alex.

With Thumper in her arms, Corky still toddling about, Betty Poling stared into the eyes of a lifetime of tasks and lessons that seemed impossible for her to face alone: diapers, training wheels, talks through adolescence, girlfriends and boyfriends, scraped knees, homework problems, balancing a checkbook, and all the heartbreaks and regrets and joys of life. It was too much. One thing helped her persist: Clark's faith. In sermon after sermon, at the pulpit, in their home, he lived his life as she did, with the determination that everything they were doing was for a higher purpose, for a life after this one. What was this mortal existence? What were humans but eternal beings out of place in the construct of time? Clark was gone for a season—a winter that would be followed by a glorious spring. He left behind a strength she added to her own, a shared vision that they would one day be together again. That dream did not fade with his death. In a letter to her father-in-law, Betty pondered her husband, "His faith and love for men and God challenged me beyond my own abilities to do what I thought was impossible."

So she did.

Life was not perfect. She raised Corky and Susan. It was nearly impossible at first. In the early months, she left Susan with Clark's parents, missing important bonding time, while she tried, as best she could, to process her grief.[1] But in time, she was able to move forward on her own. Corky became a renowned professor at Emory University; Susan a speech language pathologist. In all the years, Betty rarely talked about Clark to her children—it was just too painful.

As for Clark's father, the night he learned of Clark's death, he had a dream of that mountaintop where Clark had found himself, and where the two had embraced. It was named Wolf Hill, but when Daniel Poling awoke from his sleep, he determined it would be renamed Clark's Summit; there would be a shrine there. And "it shall tell all men that beyond all else there is a unity that transcends their differences of faith and race." And so it sits, a plaque on a mountaintop with a changed name, overlooking Clark's beloved forests in New Hampshire.

Mary Washington had given all she could. After losing three sons in the war, she rarely left her home. Her other children visited her, along with grandchildren. She remained devoted to her faith, and, after several years, she passed away, transitioning from this life in the same house where John, so many years before, had survived an illness while his mother wept and prayed over him.

At the church where Father Washington served before enlisting, his memory remains as vibrant as ever. The street next to St. Stephen's was renamed Father John P. Washington Way. Outside, a 2,000-pound bronze sculpture depicts the four chaplains, arms locked in prayer on a sinking ship. The Archdiocese of Newark declared the church to be the Sanctuary of the Four Chaplains, and the old baptistry was dedicated as a space to their memory, where pictures of each of them hang on the wall, candles glow, and benches offer spaces for reflection and prayer.

Kathleen David received word of Charles's death the same way so many others did: a telegram and condolences. She was left with little Neil, her family, Charles's father, and an assumption that he was lost at sea. He had been buried in Greenland, but the news never reached the family. They didn't even know what he had done. They assumed he was lost forever, both body and spirit. Like Theresa and Betty, Kathleen faced a world of raising her son by herself, but it was a world far more hostile to her and him than what the others faced.

She faced it the same way he had faced the water all those years before: she could thrive or let it drown her. She chose to stretch forth her arms and pull and kick. She would need work. Charles had been providing, but without his help, she was once again alone. Thankfully, the war had changed things. She was able to find work, first through odd jobs, then at A. S. Beck Shoe Company, and finally as a switchboard operator at the Bell Telephone Company. And Charles's strong family was always nearby. Kathleen turned to her father-in-law to help with Neil. The husky carpenter from Antigua, the builder of pews, the man with both presence and power—he would help her raise her son while she struggled to put food on the table.

Roughly a year later, in 1944, while the war still raged on both sides of the globe, Kathleen received a call from a newspaper reporter asking if she had a photograph of Charles. She didn't understand why. In time, the picture would become clear. Charles was receiving a special award: the Navy and Marine Corps Medal, the highest decoration awarded by the United States Navy for heroism in noncombat situations.*

Just as with the chaplains, the details of what Charles had done trickled out, layer by layer. By February 1944, he was already an inspiration to his family. On a cold day in Harlem, Kathleen sat with Neil in her apartment. With her were her sixteen-year-old brother and his friend. They had every intention of following in their brother-in-law's footsteps. A reporter asked them: Did they worry about being relegated to serving only as mess attendants? No, they didn't, not after what Charles had done.

---

* Rescue operations at sea were not considered combat situations, even if the ships were in full combat with enemy forces during the rescue.

On June 20, 1944, Kathleen dressed little Neil in a navy play-suit, put on a beautiful dress with ball-gown gloves, and traveled with him to coast guard headquarters in the historic southern tip of Manhattan, near Wall Street and Trinity Church. There she met Robert Anderson, still alive because Charles told his commander to turn the boat around and save him.

Neil David holds his father's award while Robert
Anderson (left) and Kathleen David look on

In a simple ceremony, Rear Admiral Stanley V. Parker presented Kathleen with her husband's award. Reporters stood by, clicking photos. In the room, other coast guardsmen and women stood at attention. Admiral Parker read the citation, describing Charles's sacrifice. In the middle of reading the official language, he paused and took in the room. "It must be remembered," he said, perhaps fearful that his listeners wouldn't appreciate just what Charles had endured, "that the numbing chill of the water is as great a hazard as being under fire."

When he presented the medal to Kathleen, she held the velvety box. Neil was beside her, standing on a table. He stretched forth both hands, wrapping his little fingers around the ribbon clasped to the medal, a look of wonder on his face.

Isadore Fox had gone as low as anyone could. Living without her dear, sweet George was not an option. Even thoughts of her children were not enough to pull her from her despair.

A letter from her son Wyatt was what did it.

The war did not take him. The tears he had dripped onto his bedroom floor now resolved into strength. He received news of his father's death while on the front in the Pacific. If anyone could have given up at that point, it was he. In a letter to his mom, he wrote her one sentence that changed everything: "I've just got to be the kind of a man that my father was."

That was the spark—a miniscule, almost nonexistent glow that landed in the dark but fertile recesses of Isadore's mind. It ignited a fire. Soon, burning within her was the fierce resolve that she would do what George would have wanted her to do. She returned to school. At the Boston University School of Theology, she studied to be a minister, and in 1955, she was ordained. In the years after, she served over parishes throughout New England and as a chaplain to the American Legion Auxiliary in Vermont. As she and George had done together, she continued to serve, to lift weary hands, to listen and to teach, confident her husband was looking down, proud of her work.

Eighteen months after he torpedoed the *Dorchester,* Karl-Jurg Wächter was assigned to a different U-boat: U-2503. On May 4, 1945, as he steered her through the Baltic Sea, part of a smaller convoy, he came under heavy fire. A squadron of British aircraft spied the German boats and hailed bullets and rockets upon them. Wächter's convoy wasn't huge: just three U-boats and a couple of escorts. But they were, once again, headed out to the Atlantic to sink more ships and kill more

Americans. The first U-boat was prepared to crash dive and vanished beneath the surface as soon as cannon fire penetrated its hull. Wächter scrambled his men, but they were too late. The young commander was in the control room. He issued orders the same way he had the night of the attack on the *Dorchester*. Most likely, he was screaming to get his men inside so they could seal the ship and escape into the safety of the depths.

At that moment, a British rocket somehow managed to drop right into the conning tower, detonating inside the control room. Wächter and thirteen of his men died instantly.[2]

Adolf Hitler issued two predictions when the United States entered World War II: first, that a Germany united by force under his National Socialist government would reign supreme for a millennium; second, that the United States would collapse under the strain of its vast racial and religious diversity. When he was proven wrong, he committed suicide in an underground bunker in Berlin, largely alone, only his mistress by his side, the world around him lying in literal ruins.

Meanwhile, Charles W. David Jr., Clark Poling, Alexander Goode, George Fox, and John Washington live on. Reports spread. News of their sacrifices reached their families, then the broader world. They were memorialized in paintings, books, newspapers, postage stamps, museum exhibits, chapels, movies, awards, sculptures, comic strips, and medals. The initial reports of the disaster suggested they all had been killed by a Nazi U-boat. The truth slapped that story down with vigor.

Not one of them needed to die. In the upper staterooms, as men who did not panic, who had life jackets and were fully clothed, Clark, Alex, George, and John could have stepped off the ship onto one of the first lifeboats or rafts and successfully waited, dry, to return to their families. The Nazis didn't kill them. They chose to die so others could live. So did Charles. He carried precisely zero burden to help anyone. His efforts were his choice. He was a victim to no one.

Many decades after the sinking of the *Dorchester*, Duane Cyrus, Charles W. David Jr.'s nephew, sat in a crowd in Key West, Florida. With him were five other family members, including Sharon David, the granddaughter of Charles and Kathleen. Duane couldn't help but think how much of Charles's family had been cut short because of his sacrifice. In the years since, his son and grandchildren and nephews and nieces and cousins had gone on to illustrious careers in law, education, law enforcement, activism, the military, and finance—all inspired, in part, by Charles's example, as well as that of so many others in their family who braved coming to the United States from the Caribbean. Duane himself was an eminent professor of dance at the University of North Carolina–Greensboro.

They had all been invited to a special ceremony. The coast guard had decided to name all of its new, state-of-the-art, sentinel-class cutters after the service's heroes. One of them was to be named the *Charles W. David Jr.*

But the family's numbers were few—at least relative to the rest of the crowd.

At the podium, ninety-one-year-old Dick Swanson stood to thank Charles for saving his life, for having the courage to climb back into the water to rescue him. In the audience were dozens of Swanny's descendants and family, along with dozens more of Robert Anderson's family, and of Langford Anderson's family, and of so many others' families; then there were all the families who lived but who couldn't make it to this ceremony: a sea of people of all ages.

These were the descendants John, Clark, Alex, George, and Charles had saved. Their own lines were slim, cut short by their sacrifices, but what had they left behind?

Duane surveyed the crowd—elderly folks, small children,

teenagers, middle-aged men and women, all basking under the hot Florida sun, not too far from his own family's island ancestry. He couldn't help but think: they were all there because of these good men who had given themselves to save people so different from them. They had been lost to the world for nearly three-quarters of a century, but they lived. In the faces of squealing children, families uniting over re-union meals, the eyes of children yet to be born, they lived.

A few years before that ceremony, in 2004, Dick Swanson, now in his eighties, received a phone call at his home in Nebraska.

He had lived a full life, filled with peaks and valleys and everything in between, though mostly peaks, for Dick was ever the optimist: marriage, children, the death of his first wife to cancer, a career, deep faith, a second marriage and more children in the fashion of the Brady Bunch, love, loss, gratitude, regret, grandchildren, and great-grandchildren. But through it all, his saxophone, the one he loved to play with his buddy Charles W. David Jr., never left his side. Even at that ripe old age, he could still belt out a tune.

He shared the story of Charles with anyone who would listen, the time his good friend hauled him up the cargo net when he no longer had the strength to climb it himself; he had even accepted awards on Charles's behalf because no one knew if any of his posterity was alive or where to find them. Such was the world before technology made searching for people so much easier. His friend was always there, the man who made everything that followed a possibility, the "tower of strength," a giver of lives. "He loved that man," Joan, Dick's wife of fifty-six years, would later say.[3]

But the world changed. Computers and cell phones and web pages and ancestry sites and millions of interconnected servers and satellites seemed to materialize around the Swansons as they traversed the long chronology of their lives. People became so much easier to find. And when Dick received the call, he was overwhelmed. After all the decades, with the help of new technology, Barry Sax, a researcher from the coast guard, had found some of Charles's family: his widow, Kathleen, and his granddaughter Sharon, who had developed a career in accounting. As a result of Sax's research, the coast guard had relocated Charles's remains to Long Island National Cemetery in Farmingdale, New York, where the family could now visit him. The coast guard intended to honor Charles for his heroic sacrifice. They were hoping to bring the Swansons and the Davids together after all those decades.

Dick nearly lost his breath. A wave of emotions flooded over him. He had to meet the Davids . . . and couldn't move fast enough to make it happen. He and Joan traveled with the anticipation of grandparents meeting their first grandchild, first to Washington, DC, where they borrowed their daughter's car, then to Annapolis, Maryland, where Sharon lived. The plan was for the Swansons to pick up Kathleen and Sharon there so they could drive together to an award ceremony in New Jersey.

When they pulled up to the house, Dick held his emotions in check with the thinnest of veils. How would he react when he saw Kathleen, the woman who had lost her husband so that Dick and so many others could live? What would he say? Did Kathleen know what Charles had given him? It wasn't just music and friendship in the darkness of a hull on a roiling ocean in an eon gone by. It was a reality, a world that knew no real borders, a posterity that would outstrip the timeline of any one life. That was why Dick had traveled all this way: to be the carrier of a gratitude so immense it spread like the expanding universe.

Dick and Joan stepped from their daughter's car. They approached the door. The autumn air was crisp. Fiery leaves still clung to nearby trees.

The door opened.

Whatever dams Dick had built up to hold back his emotions, they shattered with the ferocity of rushing waters. With tears spilling down his seasoned cheeks, Sharon and Joan beaming nearby, he stepped forward.

Kathleen stood there, as old as Dick—she had lived an entire life since those days with Charles in the Bronx and Harlem. She had danced at the Savoy Ballroom, auditioned with the Silver Belles, and dreamed of a career as an entertainer. All of that was on the side. From her beginning as a switchboard operator, she had worked for decades at Bell Telephone, staying on even as the company divided itself into smaller companies; she eventually retired as a supervisor. Like Dick, she had remarried, given birth to two more sons, raised her own posterity, experienced the panoply of sorrows and joys that come from living long and living well, welcomed grandchildren into the world. Her son Neil—the little boy who received his father's medal—had grown up to be a police officer, then a U.S. Marshal. This was not an easy moment for her. For over six decades, she had carried the burden of feeling Charles's death was her fault, never truly knowing that his decisions, his selflessness, had led to his all-too-soon departure to the next life. These were feelings that had faded over time, never truly gone, but buried beneath a second lifetime of caring for and raising another family. How could she be expected to deal with them all again, to have them torn back to the surface, raw and exposed in the open air of her mind?

None of that mattered to Dick. He couldn't have been aware of her complicated burden. He embraced her, a hug with a gravity so powerful, around it swirled the thankfulness of nearly a hundred families and thousands of descendants. A posterity as robust as the stars in the skies—all there because of Charles, George, John, Alex, and Clark.

They held each other for a moment: a white man, a Black woman, so different in so many ways, under the same autumn sun.[4]

AFTERWORD

The Four Chaplains have received much attention in the decades since their sacrifice. In recent years, Charles W. David Jr. has begun to receive more recognition as well, but never before has anyone included his full story in its rightful place alongside the story of the *Dorchester*. With this book, I hoped to change that, so when the David family asked me if they could include some of their own remarks, I not only agreed, I felt it was a necessity. They are his legacy. What follows is their account, in their words.

—Steven T. Collis

Life-changing events can appear before us suddenly, and our choices or actions around those events can reverberate throughout our lives—impacting future generations. As the surviving members of the David family, we acknowledge the heroism and immortal strength of our dear Charles W. David Jr. He acted out of humanity and without hesitation to save others, and his fearlessness resonates in us today! Although he died before we were born, we grew up hearing about "Charlie." That he died in the Second World War, leaving his wife and son (Kathleen and Neil) without his strong presence. We knew about his life before joining the coast guard, but little else about his time and sacrifice other than the medals, honors, and articles held by Kathleen, then passed down to Neil, and now maintained by his granddaughter, Sharon.

In 2013, Sharon had already been keeping her grandfather's legacy alive by attending memorials and events related to the sinking of the *Dorchester* when she proudly represented our family at the commissioning of the United States Coast Guard cutter *Charles W. David Jr.* in Key West, Florida. Sharon is the ship's sponsor, and several members of the family joined her in support as we toured the vessel, met the crew, and were welcomed by the servicemen at the base. Perhaps the most poignant moment of the entire event was when members of the Anderson family recognized that many in their group would not be present were it not for Charles's action on that cold and terrible night. By contrast, our group was significantly smaller. We were happy for their numbers, but painfully aware of the absence left in our own line by Charles's loss.

Our family is Caribbean in ancestry. We hail from Antigua and St. Lucia. Charles was the son of an immigrant carpenter (also named Charles). The sea is familiar to our family. Charles's uncle Richmond was a merchant marine. Charles was also the nephew of S. R. Olivia David, headmistress of a school in Antigua that now bears her name. His sister, Audrey, was a New York City nurse, and Charles's son, Neil, a NYPD officer and U.S. Marshal. Neil can be seen in our cherished family photographs from the 1940s as a small child with his mother, accepting citations in honor of his father. The importance of the moment is evident on his young face. Neil carried the tradition of selflessness for his family throughout his own life and ensured that the legacy of his father remained intact. These people are all now our beloved ancestors, and their examples of perseverance, education, and service are evidence of the fiber of fortitude running through our lineage. They are not the only ones!

How do the selfless acts of Charles W. David Jr. in 1943 resonate with us today? His granddaughter, Sharon David, has tirelessly advocated for broader recognition of his bravery—traveling to Capitol Hill to attend events and patiently working with author Steven T. Collis and other family members to bring Charlie's story to life. Dhoruba Bin Wahad, one of Charles's nephews, has fought and advocated for the rights of Black people around the world. As a former Black Panther, exonerated political prisoner, activist, and lecturer, Dhoruba exemplifies the strength of our family. Duane Cyrus, another nephew of Charles, is a choreographer and professor at the University of North Carolina. He created a performance work in 2017 titled *Hero Complexities* that celebrates his uncle's heroism and brings Charles's story to a new generation of young people through the arts. Again, we are not the only ones. We are the echo of Charles W. David Jr.'s bravery, and our strength is in action, regardless of number.

So, what do questions surrounding Charles's rescue efforts, self-sacrifice, and heroism reveal about him? Remember, he did not have to volunteer to save others in a segregated military that relegated him to steward's mate. Charles helped save men who did not necessarily see him as equal. What does it mean to be reviled and revered at the same time? And how does our society relate to and understand Charles's act of heroism while navigating present-day societal issues? How can understanding lead to healing? Other questions we ask are: What is the impact on families when servicemen are lost? What does survival mean to veterans? We do not have all of the answers, but we know that the story of Charles W. David Jr. is a necessary legacy that extends outside of military lore. His actions resonate in areas of education, art, service, healthcare, and beyond! We advocate for the ability to step forward and show up for what is human about us. We are ceaseless in our efforts to keep his legacy alive and pass it on to others.

On behalf of the David family and in loving memory of Charles W. David Jr.

— Sharon David and Duane Cyrus

ACKNOWLEDGMENTS

The creation of this book led me to cross paths with so many generous people, the space I have is not sufficient to thank them all. For those listed here, and those not, please know my gratitude extends far beyond anything I can put in print.

For research assistance into the four chaplains, Charles W. David Jr., and everyone else aboard the *Dorchester* and the other ships in its convoy, I'm thankful to all those institutions who have kept their memories alive: the Four Chaplains Memorial Foundation, the National World War II Museum, the National Archives, the American Jewish Archives, the University of Texas, the Stanford Law School Library, Saint Stephens Church, and numerous authors and historians whose work better helped me understand everything from U-boats to telegrams to Nazi spies.

A number of people tolerated a seemingly endless stream of phone calls and emails from me, always asking for a bit more information or assistance. Chief among these were Bill Kaemmer, Clark V. Poling, Susan P. Smith, Duane Cyrus, Sharon David, Erin Clancey, Joey Balfour, Adam Artigliere, Blake Boatright, Ralph and Gale Artigliere, Paul Fried, Sara Fried Rose, Joan Swanson, and Dan Ocko. I'm also immensely grateful to those who preserved interviews of the men who survived that frigid night in 1943.

To my beta readers—Tonya Wendell, Taani Secrist, Stephen Craig, Mike Berry, Jerusha Collis, and Blake Boatright—thank you for insightful comments that changed everything. Similarly, this book would not exist without my publisher and its editors: Chris Schoebinger, Emily Watts, Heidi Taylor Gordon, and the rest of Shadow Mountain's wonderful staff.

Finally, when I am deep in drafting a book, my mind is one hundred percent occupied by it when I'm writing and fifty percent even when I'm not. Thank you to my wife, Jerusha, my children, and the rest of our family for sharing that part of me during those months.

NOTES

CHAPTER 1: A DIVIDED COUNTRY

1. For details regarding Hitler's speech, see Max Domarus, ed., *Hitler: Speeches and Proclamations, 1932–1945* (London, 1990).
2. *Hitler's Secret Conversations, 1941–1944,* trans. Norman Cameron and R. H. Stevens, with an introductory essay, "The Mind of Adolf Hitler," by H. R. Trevor-Roper (New York, 1961), 154–55.
3. Douglas Laycock, "Religious Liberty as Liberty," *Journal of Contemporary Legal Issues* (1996), 7, 313, 353; Douglas Laycock, "Remarks on Acceptance of National First Freedom Award from the Council for America's First Freedom," January 15, 2009; John Corvino, Ryan T. Anderson, and Sherif Girgis, *Debating Religious Liberty and Discrimination* (New York, 2017), 5, 233–34.
4. Douglas Laycock, "Continuity and Change in the Threat to Religious Liberty: The Reformation Era and the Late Twentieth Century," 80 Minn. L. Rev. (1996), 1047, 1049–66; Laycock, "Religious Liberty as Liberty," 317; Will Durant, *The Reformation* (New York, 1957), 438–41; William S. Maltby, *Alba: A Biography of Fernando Alvarez de Toledo, Third Duke of Alba, 1507–1582* (1983), 153–58; *North American Indigenous Warfare and Ritual Violence,* eds. Richard J. Chacon and Rubén G. Mendoza (Tucson, 2007).

CHAPTER 2: TRAINING FOR THE HUNT

1. Short for "Technical Training Group for Front-line U-boats" (*Technische Ausbildungsgruppe fur Front U-Boote*). Dennis Haslp, *Britain, Germany, and the Battle of the Atlantic: A Comparative Study* (New York, 2013).
2. Bernard Edwards, *The Twilight of the U-Boats* (New York, 2004), 16–17; https://uboat.net/men/commanders/1311.html.
3. https://uboat.net/men/commanders/1311.html.
4. Lawrence Paterson, *U-Boats in the Mediterranean: 1941–1944* (New York, 2007), 233.
5. A vocal anti-Semite, Dönitz would eventually rise high enough in the Nazi regime

that he became the interim ruler of Germany immediately after Hitler's death and after the war.

6. Karl Dönitz, *Die U-Bootswaffe* (Berlin, 1939), 26–67.

7. Dönitz, *Die U-Bootswaffe,* 26–67.

8. Terence Robertson, *The Golden Horseshoe: The Wartime Career of Otto Kretschmer, U-Boat Ace* (London, 2006), 14.

9. Timothy P. Mulligan, *Neither sharks nor wolves: the men of Nazi Germany's U-boat arm, 1939–1945* (Annapolis 2011), 73–74, 131–33.

10. Edwards, *Twilight,* 15.

11. David Westwood, *The U-Boat War: The German Submarine Service and the Battle of the Atlantic, 1935–1945* (London, 2005), 160–61 (photo inserts).

12. Edwards, *Twilight,* 15.

CHAPTER 3: FROM THE RUBBLE

1. U-223 was finishing its training at the Agru-Front on July 31, 1942, and continued various training and preparation exercises into August. Alexander and George reported to their training on August 4, 1942.

2. Isadore Fox, *The Immortal Chaplain: The Story of Rev. George L. Fox (1900–1943)* (New York, 1965), 9.

3. Fox, *Immortal Chaplain,* 9, 15–17.

4. Photos were used for a description of George; for the detail regarding his eyebrows, see Fox, *Immortal Chaplain,* 76.

5. "Weather," *Boston Globe,* Aug. 4, 1942, 22.

6. Isaac Klein, *The Anguish and the Ecstasy of a Jewish Chaplain* (New York, 1974), 20.

7. Klein, *Anguish and Ecstasy,* 20.

8. The details of the chaplains' first days in drills at Harvard come from an interview with Lyman C. Berrett by Richard Maher on October 10, 1975, for the Western Studies, Oral History Project, LDS Chaplains of World War II, as recorded in Richard Maher, *For God and Country: Memorable Stories from the Lives of Mormon Chaplains* (Bountiful, UT, 1976), 51–52.

9. https://www.ocregister.com/2013/06/07/final-lesson-lives-on-of-wwiis-immortal-chaplains/.

10. Fox, *Immortal Chaplain,* 9.

11. Fox, *Immortal Chaplain,* 11–14.

12. Fox, *Immortal Chaplain,* 13.

13. Fox, *Immortal Chaplain,* 15.

14. Fox, *Immortal Chaplain,* 20–80.

15. Fox, *Immortal Chaplain,* 75.

16. https://www.ocregister.com/2013/06/07/final-lesson-lives-on-of-wwiis-immortal-chaplains/.

17. Fox, *Immortal Chaplain,* 17.

18. Fox, *Immortal Chaplain,* 78.

CHAPTER 4: A NEW ERA OF HUMANITY

1. Isaac Klein, *The Anguish and the Ecstasy of a Jewish Chaplain* (New York, 1974), 20.
2. Frances Beauchesne Thornton, *Sea of Glory: The Magnificent Story of the Four Chaplains* (New York, 1953), 75–78.
3. Harry N. Price, "End All War, Pleads Harding Over Tomb," *Washington Post*, Nov. 12, 1921, 1; Lieut. Col. Repington, "Finds Pilgrim Echo in Honors to Dead: Scenes in Washington at Burial of the Unknown Warrior," *New York Times*, Nov. 12, 1921, 3.
4. H.G. Wells, "First Photographs of the Burial of America's Unknown Soldier," *St. Louis Post-Dispatch,* Nov. 13, 1921, 3.
5. From the Alexander Goode Papers, courtesy of the National Jewish Archive, Columbus, Ohio.
6. Alexander Goode Papers.
7. Thornton, *Sea of Glory,* 79.
8. Thornton, *Sea of Glory,* 67.
9. See "Suicides of Idle Cited in Plea for Congress Call," *New York Herald Tribune,* Sept. 7, 1931, 7; Associated Press, "Two Suicides Shake Nerve of Markets," *Washington Post,* Mar. 15, 1932, 1; Milton L. Randolph, "Pretty Atlanta Grad School Co-Ed Commits Suicide," *Pittsburgh Carrier,* Mar. 11, 1933, 1; "Penny Cafeteria Will Feed 500," *Washington Post,* Nov. 17, 1933, 15.
10. Thornton, *Sea of Glory,* 90.
11. Alexander Goode to Theresa Flax, April 3, 1933, in *War Letters: Extraordinary Correspondence from American Wars,* edited by Andrew Carroll (New York, 2001), 180–81.
12. Thornton, *Sea of Glory,* 109.

CHAPTER 5: NEVER SEEN A JEW

1. Isaac Klein, *The Anguish and the Ecstasy of a Jewish Chaplain* (New York, 1974), 24.
2. Klein, *Anguish and Ecstasy,* 25.
3. Klein, *Anguish and Ecstasy,* 25.
4. Klein, *Anguish and Ecstasy,* 26.
5. Klein, *Anguish and Ecstasy,* 22.
6. See generally Ronit Y. Stahl, *Enlisting Faith* (Cambridge, MA, 2017).
7. Robert Gellately, *Lenin, Stalin, and Hitler: The Age of Social Catastrophe* (New York, 2008); Robert Conquest, *The Great Terror: A Reassessment* (Oxford, 2007).
8. Stahl, *Enlisting Faith,* 77.
9. Reverend George Aki Application, November 17, 1943, Box I, Folder: Chaplains Aiken-Allenby, CCCA.
10. Stahl, *Enlisting Faith,* 77–78.
11. Stahl, *Enlisting Faith,* 10 and corresponding notes.
12. Stahl, *Enlisting Faith,* 30.
13. Stahl, *Enlisting Faith,* 10.
14. Ann Braude, "Women's History is American Religious History," in *Retelling US Religious History,* ed. Thomas Tweed (California, 1997), 87–107.
15. Stahl, *Enlisting Faith,* 11.

16. Letter from Mary Elizabeth Dibble to the Christian Science Board of Directors, September 30, 1942; Letter from Arthur Eckman to Mary Elizabeth Dibble, October 15, 1942, Box 14669, Folder 1476, housed at the Mary Baker Eddy Library.

17. Letter from Edwin B. Nylen to Clark Poling, sent to his father Daniel Poling after Clark's death, August 5, 1943, in possession of the author.

18. Klein, *Anguish and Ecstasy*, 23.

19. Klein, *Anguish and Ecstasy*, 24.

20. Klein, *Anguish and Ecstasy*, 20.

21. Klein, *Anguish and Ecstasy*, 20.

22. Klein, *Anguish and Ecstasy*, 24.

23. Isadore Fox, *The Immortal Chaplain: The Story of Rev. George L. Fox (1900–1943)* (New York, 1965), 81.

24. For a description of the graduation ceremony and the receiving of assignments, see Klein, *Anguish and Ecstasy*, 28–29.

25. For a description of Alex facing anti-Semitism during his first assignment, see Dan Kurzman, *No Greater Glory: The Four Immortal Chaplains and the Sinking of the Dorchester in World War II* (New York, 2005), 20–21.

CHAPTER 6: TIDINGS OF DAYS TO COME

1. Letter from T.M. Torrey to Messrs. F.W. Lafrentz & Company, February 18, 1943, copy on file with the author, courtesy of the National Archives.

2. Memo from D.F. Houlihan and William Radner to T.M. Torrey, July 15, 1942, copy on file with the author, courtesy of the National Archives.

3. https://uboat.net/allies/merchants/ship/2093.html.

4. Just before Christmas in 1940, Winston Churchill sent a letter to President Franklin Roosevelt, hoping to persuade the United States to come to Britain's aid against the Nazis. In it, he wrote: "The danger of Great Britain being destroyed by a swift, overwhelming blow has for the time very greatly receded. In its place there is a long, gradually maturing danger, less sudden and less spectacular, but equally deadly. This mortal danger is the steady and increasing diminution of sea tonnage. . . . Unless we can establish our ability to feed this island . . . we may fall by the way, and the time needed by the United States to complete her defensive preparations may not be forthcoming. It is, therefore, in shipping and in the power to transport across the oceans, particularly the Atlantic Ocean, that in 1941 the crunch of the whole war will be found" (Letter from Winston Churchill to Franklin D. Roosevelt, December 8, 1940, available at the Sir Winston Churchill Archive Trust).

5. David Westwood, *The U-Boat War: The German Submarine Service and the Battle of the Atlantic, 1935–1945* (London, 2005), 151; Edwin P. Hoyt, *The U-Boat Wars* (New York, 1984), 134.

6. Michael Gannon, *Operation Drumbeat* (New York, 1990), xv–xviii.

7. Hoyt, *The U-Boat Wars*, 136–37.

8. Gannon, *Operation Drumbeat*, 389–90.

9. Nathan Miller, *War at Sea: A Naval History of World War II* (Oxford, 1997), 295. The "First Happy Time" was during the early years of the war, before the United States got involved. Between July and October 1940, the Germans enjoyed immense success attacking Allied ships, particularly those of Britain.

10. Lieutenant N.A. Lindsay Jr., "Report of Action," Jan. 27, 1945, available at National Archives.
11. https://uboat.net/allies/merchants/ship/2093.html.
12. Lindsay Jr., "Report of Action," note 8.
13. "Attached report on attacks on SG 6 complied for the interest of Commander Task Force 24," n.d., "Convoy Sg-6 Record of Despatches," Records of Naval Operating Forces, RG 313, Red, CTF 24, box 8702, Washington National Records Center, Washington, D.C., National Archives and Records Administration.
14. Reports vary on how many men the *Chatham* lost. Some indicate fourteen men, some fifteen, and at least one source suggests as many as twenty-six. See Dan Kurzman, *No Greater Glory: The Four Immortal Chaplains and the Sinking of the Dorchester in World War II* (New York, 2005), 7; also https://uboat.net/allies/merchants/ship/2093.html.

CHAPTER 7: PREPARATION OF AN ANSWER TO PRAYERS

1. Ransford Palmer, *Pilgrims from the Sun: West Indian Migration to America* (New York, 1995).
2. Palmer, *Pilgrims from the Sun*.
3. Interview with Sharon David and Duane Cyrus, July 17, 2020.
4. Nancy Foner, ed., *Islands in the City: West Indian Migration to New York* (Berkeley, CA, 2001).
5. World War I Draft Registration Card of Charles David.
6. Interview with Sharon David and Duane Cyrus, July 17, 2020.
7. Eugene Gordon, "Negro Hero's Wife Sums It Up; Bill Knew Why He Was Fighting," *The Daily Worker,* Feb. 24, 1944, 3.
8. Interview with Sharon David and Duane Cyrus, July 17, 2020.
9. Gordon, "Negro Hero's Wife," 3.
10. Gordon, "Negro Hero's Wife," 3.
11. https://coastguard.togetherweserved.com/uscg/servlet/tws.webapp.
12. "The Four Chaplains: U-Boat Attack Leads to Heroic Sacrifice," *America in WWII* (Feb. 2008); "Negro Honored for Saving 100 in Icy Atlantic," *New York Herald Tribune,* June 21, 1944, 15.
13. Interview with Joan Swanson, June 18, 2020; Interview with Dick Swanson, courtesy of Patriot Features, https://www.patriotfeatures.org/portfolio/dick-swanson/.
14. Cammy Clark, "New Coast Guard cutter honors African-American ship cook and hero Charles David Jr.," *Miami Herald,* (Nov. 18, 2013), available at: https://www.miamiherald.com/news/nation-world/article1957551.html; Interview with Joan Swanson.
15. Clark, "New Coast Guard cutter."
16. Clark, "New Coast Guard cutter."
17. Gordon, "Negro Hero's Wife," 3.

CHAPTER 8: LOST ON A MOUNTAINTOP

1. The details about Clark's time waiting to receive his orders come from Betty's letters to Daniel Poling, date unknown. In the possession of the author, courtesy of Clark V. Poling ("Corky").

2. Daniel Poling, *Your Daddy Did Not Die* (New York, 1944), 28, 119.

3. https://www.cdc.gov/pertussis/about/faqs.html.

4. Poling, *Your Daddy*, 11.

5. Poling, *Your Daddy*, 20–22, 30–31.

6. Poling, *Your Daddy*, 31, 10–11.

7. Poling, *Your Daddy*, 9.

8. Poling, *Your Daddy*, 50.

9. Poling, *Your Daddy*, 51.

10. https://www.oakwoodfriends.org/about/history/.

11. Poling, *Your Daddy*, 11.

12. Poling, *Your Daddy*, 100.

13. Poling, *Your Daddy*, 91.

14. Poling, *Your Daddy*, 108.

15. Poling, *Your Daddy*, 105.

16. Photo in the possession of the author, courtesy of Clark V. Poling ("Corky").

17. Poling, *Your Daddy*, 110–11.

18. Poling, *Your Daddy*, 113.

19. Francis Beauchesne Thornton, *Sea of Glory: The Magnificent Story of the Four Chaplains* (New York, 1953), 164.

20. Letter from Arch Wemple, as recorded in Thornton, *Sea of Glory*, 157.

21. Poling, *Your Daddy*, 56.

22. Photograph of Clark's farewell dinner. In possession of the author, courtesy of Clark V. Poling ("Corky") and Susan Smith.

23. The details of Betty's thinking during this time are in her letters to Daniel Poling, date unknown. In the possession of the author, courtesy of Clark V. Poling ("Corky").

24. The details related to Clark's reunion with his wife and son come from a letter from Betty Poling to Daniel Poling, date unknown, in possession of the author.

CHAPTER 9: SOMETHING DEEPER BENEATH

1. The details of John Washington's early life come largely from Francis Beauchesne Thornton, *Sea of Glory: The Magnificent Story of the Four Chaplains* (New York, 1953), 173–226; and Dan Kurzman, *No Greater Glory: The Four Immortal Chaplains and the Sinking of the Dorchester in World War II* (New York, 2005) 28–31, 105–10. They also come from records housed in the archives at St. Stephen's Church, Kearny, New Jersey.

2. At the time, this rite would have been known as "extreme unction," a term rarely used now.

CHAPTER 10: SHEPHERDS IN DEATH'S SHADOW

1. The details regarding Aloysius Schmitt's sacrifice come from Jerry D. Lewis, "Salute the Chaplain!" *New York Herald Tribune*, Dec. 20, 1942, SM10; Casper Nannes, "Boys in Service Idolize Chaplains in War Zones," *The Daily Boston Globe*, Dec. 19, 1943, B1; Kelly McGowan, "'For God and Country': Navy

Chaplain lived and died serving others," *Des Moines Register,* Dec. 2, 2016; Craig Nelson, *Pearl Harbor: From Infamy to Greatness* (New York, 2016), 270.

2. "William F. Davitt," *Holy Cross College Service Record: War of 1917* (Worcester, MA, 1920), 16–17; "The Front as a Rest Area," *New York Tribune,* Jan. 19, 1919, C8.

3. Lyle W. Dorsett, *Serving God and Country: United States Military Chaplains in World War II* (New York, 2012), 54; Robert L. Gushwa, *The Best and Worst of Times: The U.S. Army Chaplaincy, 1920–1945,* Vol. IV (Washington, D.C., 1977), 215–16; Clifford M. Drury, *The History of the Chaplain Corps, U.S. Navy,* Vol. II (Washington, D.C.), 155–59.

4. Roy John Honeywell, *Chaplains of the United States Army* (Washington, D.C., 1958), 183; Annessa C. Stagner, "Healing the Soldier, Restoring the Nation: Representations of Shell Shock in the USA During and After the First World War," *Journal of Contemporary History,* Vol. 49, No. 2 (April 2014), 259.

5. Duane P. Schultz, *The Last Battle Station: The Story of the U.S.S. Houston* (New York, 1985); https://www.usswestvirginia.org/veterans/personalpage.php?id=2608. Just as remarkable was how Chaplain Rentz died. In a different battle, after the *Houston* was finally sunk, a number of men found themselves floating in the water, clinging to a pontoon from a shot-down plane. Rentz was among them. More and more men climbed onto the makeshift life raft. Seeing that it was taking on water and couldn't support them all, he said, "You men are young, I have lived the major part of my life and I am willing to go." He tried to give up his spot on the pontoon and to force his life jacket on some of the younger, more injured sailors. They refused. He insisted. They would not accept it. Finally, Rentz said a prayer, took off his life jacket, and offered it to a young seaman named Walter Beeson, who declined to put it on. The men continued to debate what to do next. When Beeson and others looked back, Rentz was gone, as if he had just disappeared. They then realized what had happened. While no one was looking, to ensure others would use his life jacket and his space on the pontoon, Rentz had quietly pushed himself away from safety and disappeared into the water. He was fifty-nine years old. See Duane P. Schultz, *The Last Battle Station: The Story of the U.S.S. Houston* (New York, 1985); James D. Hornfischer, *Ship of Ghosts: The Story of The* U.S.S. Houston, *FDR's Legendary Lost Cruiser, and Epic Saga of Her Survivors* (New York, 2006), 156–57; https://www.usswestvirginia .org/veterans/personalpage.php?id=2608.

6. Nicholas Arata, "How the Christian Faith Helped World War I Soldiers on the Western Front Cope with Shell-Shock," *James Blair Historical Review,* Vol. 9, No. 2 (2019).

7. Letter of Hiro Higuchi to his wife, July 8, 1944. On file with the author, courtesy of The University of Hawai'i at Manoa Libraries. "Japanese American Veterans Collection Digital Resources: Chaplain Higuchi Wartime Correspondence."

8. Letter of Hiro Higuchi to his wife, October 18, 1944. On file with the author, courtesy of The University of Hawai'i at Manoa Libraries. "Japanese American Veterans Collection Digital Resources: Chaplain Higuchi Wartime Correspondence."

9. Russell Cartwright Stroup, *Letters from the Pacific: A Combat Chaplain in World War II* (Columbia, MO, 2000), 78.

10. Stroup, *Letters*, 99.

11. Donald F. Crosby, *Battlefield Chaplains: Catholic Priests in World War II* (Kansas, 1994), 200–201.

12. Crosby, *Battlefield Chaplains*, 226.

13. Crosby, *Battlefield Chaplains*, 226.

14. Many other details related to the duties and burdens of chaplains came from interviews with Blake Boatright, who served as a military chaplain for twenty-four years in multiple battlefronts.

CHAPTER 11: THE FINAL GOODBYES

1. Letter from Betty Poling to Daniel Poling, in possession of the author, courtesy of Clark V. Poling.

2. Interview with Clark V. Poling.

3. Exchanges with Susan "Thumper" Smith.

4. Alexander Goode Papers, National Jewish Archives.

5. "Joint Declaration," announced simultaneously on December 17th, 1942, in London, Moscow, and Washington.

6. Interview and email exchange with Sharon David, on file with the author.

7. Bernard Edwards, *The Twilight of the U-Boats* (New York, 2004), 2.

8. Edwards, *Twilight*, 15.

9. From Edwards, *Twilight*, 17–23.

10. Letter from Betty Poling to Daniel Poling.

11. Details related to George and Isadore's final goodbye come from her book *The Immortal Chaplain: The Story of Rev. George L. Fox (1900–1943)* (New York, 1965).

12. Details related to U-223 and their course and activites are taken from the service journal of Karl-Jurg Wächter and from Edwards, *Twilight*, 17–23.

13. Interview with Paul Fried.

14. Details related to Theresa and Alex's goodbye come from Dan Kurzman, *No Greater Glory: The Four Immortal Chaplains and the Sinking of the Dorchester in World War II* (New York, 2005).

15. The details of Betty receiving multiple calls and the telegraph come from a letter she wrote to Daniel Poling.

16. This section is based on Kurzman, *No Greater Glory*, 32.

CHAPTER 12: ENTERING DANGEROUS WATERS

1. "Summary of Statement by Survivors SS DORCHESTER, Passenger-Cargo Vessel, 5654 G.T., . . ." courtesy of National Archives.

2. Interview with James McAtamney, courtesy of the Four Chaplains Memorial Foundation.

3. Interview with James Perkins, Feb. 26, 1998, courtesy of Chapel of the Four Chaplains.

4. Scenes related to the boarding of the *Dorchester* come from a variety of sources: documents in possession of the author from the National Archives; Bernard Edwards, *The Twilight of the U-Boats* (New York, 2004), 20–21; Chester J.

Szymczak, *The Men, The Ship* (Chicago, IL, 1976), 15–16; Dan Kurzman, *No Greater Glory: The Four Immortal Chaplains and the Sinking of the Dorchester in World War II* (New York, 2005), 2–10.

5. Daniel Poling, *Your Daddy Did Not Die* (New York, 1944), 132–33.
6. Edwards, *Twilight,* pg. 22.
7. McAtamney Interview.

CHAPTER 13: THE SPIES OF THE FIFTH COLUMN

1. "Destruction by Fire of Knights of Columbus Hostel, St. John's, December 12th, 1942, with loss of 99 lives," Report of Justice Brian Dunfield (St. John's, 1943).
2. Robert G. Thorne, *A Cherished Past* (2004), 131.
3. Gehard P. Bassler, *Vikings to U-Boats: The German Experience in Newfoundland and Labrador* (Montreal, 2006), 285–92.
4. Letter from Clark to Betty, as recorded in Daniel Poling, *Your Daddy Did Not Die* (New York, 1944), 133.
5. All details related to U-223's whereabouts and activities come from Wächter's captain's journal, in possession of the author. The same is true for the weather. Details regarding the moon and sun data are available at Uboatarchive.net and are taken from U.S. Naval Observatory Data.

CHAPTER 14: INTO THE DARK

1. Details relating to the conflict with the cook came from an interview with William Kramer, courtesy of the Chapel of the Four Chaplains.
2. For details relating to the storm and the ice, see Chester J. Szymczak, *The Men, The Ship* (Chicago, IL, 1976), 63; Bernard Edwards, *The Twilight of the U-Boats* (New York, 2004), 25–26; Michael G. Walling, *Bloodstained Sea* (Camden, ME, 2004), 112–13; Dan Kurzman, *No Greater Glory: The Four Immortal Chaplains and the Sinking of the Dorchester in World War II* (New York, 2005), 101.
3. Interview with Dick Swanson, courtesy of the National World War II Museum and Patriot Features.
4. https://coastguard.dodlive.mil/2015/09/long-blue-line-an-african-american -hero-serving-in-a-segregated-service/; "Report from Lieutenant Commander Ralph Curry," 1.
5. Kurzman, *No Greater Glory,* 101.
6. Interview with Anthony Naydyhor, Feb. 27, 1998, courtesy of the Chapel of the Four Chaplains.
7. The details relating to hypothermia largely stem from research on hypothermia compiled by Minnesota Sea Grant and researchers at the University of Minnesota. In particular, helpful information is located at "Hypothermia Prevention: Survival in Cold water," available at http://www.seagrant.umn.edu/coastal_communities/ hypothermia#torso.
8. For detail regarding the *Laconia* incident, see James P. Duffy, *The Sinking of the Laconia and the U-Boat War: Disaster in the Mid-Atlantic* (Nebraska, 2013); J. Hood, *Come Hell and High Water: Extraordinary Stories of Wreck, Terror and Triumph on the Sea* (Ithaca, NY, 2006).

9. Video interview with James McAtamney, courtesy of the Chapel of the Four Chaplains.
10. Kurzman, *No Greater Glory,* 55.
11. Interview with Daniel O'Keefe, courtesy of the Chapel of the Four Chaplains.

CHAPTER 15: FULLY CLOTHED WITH LIFE JACKETS ON

1. Wächter Captain's Journal, entries from January 30–February 2, 1943, copy in possession of the author; also available at http://uboatarchive.net/U-223/KTB223-1.htm.
2. https://coastguard.dodlive.mil/2015/09/long-blue-line-an-african-american-hero-serving-in-a-segregated-service/.
3. Reports of the captain's command over the speakers comes from interviews at the Four Chaplains Memorial Foundation and also from Chester Szymczak's firsthand account of his survival (see Chester J. Szymczak, *The Men, The Ship* [Chicago, IL, 1976]). Szymczak attributes the orders to someone other than Danielson, but I was not able to confirm his account.
4. Dan Kurzman, *No Greater Glory: The Four Immortal Chaplains and the Sinking of the Dorchester in World War II* (New York, 2005), 115.
5. Video interview with Kurt Roser, courtesy of the Four Chaplains Memorial Foundation.

CHAPTER 16: A MUFFLED EXPLOSION AND AMMONIA

1. Report of William H. Arpaia to The Vice Chief of Naval Operations, "U.S.A.T. DORCHESTER—Sinking of," date unknown, para. 8, in possession of the author.
2. Details related to Roy Summers's experience when the torpedo struck and his background come from Dan Kurzman, *No Greater Glory: The Four Immortal Chaplains and the Sinking of the Dorchester in World War II* (New York, 2005), 122–23.
3. Report of William Arpaia.
4. Several survivors explained the experiences below deck the moment the torpedo struck in videotaped interviews, courtesy of the Four Chaplains Memorial Foundation; the official report from the Office of the Chief of Naval Operations ("Summary of Statements by Survivors SS Dorchester") also provided valuable details regarding what happened below deck immediately after the attack. The "Memorandum to Major Harold R. Greenlee of Survivors Samuel I. Dix, Irwin White, Harold Beach, and James Caulley" also provided valuable information regarding the torpedo's damage and what it caused below deck.
5. Interview with David Labadie, date unknown, courtesy of the Chapel of the Four Chaplains; interview with Henry Goguen, date unknown, courtesy of the Chapel of the Four Chaplains.

CHAPTER 17: TWENTY-FIVE MINUTES IN FEBRUARY

1. Chester J. Szymczak, *The Men, The Ship* (Chicago, IL, 1976), 266–67.
2. Report of William H. Arpaia to The Vice Chief of Naval Operations, 165.

3. Details related to Roy Summers come from his videotaped interviews, courtesy of the Four Chaplains Memorial Foundation, as well as from Dan Kurzman, *No Greater Glory: The Four Immortal Chaplains and the Sinking of the Dorchester in World War II* (New York, 2005), 130.

4. Memorandum to Chief of the Casualty Branch, April 4, 1943, "Determination of Status, SS Dorchester," in possession of author, courtesy of the National Archives.

5. http://www.americainwwii.com/articles/the-faithful-four/.

6. Memorandum, April 4, 1943, 2.

7. Memorandum, April 4, 1943, 2.

8. Interview with Edward Dionne, courtesy of the Four Chaplains Memorial Foundation.

9. Written eyewitness statement from Donald C. Kant, housed in the National Archives, courtesy of the Chapel of the Four Chaplains.

10. Interview with Edward Dionne, courtesy of the Four Chaplains Memorial Foundation.

11. "The Heroism of the Four Chaplains," James A. Cox, *Marine Corps League Magazine,* Autumn 1989.

12. Memorandum, April 4, 1943, 3.

13. Memorandum, April 4, 1943, 3.

14. It's possible this chaplain could have been someone other than Clark. The eyewitness accounts are not perfectly clear. One eyewitness said he heard a strange laugh from the chaplain during this particular moment, and Clark's father later suggested that Clark had a strange laugh when he got angry or overly excited. But we may never know precisely which chaplain performed this particular heroic act. Because we know George gave his jacket to a different soldier, and we have eyewitness accounts for when the other chaplains all gave up their jackets, I have chosen to assume that Clark was the one acting in this instance, but I do so with a caveat.

15. The encounter with the young man to whom Clark gave his life jacket was recounted by Grady Clark, who was the witness and who survived by swimming to the boat. He recounted the story to Dr. Daniel Poling, as reported in the *Eagle* magazine, October 1950.

16. References to the ship going down bow-first came from a number of interviews, including interview of William Kramer, courtesy of the Chapel of the Four Chaplains.

17. Statement to the army by Joseph D. Haymore.

CHAPTER 18: HELP IN THE DARK

1. Memorandum to Chief of the Casualty Branch, April 4, 1943.

2. http://www.seagrant.umn.edu/coastal_communities/hypothermia#symptoms.

3. "Report to Commander," Task Unit 24.8.3, Feb. 5, 1943.

4. Log of Lt. Com. Carl U. Peterson, Feb. 3, 1943.

5. "Screening Instructions for Escort of Convoy Operations," Nov. 14, 1942.

CHAPTER 19: ALONE

1. Purchase Supply Sheet, February 10, 1942, courtesy of the National Archives.
2. Dan Kurzman, *No Greater Glory: The Four Immortal Chaplains and the Sinking of the Dorchester in World War II* (New York, 2005), 154.
3. Ron Grossman, "4 Chaplains' Deeds in '43 Still Inspire," *Chicago Tribune*, Feb. 4, 2005.

CHAPTER 20: THE WORST DISASTER

1. War Department, "Memorandum for Major Louis Lippman, Search for Dorchester Survivors," March 26, 1943.
2. Information related to the clerical mistakes comes from Daniel Poling, *Your Daddy Did Not Die* (New York, 1944).
3. All of the information related to Ms. Swanwick is from a letter written to her by J.A. Ulio, who explained the entire situation and offered his sympathies. It was recovered from the National Archives.
4. All of the information related to Isadore Fox learning of her missing husband is from Isadore Fox, *The Immortal Chaplain: The Story of Rev. George L. Fox (1900–1943)* (New York, 1965), 82–83.
5. Dan Kurzman, *No Greater Glory: The Four Immortal Chaplains and the Sinking of the Dorchester in World War II* (New York, 2005), 181.
6. The details related to Kathleen's feelings came from an interview with Sharon David and Duane Cyrus, July 17, 2020.
7. The details of Isadore's grief come from Fox, *Immortal Chaplain*, 83.
8. R. Alton Lee, "The Army 'Mutiny' of 1946," *Journal of American History*, Vol. 53, No. 3 (Dec. 1966), 557.
9. Headquarters of the Commander in Chief, United States Fleet; Commander, Tenth Fleet. Naval History & Heritage Command. United States Navy, "United States Naval Administration in World War II History of Convoy and Routing" (Washington, DC, 1945), 62; https://www.history.navy.mil/research/library/online-reading-room/title-list-alphabetically/h/history-convoy-routing-1945.html.

CHAPTER 21: A LIGHT IN THE DARK

1. Memorandum for File, "Summary of Statement by Survivors SS DORCHESTER," March 1, 1943.
2. Norris Burkes, "Spiritual Care: Remember Those on Memorial Day," http://www.egcitizen.com/lifestyle/spiritual-care/article_e8161126-7e60-11e9-9114-6fef6669c192.html.
3. Statement from Ben Epstein in Bob Smietana, "If We Can Die Together, Can't We Live Together?" *Covenant Companion*, May 2003; https://covenantcompanion.com/2019/02/03/four-chaplains-day-commemorates-fallen-heroes-2/; interview with Ben Epstein, March 26, 1998, courtesy of the Chapel of the Four Chaplains.
4. Interview with James Eardley, March 2, 1998, courtesy of the Chapel of the Four Chaplains.

CHAPTER 22: STEPPING FORWARD

1. Interview with David Labadie, date unknown, courtesy of the Chapel of the Four Chaplains.
2. Interview with David Labadie.
3. Interview with Henry Goguen, date unknown, courtesy of the Chapel of the Four Chaplains.
4. Interview with Paul Jorgensen, March 28, 1998, courtesy of the Chapel of the Four Chaplains.
5. Interview with Gale and Ralph Artigliere, September 24, 2020.
6. Interview with Anthony Naydyhor, Feb. 27, 1998, courtesy of the Chapel of the Four Chaplains.
7. William H. Thiesen, "The Long Blue Line: An African-American Hero Serving in a Segregated Service," https://coastguard.dodlive.mil/2015/09/long-blue-line-an -african-american-hero-serving-in-a-segregated-service/.
8. https://www.miamiherald.com/news/nation-world/article1957551.html.
9. Interview with Gale and Ralph Artigliere, September 24, 2020.
10. Letter from Robert Anderson to Muriel Anderson, November 12, 1942, on file with the author, courtesy of Adam Artigliere; the details of Robert and Muriel's plans in Boston come from an interview with Gale and Ralph Artigliere, September 24, 2020.
11. https://www.miamiherald.com/news/nation-world/article1957551.html.
12. Interview with David Labadie.
13. "He was not alone." See Dan Kurzman, *No Greater Glory: The Four Immortal Chaplains and the Sinking of the Dorchester in World War II* (New York, 2005), 221–23.
14. Interview with Richard Swanson, courtesy of the National World War II Museum; Interview with Richard Swanson, courtesy of Patriot Features.
15. Interview with Richard Swanson, courtesy of the National World War II Museum; Interview with Richard Swanson, courtesy of Patriot Features.
16. For additional information regarding the lifeboat the *Escanaba* rescued, see Ray Kisonas, "Monroe man is only person remaining from World War II transport ship," *Monroe News*, Aug. 15, 2015; https://www.monroenews.com/article/20150815 /NEWS/308159989.

CHAPTER 23: LEGACY

1. Author correspondence with Clark V. Poling and Susan Smith, throughout 2020.
2. Lawrence Paterson, *Black Flag: The Surrender of Germany's U-Boat Forces on Land and at Sea* (Barnsley, UK, 2009), 87.
3. Interview with Joan Swanson, June 18, 2020.
4. The details of Dick Swanson's and Kathleen David's reunion come from an interview with Joan Swanson, June 18, 2020.

INDEX